OLDEST CITY
The History of Saint Augustine

St. Augustine Historical Society
St. Augustine, Florida

Fireworks light the sky over Matanzas Bay during St. Augustine's 450th birthday celebration. With permission of The St. Augustine Record.

OLDEST CITY

THE HISTORY OF SAINT AUGUSTINE

Edited by
Susan Richbourg Parker

ST. AUGUSTINE HISTORICAL SOCIETY

St. Augustine Historical Society
St. Augustine, Florida

Published in the United States of America
by St. Augustine Historical Society

This book may be available in electronic edition.

Oldest City, the history of Saint Augustine
edited by Susan Richbourg Parker
layout and design by Robert Parker
(includes index)

ISBN 978-0-578-41179-8

Illustrations not otherwise credited are from the collections of the St. Augustine Historical Society.

Cover: Post card view of San Agustín Bastion (southeast bastion), Castillo de San Marcos National Monument
Page v: Photograph of Michael Gannon by Jerry Uelsmann with permission

St. Augustine Historical Society
271 Charlotte Street
St. Augustine, FL 32084

This history of St. Augustine is

dedicated to Michael Valentine Gannon

(1927 - 2017)

Teacher, Historian, Humanist, Raconteur

Contents

Preface

"This book is about St. Augustine." Those words introduced the story of St. Augustine in the preface of *The Oldest City, St. Augustine: Saga of Survival,* the 1983 history published by The Saint Augustine Historical Society.

Now the Society offers a new history: *Oldest City: The History of St. Augustine.* Like its predecessor, this work endeavors to "present the broad picture at a popular level, yet without sacrificing historical accuracy." To provide a more authoritative voice and assist readers, this book includes end-of-chapter notes, which cite the specific sources used by the authors. Earlier histories of St. Augustine--Fairbanks, Dewhurst, Waterbury, ed.--did not offer this level of detail about sources.

There are many history books and articles about the history of St. Augustine, yet a surprisingly small number encompass the entire period of St. Augustine's written past, from the 1560s forward. *The History and Antiquities of the City of St. Augustine, Florida*, by George R. Fairbanks was published in 1858, three years before the U.S. Civil War began. He was the first to make major use of Spanish documents and the first serious historian to study St. Augustine. The Spanish explorations and settlements fascinated Fairbanks, who devoted almost half of his book--95 of 200 pages--to the French-Spanish contest in the Southeast between 1564 and 1568. In 1881, W. W. Dewhurst published his work, *The History of St. Augustine, Florida.* The book appeared before Henry Flagler had visited the city and initiated major changes to the ancient town. Dewhurst brought his history to within a few years of its publication date by including the story of the Plains Indians held as captives at the old fortress (1875-1878). Yet he left out for the most part the story of the Civil War, which he called the "Rebellion," commenting "it is perhaps too soon after the close of the struggle to discuss the events of that period."

A century later, in 1983, Dewhurst's grand-daughter Jean Parker Waterbury presided over the multi-author compilation of a history published by the Historical Society. She relied on eight experts and specialists in St. Augustine's time periods.

Thirty-five years later the Society has published this new history. Events in the past do not change, but the questions that we ask do. Herein eleven authors present their research and interpretations of St. Augustine's past, relying upon the some of the same documents used for previous histories, but also upon documents and other information that were not known in 1983.

Kathleen Deagan deserves the most thanks and recognition in the shaping of this book. She shared her experience, expertise, and wisdom as a writer and editor to guide the creation of the book. In addition she brought her knowledge and insight about St. Augustine's past. James Cusick, Curator at the University of Florida's P. K. Yonge Library of History, assisted with requests for images and information and offered the often-elusive qualities of wisdom and insight. The St. Augustine Record through Executive Editor Craig Richardson has been gracious and generous with permitting the use of its photographs. Barbara Golden of the St. Johns County Visitors and Convention Bureau provided access to hundreds of pictures and images. Many other persons shared their illustrations; their names appear in the images' credits. Ronnie Lovell copyedited an early version of the book and Greg Smith copyedited the final version. As this is a work by humans, there is no doubt that errors remain.

River
Santa E
GUALE
Altamaha River
Atlantic
Ocean
MOCAMA
TIMUCUA
River
St.
Marys
WESTERN
TIMUCUA
SALT WATER
TIMUCUA
St. Augustine
Apalache
River
Suwannee
Gulf of Mexico
150

1

The People Who Met Menéndez

AD1500 - 1565

Kathleen Deagan and Carl Halbirt

One can only imagine what the native Timucuan people of today's St. Augustine felt in September of 1565 when they saw the sails of Admiral Pedro Menéndez de Avilés' five ships off their shores. Curiosity, certainly! There was probably also a sense of foreboding. These were not the first Europeans the Timucua had seen arrive in ships. Spaniards had cruised the Florida coast since the first decade of the sixteenth century in search of slaves and new lands.[1] In 1564 the French had established Fort Caroline just 40 miles north of where Menéndez came ashore. Relations with the Timucua were initially amicable, but conflicts soon emerged.[2] Demands for food, introduction of European diseases to which the Florida natives had no immunity, and unstable Native American political alliances resulted in acrimonious relations that were undoubtedly known to St. Augustine's indigenous population. The Timucua had good reason to be apprehensive.

Who were these people whose land the Spaniards invaded? The Timucua--the name of the linguistic group by which modern researchers refer to them--had been living in northeastern and north central Florida and southeastern Georgia for thousands of years when Menéndez arrived in Florida in 1565. Their ancestors had been here for thousands before them. By the mid-sixteenth century, the people known today as the Timucua were actually a number of different tribes that were loosely allied into at least seven independent and often warring confederacies, recognized by the Spaniards as chiefdoms, or *cacicazgos*. Each was headed by a paramount chief (*cacique*), to whom a series of regional and local

LEFT: Timucua groups in the Sixteenth Century.

chiefs was subject. Although they all shared the general language group known as "Timucua," these chiefdoms each had well-defined territories, distinctive dialects and recognizably distinct kinds of pottery.[3]

Most of what we know about the Timucua and their culture comes from French and Spanish accounts of the mid-sixteenth century and the accounts of Catholic missionaries who lived among them after the late sixteenth century. Researchers today acknowledge that most of these written accounts have to be used with caution, since they were produced for a reason (such as justifying Spanish actions), and they contain biases of language and misunderstandings. They are, however, among the earliest and most detailed accounts of a North American cultural group at the dawn of European colonization. When combined with archaeological evidence these accounts offer a rich, if still incomplete, picture of Timucuan society.

First Impressions

Both French and Spanish observers described the appearance of the Saltwater Timucua in some detail.[4] Furthermore, Theodore DeBry's engravings of the Timucua under Saturiwa (based on paintings by Frenchman Jacques Le Moyne, an artist on the Fort Caroline expedition) are some of the earliest images of Native Americans in North America and are widely published.[5] Many of DeBry's engravings of Timucua are clearly based on earlier depictions of South American Indians and are thought to be inaccurate , but some of them correspond to written descriptions of Timucua appearance.[6] These descriptions all note the absence of much clothing among the Timucua, as well as the widespread use of tattoos and body painting. What clothing was worn seems to have been restricted to breechclouts or loincloths made of skins or woven palm among men, and skirts made of Spanish moss or skins for women. Intricately painted deerskin mantles or cloaks were associated with members of the chiefly class. Most Europeans observed that Timucua men and women were tall, strong, ruddy in complexion and had very long hair. Men wore theirs gathered

RIGHT: Timucuan Woman, Theodore De Bry.

and bound atop the head, and women's hair was loose and "well combed". Sadly, no accounts by Timucuas describing the Spaniards exist, and we can only imagine their impressions of the heavily-clothed, light-skinned, and infrequently-bathed newcomers.[7]

St. Augustine is located in the Timucua territory and dialect region known to the Spaniards as the "Saltwater (*Agua Salada*) Timucua." The paramount chief in 1564 was called Saturiwa (or Saturiba), whose seat was near the mouth of the St. Johns River. According to Spanish and French accounts of the 1560s, the local cacique of the St. Augustine area, Seloy (or Soloy), was subject to Saturiwa. Saturiwa's domain extended southward from the south side of the St. Johns River's mouth to at least present day Daytona Beach, and westward from the Atlantic coast to the St. Johns River. The Ais Indians lived to the south of this territory, the Mocama Timucua lived to the north of the St. Johns River, and the Utina, Potano, and Acuera Timucua groups occupied the territory to the west of the river. Early European accounts relate that Saturiwa and Utina (the cacique of the Utina Timucua) were fierce rivals, although it is not known if the rivalries were over territorial expansion, riverine transportation and communication routes, or ancient feuds. Each of these caciques tried to enlist European support in fighting the other: the Saltwater Timucua, under Saturiwa, allied with the French against the Utina, and the Spaniards later allied with the Utina against Saturiwa.

The Timucua were described as having matrilineal clans (that is, a hereditary kinship group who traces descent through the mother rather than the father). These clans were ranked in terms of social importance, and caciques came from a specific hereditary family group. Caciques wielded considerable power and privilege, commanding a series of less-powerful sub-regional and local, caciques. They could apparently call on their subjects for warfare, labor, and food production. A hierarchical organization of power was familiar to the Spaniards, and their engagements with the Timucua became structured through that system. The Spaniards acknowledged the clans and their caciques as nobles, and accorded the caciques special gifts and privileges well into the eighteenth century. Through them, the Spanish could gain access to native labor and food production, and encourage conversion to Christianity.

Before the Spanish arrived

The Timucua in the vicinity of St. Augustine lived mostly along the intracoastal and inland waterways at places that were occupied--sometimes continuously--for thousands of years.[8] The Timucua and their ancestors developed an economy and a way of life based on fishing, hunting, and especially shellfish gathering. Their occupation sites occur principally along coastal estuaries where access to marine resources, land resources, and routes of communication were all at hand. Although craft traditions, social expression, and ritual practices changed over the millennia, their choice of places to live generally did not. Some very large and dense marine shell midden sites in the vicinity of St. Augustine, such as the Shell Bluff Landing site (8SJ32),[9] reflect this long-term occupation. The Shell Bluff Landing site, about ten miles north of St. Augustine, extends for about 450 meters along the Tolomato River and is from 150 to 250 meters wide. Artifacts show that this area was regularly occupied by native people from about 2,000 BC into the eighteenth century.

The earliest archaeologically known Native American occupation of the coastal region around St Augustine is known today as the "Orange Period Archaic" culture, named after their style of pottery ("Orange Fiber Tempered"). Fiber-tempered pottery was being made by about 2,500 BC (4,500 years ago) and was some of the earliest pottery ever made in North America. During this period people usually lived in seasonal or temporary camps along the waterway. Orange Period sites have been located extending from several miles north of St. Augustine southward to well below the Matanzas Inlet. Most Orange period sites are shell middens (deposits of refuse spread over an area of occupation and built up over a period of time) comprising oysters, conchs, moonsnails, and large numbers of tiny coquina (periwinkle) shells. Fish and terrestrial animal bones, fiber-tempered pottery, and other stone and bone artifacts are dispersed throughout these shell deposits.

Although most recorded Orange Period Archaic sites are small and were seasonally occupied, a few large village sites have been found in what were apparently stable settlement locations. On the west side of Anastasia Island near the St. Augustine Alligator Farm, for example, extensive Orange Period deposits of periwinkle shells have been found along with fire pits and evidence for structures. At least one very large Orange Period Archaic village site, the Summer Haven site (8SJ46), has been located to the south of St. Augustine on the south side of the Matanzas Inlet. It is a very large shell midden containing hearths, human burials, trash pits and structures.[10]

A very distinctive kind of Orange period shell sites is the shell "ring." Raised accumulations of shell in roughly ring or arc shapes are found along the coasts of South Carolina, Georgia and Florida, dating to the late Archaic period (which in Florida is roughly between 4,000 and 2,500 years before present). These were purposefully planned constructions, built around a central plaza area that is usually free of shell or other debris. Archaeologists continue to debate the question of whether these were specialized ceremonial sites, domestic living sites arranged in a circle or arc, or a combination of both.[11] Only one such site has been identified in the St. Augustine vicinity, known as the Guana Shell Ring (8SJ2554) located about twelve miles north of the city. It is formed in the shape of a "C" measuring 170 meters in diameter and about 1.3 meters in height, and appears to have been in use around 3,500 years ago. A large Orange period midden is located adjacent to the ring.

Abundant shellfish and coastal resources sustained this hunting and gathering way of life up until about 500 BC, when a number of conspicuous changes took place. These changes marked the beginning of what is known as the "St. Johns I" cultural tradition in northeast Florida. St. Johns I settlements were generally larger than those of the Orange Archaic period, and they occurred in a wider range of environments. They may have been occupied year round, or during the same season of each year. People began to bury some of their dead in low earth mounds, rather than in the middens associated with occupation sites, perhaps indicating a change in belief systems.

People of the St. Johns I period appear to have had wider trade networks throughout the southeastern United States, exchanging such Florida resources as marine shell and alligator teeth for exotic materials (mica, copper, greenstone) and pottery from outside the area. Most archaeologists think that some plant cultivation–perhaps grasses, beans and squashes - may have taken place during the St. Johns I period, but it seems to have been a relatively minor addition to the basic pattern of hunting-and-gathering lifestyle. Cultivation may have supported some population stability, but there is so far no archaeological evidence that it was a major economic contribution.

The principal defining archaeological characteristic of the St. Johns cultural tradition is the production and use of St. Johns pottery: a smooth, chalky-textured ceramic that is much thinner, harder and more durable that the earlier Orange Fiber tempered pottery. Some of the early St. Johns pottery is decorated with designs that are very similar to those used earlier on Orange Period ware, and most archaeologists believe that the changes introduced in the St. Johns period represent local developments rather than the arrival of a new group of people. Wetland sites (both freshwater and estuarine) continued to be the principal areas of habitation, and the focus on fish and shellfish continued as the dietary base (although

Orange period pottery. Courtesy of Florida Museum of Natural History.

the periwinkle shells so frequent on Orange period sites were no longer used in a major way by St. Johns period people).

St. Johns I society persisted in this area for 1,250 years, until about AD 750 - 800. At about that time, archaeologists recognize an elaboration and intensification of some cultural practices, but not an abrupt change. The St. Johns II Period was marked by the introduction of check stamping on ceramics (produced by stamping clay pots with a carved paddle before firing). Concurrently, villages became larger, more numerous and were perhaps occupied year round. Plant cultivation may have intensified, but although corn was introduced to the region during this period, it does not seem to have become a major part of the St. Augustine Timucuan diet until sometime after AD 1400.

During the St. Johns II period burial mounds became much larger and were used over longer periods of time, and individual burials (including children) were treated differentially–some were accompanied by specialized and valuable grave goods, others were not, and some people were buried in the middens at village sites. This implies increased social inequality–elites with inherited special privileges and others without them.

St. Johns Pottery. Courtesy of Florida Museum of Natural History.

During the later St. Johns II period (from about AD 800 until the early sixteenth century) Indians throughout much of the greater Southeastern United States were engaged in a phenomenon known as the "Mississippian" culture. Mississippian in general refers to a complex of centralized ceremonial earthworks and temple mounds, a set of ritual symbols found on shell, pottery, wood, and copper artifacts, wide-ranging trade networks and intensified corn agriculture.[12] The symbolic and ritual aspects of the Mississippian tradition were practiced across a variety of local cultural traditions, however they are largely absent in the Saltwater Timucua area. Archaeologists have speculated that the isolation from major riverine (and therefore transportation and communication) systems and the absence of land that could support intensive corn agriculture may have been factors in this absence.

Some nearby St. Johns II Timucua groups did construct platform mounds and earthworks upon which special structures were built as temples or residences for chiefs, although these are quite small compared to those in the classic Mississippian sites. None have been recorded in the vicinity of St. Augustine. Mound and earthwork complexes in Duval, Putnam, and Volusia counties all have close proximity to the St. Johns River, and they contain ritual symbology and exotic goods (mica, galena, greenstone, copper) typical of the Mississippian tradition. These mound complexes probably served as centralized regional ritual centers for the surrounding areas, and possibly as centers for trade.[13]

Like the earlier Orange period village sites, St. Johns sites in the St. Augustine vicinity are most commonly shell middens. During the late prehistoric St. Johns period however, small scattered shell midden deposits, perhaps reflecting households, are more common. Discrete shell midden sites measuring from 10 to 20 square meters in area are dispersed for several miles to the north and south of the present day city along the intracoastal waterways. Little is known archaeologically about how these occupation areas were internally organized, or whether they were parts of villages with a shared public area. Not only has there been only limited study of these sites, but many of them have also been destroyed by modern development. The occupation middens are known, however, to contain buildings, cooking and trash pits, and both human and dog burials .

One of the best-preserved and extensively investigated Timucua settlement areas in St. Augustine is the Fountain of Youth Park Site (FOY) (8SJ31) and the waterfront areas to the north of the present day tourist attraction.[14] Excavations at the Fountain of Youth Park site have revealed two principal oyster shell middens separated by an open, relatively refuse-free and shell-free area about 45 meters in diameter. The open area was probably a central plaza or public space. The middens and open space cover an area of approximately 75 meters north to south, 50 meters east to west, and extend from 25 to 50 centimeters in depth (the depth and configuration of the midden may have been altered by modern farming activities and flood-related soil erosion). The shell middens were initially deposited around AD 900, and were occupied from that time until the arrival of Pedro Menéndez in 1565.

Houses were located around the plaza, at the inner edge of the midden itself. These were circular or oval post-and-thatch buildings, averaging four meters in diameter, although two structures opposite one another across the plaza are some nine meters in diameter. Sixteenth-and seventeenth-century accounts describe large council houses in many large villages, often capable of sheltering hundreds of people; however, such a structure has not yet been found at the Fountain of Youth Park site or elsewhere in St. Augustine.

Hearths and trash pits were most often located outside of buildings, although examples of hearths and cooking pits have been documented inside houses. The Timucua at the village principally used and made St. Johns chalky-ware pottery, but ceramics made by people from interior Florida and what is today the Georgia coast are also present. This indicates that the St. Augustine Timucua had at least limited exchange relationships with Indian groups in those distant areas, possibly exchanging shell and shell items for stone or other non-locally available goods. Dozens of shell beads, awls, scrapers, hammers and picks have been recovered from the site, many in partially finished production stages. Several Timucuan dogs have been excavated from the Fountain of Youth Park site and

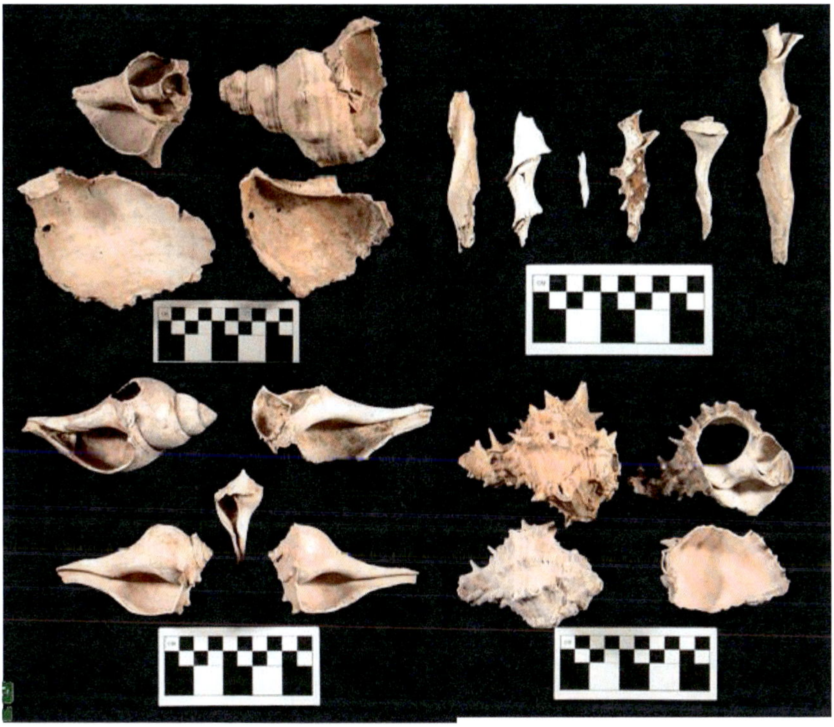

Shell tools. Courtesy of Florida Museum of Natural History.

the surrounding area dating to between about AD 900 and 1100. The dogs were carefully buried in pits, with no indication that they served as food or as work animals. They rather appear to have been pets or companions.

Food remains from the site show that fish and shellfish were the major staples of the diet, accounting for 85 percent of the meat weight. The sizes and quantity of fish bone at sites of the period suggest that most were caught using such mass capture methods as nets and weirs. Small mammals, birds, turtles, reptiles, and deer were also caten. A few plants such as squash, beans, and corn were cultivated, but made up only 19 percent of all recovered plant remains. The rest were wild fruits and nuts. Farming, although practiced, does not seem to have been become an important part of the Saltwater Timucuan diet until after about AD 1400, when corn cultivation began.[15] Timucua hunting and fighting were done with bows and arrows, using small triangular arrowheads made from

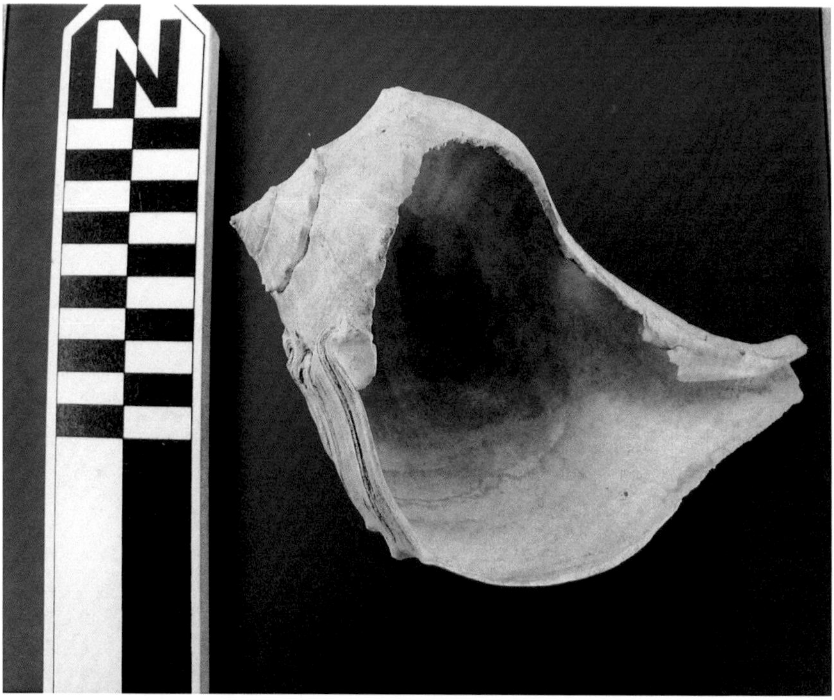

Busycon shell cup made by the Timucuans and used by the Spanish. Courtesy of Florida Museum of Natural History.

chert, as well as sharpened bone and shell. Timucua arrows were described later by the Spaniards as extremely powerful, penetrating brigandine (body armor or scales or plates) and chain mail armor.

The first Spaniards of St. Augustine under Pedro Menéndez had a number of occasions on which to experience Timucan weaponry. Their intial 1565 settlement was established at a village in territory under the control of Seloy, a local cacique subject to Saturiwa. Hostilities between the Spaniards and Seloy's Timucua quickly developed, and nine months later in 1566, the Indians forced the settlers to abandon the first settlement and move across the Matanzas River to the relative safety of Anastasia Island.

Saturiwa was a bitter enemy of the Spaniards, and remained violently hostile well after other Timucua caciques had come to terms with Menéndez. For six years hostilities or the threat thereof governed relations between the Saltwater Timucua and the Spaniards. It was not, apparently, until 1572 that the Saltwater Timucua in the St. Augustine region were either sufficiently peaceable or sufficiently vanquished by disease and warfare to allow the Spaniards to move back to the mainland and establish St. Augustine in an area south of the downtown plaza.[16].

Christianity and Change

The Spanish goal of converting Florida's native people to Catholicism was the most profound influence shaping Timucua life after 1565. Starting in 1567, Jesuit missionaries had briefly and unsuccessfully attempted to convert the Calusa people of South Florida and the Guale people of coastal South Carolina. Native resistance to their presence caused them to abandon their efforts in 1570 and leave La Florida. It was not until 1587 that a formal mission was established among the Timucua. That year the Franciscan mission of Nombre de Dios was founded at an Indian town just north of the Spanish settlement. The community of Nombre de Dios was led in 1600 by Cacica Doña Maria, who was a Christian, and was married to a Spanish soldier. Her mother had been Cacica before her, and was also a Christian. From the earliest days of Spanish colonization, intermarriage between Indian women and Spanish men took place, and native practices had considerable influence on household life in St. Augustine. Nombre de Dios persisted as a mission at St. Augustine until the end of the first Spanish period in 1763, although it had moved at least three times over the course of its 176 year history, particularly as English raids on St. Augustine increased during the eighteenth century.

As missions were established throughout the frontier of La Florida during the seventeenth century, the Timucua became organized through their own caciques and the mission friars to provide food and labor for the Spaniards in St. Augustine. Non-elite Indians from the mission communities were obliged to serve labor drafts of several months in St. Augustine building fortifications and growing food, and were an ever-present part of the town's population.[17]

The establishment of Charleston by the English, along with anti-Spanish revolts by mission Indians and shifts in internal politics among non-Christian Indians all combined by the late seventeenth century to make the Spanish mission system unstable. Threatened

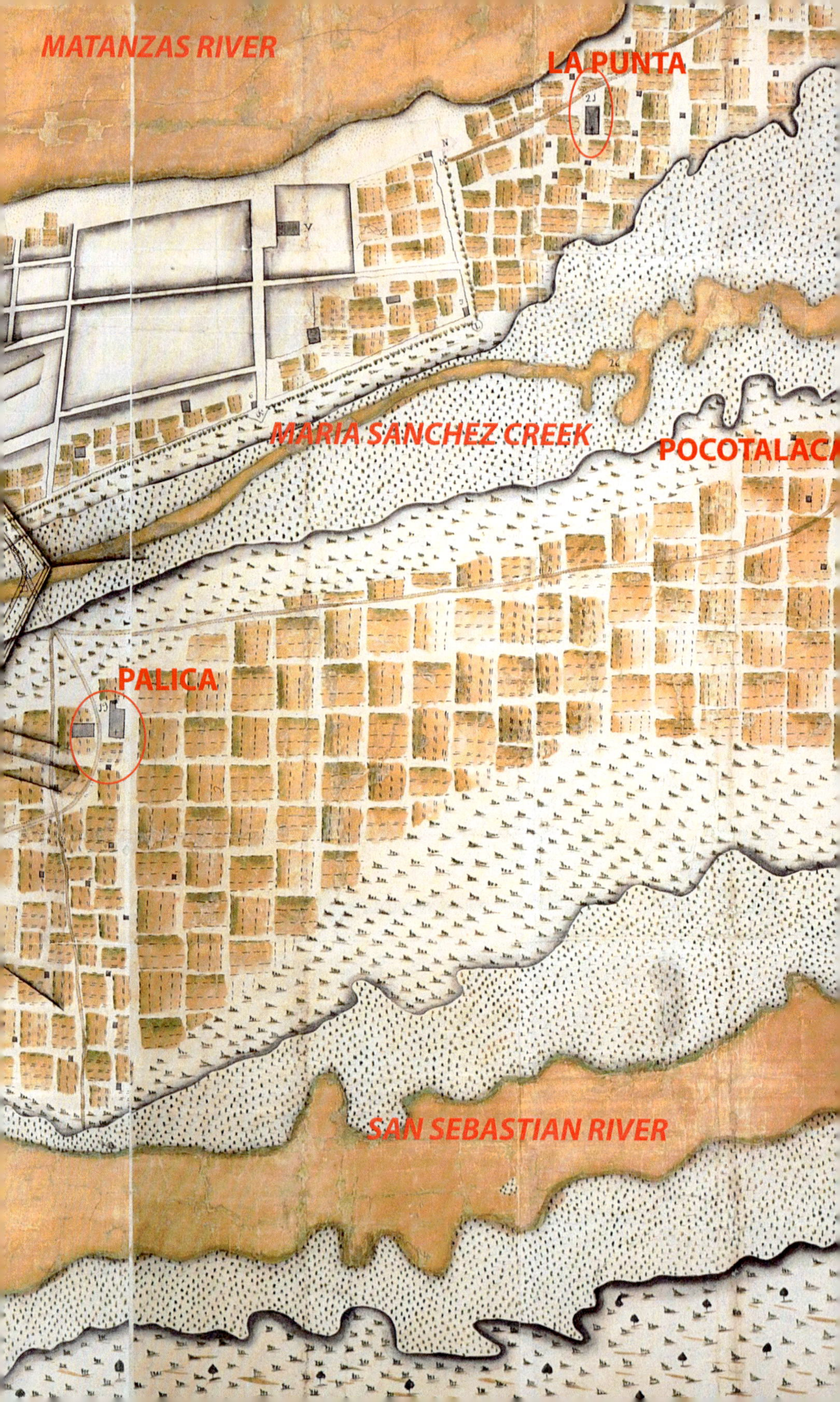

MATANZAS RIVER
LA PUNTA
MARIA SANCHEZ CREEK
POCOTALACA
PALICA
SAN SEBASTIAN RIVER

by the English and their Indian allies, mission communities in Georgia gradually relocated toward St. Augustine. In 1702 and1704 the entire frontier mission system was attacked and essentially destroyed by Colonel James Moore of South Carolina, intent on capturing slaves and cattle.

Christian Indians from the entire mission frontier region found refuge in St. Augustine. Refugees included Saltwater Timucua, Mocama and Potano Timucua, Guales, Apalachees, Yamasees, Mayacas, Ais, Jororos, and others. Those Indians not assimilated into Spanish society lived together in several small mission communities on the outskirts of the Spanish town. Some mission communities consisted of dispersed farmsteads with a nearby church and occasionally a strong house or *casa fuerte* for defense. Others were not much more than clusters of houses close to the fort. These refugee sites represented the last vestiges of the once-extensive Franciscan mission system.

The Antonio Arredondo Map of 1737 illustrated six mission communities on the outskirts of the Spanish town: Nombre de Dios, Ais, Tolomato, Palica, Pocotolaca, and La Punta. The most intensively investigated (and one of the largest) of these eighteenth-century mission communities is *Nuestra Señora del Rosario de la Punta* (Our Lady of the Rosary at the Point) located on the St. Augustine peninsula south of the colonial city. Spanish census figures for La Punta between 1736 and 1752 indicate that there were between 34 and 62 people living at the mission community. Most of them were Yamassee Indian refugees. The 1737 map shows the La Punta mission community as consisting of 20 farmsteads dispersed over approximately 30 acres.[18] Farmsteads included structures following both Native American (circular) and European (rectangular) architectural styles. A well house covering a large barrel well was found near a cluster of structures.

A small church and cemetery were centered within the La Punta occupation area The church measured 46 feet (east-west) by

RIGHT: Detail of the southern end of St. Augustine in 1737, showing mission communities. *Plano de San Agustín de la Florida y su entorno.* Archivo General de Indias, MP-FLORIDA_LUISIANA, 40.

27 feet (north-south), with possibly as many as 75 burials interred under the church floor. These burials were positioned with their feet directed toward the altar and their heads toward the church entry at the east, looking toward the altar. These were most likely shroud burials as no evidence for coffins or burial goods was recovered.

La Punta mission village as drawn by Elsbeth K. Gordon. With permission.

One man in his thirties was buried outside the northeast corner of the church. He was oriented in a northeast to southwest direction and was the only burial accompanied by grave goods, including a stone celt (a small ax), and a necklace of carved shell beads. This suggests that he may not have been converted to Christianity when he died. A small pit containing the remains of four piglet hooves was found 12 feet east of the church roughly at the midpoint of the eastern wall. What this pit may have represented is unclear; however it undoubtedly had cultural relevance and symbolic importance to the mission population.

Eighteenth-century Spanish documents frequently portrayed the Native Americans at these mission communities as living in a state of drunkenness, spiritual decadence, and more interested in hunting and waging war than in farming. The extent to which this actually described the mission Indians is unclear, but the English attacks, relocation to a strange place, and disease outbreaks must have caused serious cultural and social disruption. The archaeological record reveals a community adapting to Spanish culture while maintaining aspects of their traditional lifeways. Architecture and burial practices, for example, showed elements of both cultures, while diet was principally governed by traditional foodways.[19]

The Exodus

By 1759 the effects of relocation and diseases--exacerbated by the consolidation of many groups near the Spanish town--had reduced the Native American population of these mission settlements to 95 people living in two villages: Nombre de Dios and Tolomato. Only seven Timucua speakers had survived. Four years later, in 1763, Spain ceded Florida to the British in exchange for Havana, which had been captured by Great Britian during the Seven Years War. All of the remaining 89 Indians in St. Augustine agreed to emigrate to Cuba along with the rest of the town residents rather than remain under Protestant British rule. It had been 198 years since the Timucua first encountered Pedro Menéndez de Avilés, and although much of the Spaniards' survival was due to adopting Indian practices, the consequences of encounter had been disastrous for the Timucua. No descendants of the original Timucua inhabitants remain in Florida today.

NOTES

1 A summary of the Spanish explorations in Florida before 1565 is provided in Michael Gannon, "First European Contacts," in *The History of Florida*, ed. Michael Gannon (Gainesville: University Press of Florida, 2013), 18-40.

2 For more in-depth information about the French enterprise in Florida see John T. McGrath, *The French in Early Florida: In the Eye of the Hurricane* (Gainesville: University Press of Florida, 2000); Charles Bennett, *Three Voyages*. (Tuscaloosa: University of Alabama Press,1968).

3 General sources for the Timucua include John Hann, A *History of the Timucua Indians and their Missions* (Gainesville: University Press of Florida, 1996); Jerald T. Milanich, *The Timucua* (New York : Blackwell Press, 1996); John Worth, *The Timucuan Chiefdoms of Spanish Florida* (Gainesville: University Press of Florida, 1998).

4 For a compilation of these descriptions see John Hann, *A History of the Timucua Indians,* 21-26.

5 The complete series of De Bry engravings from Le Moyne's Fort Caroline paintings can be seen in Paul Hulton, *The Work of Jacques Le Moyne de Morgues: A Huguenot Artist in France and Florida*, 2 vols. (London: British Museum Publications, 1977). For more information about Le Moyne and his paintings see Miles Harvey, *Painter in a Savage Land: The Strange Saga of the First European Artist in North America* (New York: Random House, 2008).

6 Critique of the engravings' accuracy is found in Jerald Milanich, "The Devil in the Details," *Archaeology* 58 (3) (May 2005). Stable URL: http://archive.archaeology.org/0505/abstracts/florida.html, accessed 7/15/2014.

7 Kathleen Deagan, *Timucua 1580: Research and Exhibit Plan for a 1580 Timucua Village near St. Augustine, Florida* (St. Augustine: St. Augustine Foundation, Inc., 1979).

8 Some basic sources for prehistory in the Saltwater Timucua region include John Goggin, *Space and Time Perspective in Northern St. Johns Archaeology, Florida.* Yale University Publications in Anthropology 47 (New Haven: Yale University Press, 1952); Jerald T. Milanich, *The Archaeology of Precolumbian Florida* (Gainesville: University Press of Florida, 1994).

9 "8SJ32", for example, is the Florida Master Site File number for The Shell Bluff Landing Site. "8"refers to Florida (8th state in alphabetical order), "SJ" to St. Johns County, and "32" to the 32nd site to be recorded in that county. The Fountain of Youth Site is 8SJ31.

10 Randy V. Bellomo, "Archaeological Investigations at the Summer Haven Site (8SJ46), an Orange Period and St. Johns Period Midden Site in Southeastern St. Johns County, Florida," Florida Department of Transportation. District Two, (St. Petersburg, FL: Janus Research, 1995).

11 Michel Russo, *Archaic Shell Rings of the Southeast. U.S. National Historic Landmarks Historic Context Study* (Tallahassee: Southeast Archaeological Center, 2002). http://www.nps.gov/nhl/learn/themes/ArchaicShellRings.pdf, accessed 6/16/2014.

12 For more information about Florida Indian expressions of the Mississippian tradition, see Keith Ashley and Nancy White eds., *Late Prehistoric Florida: Archaeology at the Edge of the Mississippian World* (Gainesville: University Press of Florida, 2012).

13 See Milanich, *Archaeology of Precolumbian Florida,* 169-272; and Keith Ashley, "Early St. Johns II Interaction Exchange and Politics," in Ashley and White, eds., *Late Prehistoric Florida,* 100-125.

14 Summaries of the excavations at the Fountain of Youth Park can be found in Kathleen Deagan, *Fifty Years of Archaeology at the Fountain of Youth Park site (8-SJ-31). St. Augustine* (Florida Museum of Natural History Miscellaneous Project Report Series # 59. University of Florida, Gainesville, 2008), http://www.flmnh.ufl.edu/histarch/foy_site_reports.htm, accessed 6/20/2014.

15 Ashley and White, eds., *Late Prehistoric Florida.*

16 See Eugene Lyon, Chapter 2, this volume

17 See Bushnell, Chapter 3, this volume.

18 Andrea P. White, "Living on the Periphery: A Study of an Eighteenth-Century Yamasee Mission Community in Colonial St. Augustine" (MA thesis, The College of William and Mary in Virginia, 2002).

19 Ibid.

LA FLORIDA
DE MEXICO

2

On the Edge of History: The Oldest City

1565 - 1600

Eugene Lyon

Rivalries, intrigues and deceits, devotion, daring and sacrifice all played a part in the founding of the city of St. Augustine. Thus did Pedro Menéndez de Avilés leave his mark on the history of the United States and of the world.

Menéndez was the first to succeed in establishing a permanent settlement in North America—St. Augustine, Florida. A long line of failed would-be conquerors preceded him--Juan Ponce de León, Lucas Vázquez de Ayllón, Pánfilo de Narváez, Hernando de Soto, Father Cáncer de Barbastro,Tristán de Luna, Ángel de Villafañe, and the second Lucas Vázquez de Ayllón.

Menéndez was a lifelong seaman and a native of Asturias, Spain, who headed a coterie of affiliated Asturian families.[1] As Menéndez advanced in standing with the king of Spain, he came to command several Spanish fleets that sailed between Spain and the West Indies. By early 1565, he was negotiating for a license from the crown to conquer *La Florida*. On March 20, he and Philip II signed an agreement framed as an *adelantamiento,*[2] which was a system in which conqueror-settlers would bear the main costs of their endeavors in return for titles, benefits and revenues shared with the crown.

LEFT: Portrait in ceramic tile of Pedro Menéndez de Avilés.
Tile portrait is located on east wall of Webb Building, 18 St. Francis Street (Oldest House complex). Created by Manuel Real Alarcón in Valencia, Spain, in 1958 for the St. Augustine Historical Society and arrived at SAHS in August of 1959. Photograph by James Quine, 2014.

Menéndez agreed to sail his new 900-ton galleass, *San Pelayo*, to Florida along with ten other vessels with one hundred farmers and other armed and skilled men and sailors. Upon arrival, Menéndez was to explore the coasts of La Florida--from St. Joseph's Bay (in the Florida panhandle) around the Florida Keys to Newfoundland. He was to found two or three towns and would have ten to twelve secular priests and four Jesuits to instruct the Indians in the Catholic faith. Menéndez would receive the title of a*delantado* in perpetuity. He could choose a lieutenant and distribute lands in Florida, as long as he did not impede the rights of the Indians. His estate would be 25 leagues squared–5,500 square miles. Successful completion of his contract would entitle him to the title of marquis, which Hernán Cortés and Francisco Pizarro had enjoyed. He would have two fisheries, exemption from certain dues and taxes, and permission to put ships into the Indies trade.

Earlier, in 1562, the French rulers and Admiral Gaspard de Coligny had sent the Huguenot (French Protestant) Jean Ribault to found a colony at Port Royal in present-day South Carolina in Spanish-claimed La Floridá. In doing this, the French had ignored the Treaty of Tordesillas, which had been established by Papal Bull and agreed to by Spain and Portugal in 1494. The treaty established territorial boundaries in the Americas, with Spain given rights to lands west of an arbitrary line at approximately 45 degrees longitude, and Portugal gaining rights to land east of the line. When Ribault failed to send supplies to the Florida colonists they deserted, leaving behind just one man, Guillaume Rouffi. A Spanish search vessel found Rouffi and took him to Havana.[3] But the French threat to Spain's New World possessions had not ended.

On April 22, 1564, René de Laudonnière left France with reinforcements and instead of going to Port Royal, he arrived at the mouth of the St. Johns River, which he named the River May. He built Fort Caroline upriver. The French established good relations with the Native Americans subject to Saturiba, the principal chief of the Timucuan groupings in the vicinity of present-day Mayport. Up the St. Johns River were Calibay and Utina, the latter a strong rival of Saturiba. Menéndez would describe the customs of the northeastern Florida Indians: "The ceremonies of these Indians...

are to worship the sun and moon; they have dead stags and other animals as idols. Each year they make... feasts for their devotions. ...He who is weak, who cannot suffer this, is taken for a bad Indian, and goes about scorned by the noble people. He who passes best is taken for principal and given the most courtesy. They are a people of many strengths, swift and great swimmers. They have many wars with each other, and no chief among them is recognized as powerful."[4]

Things went well for the French settlers for a short time, until the men at Fort Caroline mutinied. Eleven men seized a small boat and sailed for the Caribbean. On December 18, 1564, 70 more mutineers held Laudonnière hostage, took two small ships and sailed south. After raiding Hispaniola and Cuba, the second group was captured in Spanish Jamaica.[5] During interrogation, one of the captives, Stefan de Rougement, alleged that Pedro Menéndez's son, Juan, had been shipwrecked in 1563 near Cape Canaveral.[6]

Thus the Spanish learned about the French presence in Florida and the existence of Fort Caroline from the captured mutineers. They also found out about Jean Ribault's plans to bring reinforcements from France. The King of Spain was immediately advised about the French plans. Word was received in Seville by March 30, 1565.[7]

In the face of this news, Menéndez's approved Florida enterprise was quickly and substantially changed. First the King ordered Menéndez to keep his departure secret and to leave by the first of May. Philip II also promised to pay for 300 additional troops.[8] La Florida had become a joint venture between the King and his adelantado.

Spain's King Philip II sent a skilled spy, Dr. Gabriel de Enveja, to investigate the French ports where Ribault's reinforcement fleet was in preparation. Enveja's report was in Madrid by June 2, and was so startlingly complete that it gave Philip and Pedro Menéndez a real advantage. Enveja reported that Jean Ribault had seven ships with 900 to 1,000 persons, including soldiers, their wives and their children, many of whom were Lutherans (a general term for Protestants in the sixteenth century).[9] Ribault sailed about May 26, 1565.

The Spanish contingents left later. Pedro Menéndez's own ships sailed from the ports of Cádiz in southwest Spain, from Santander in northwest Spain and from other ports in Asturias. The Cádiz ships carried substantial supplies purchased with both royal money and through Menéndez's own account.[10] The Cádiz ships left June 27 carrying, as Menéndez claimed, 1,504 persons. The House of Trade reported only 995 persons aboard.[11] At last, the adelantado's Florida fleets were underway. He was in a desperate race to reach his goal before French rival, Jean Ribault and his reinforcement ships.

The vessels from Northern Spain, however, missed the planned rendezvous at the Canary Islands, while the Cádiz group, including the *Capitana San Pelayo*, ran into a heavy Atlantic storm. Several ships were lost. After crossing the Atlantic, the surviving vessels put into San Juan, Puerto Rico. There the namesake and descendant of Juan Ponce de León helped Menéndez obtain a ship and recruit sailors. Underway again on August 17, the adelantado reorganized his soldiery under the command of *Maestre de Campo* (second in command) Pedro de Valdés, his future son-in-law.

On August 25 or 28, depending on the source, the Spanish fleet sighted Florida at Cape Canaveral. But Jean Ribault's ships had won the race; they had already arrived at the mouth of the River May (St. Johns) and begun unloading their cargoes for Fort Caroline.

On September 4, the Spaniards arrived at the great river mouth and attacked their Huguenot enemy. The French ships cut their anchor lines, raised their sails, and sailed into the open ocean. Pedro Menéndez decided to sail southward to where he had already scouted out an inlet and harbor to prepare for a long campaign. He named that place St. Augustine. He and his men went ashore on September 8 to take formal possession of the land for the King of Spain. Menéndez had "a solemn mass said," then "had the Indians fed and dined himself." The Spanish met a Timucuan *cacique* (chief) named Seloy who gave them a longhouse which they prepared for use as a fort.[12]

Ribault's French fleet decided to give chase, to attack the Spaniards whom they found at St. Augustine. Instead a powerful storm, likely a strong northeaster, struck the French ships, driving them further south and onto shore near Cape Canaveral.

Every nautical instinct told sailor Pedro Menéndez that his enemy's fleet had been driven south, leaving Fort Caroline unprotected.[13] It was time for him to strike. Guided by a French prisoner and directed by Florida Indians, the adelantado led 500 arquebusiers and axemen from St. Augustine through tangled woods and vines in pouring rain up the North River and then across to Fort Caroline. As dawn came on September 20, the Spanish forces broke through Fort Caroline's gate and vanquished the sleeping French garrison.

The Spanish took over Fort Caroline and renamed it San Mateo. In Jean Ribault's apartment in the fort the Spanish found a strongbox containing "all his [Ribault's] papers, provisions and titles (as) Captain-General and Viceroy". There were six decrees signed by the France's Admiral Coligny.[14]

Said Menéndez: "We cut the throats of one hundred thirty-two." He had called out to spare all women and the children under fifteen years of age. Fifty were spared. Later, Menéndez noted that ten other Frenchmen had been found in the forest.[15] Jean Mennin, a young musician from La Rochelle, made a deposition to French King Charles IX's ambassador to the Spanish court, and swore that he was present at Fort Caroline when the Spaniards struck, stating: "They made a pretty butchery of it, except for a small Number, among which were the deponent, three drummers, (one from Dieppe and the other two from Rouen) and four trumpeters (three from Normandy and the other, named Jacques DuLac, from Bordeaux)."[16] Jean Ribault's son Jacques escaped and made his way back to France. Pedro de Bustinçury, a Vizcayan from Spain, escaped with Jacques Ribault during the attack. Bustinçury had been shipwrecked as a youth about twenty years earlier near Cape Canaveral and was rescued from the Ais Indians by Laudonniere in 1564. From Fort Caroline, Bustinçury made it first to France, and then escaped to the Spanish court to tell the story of Menéndez's victory over the French. He made such an impression on Philip II that he was sent back to Florida to serve Pedro Menéndez.[17]

Survivors from the French shipwrecks came to land, some to build a vessel for escape. Others began a march northward toward Fort Caroline, disbanding into several parties. On September 28, Indians told Pedro Menéndez that Frenchmen had gathered at an inlet some eighteen miles south from St. Augustine. At dawn of the next day the adelantado proceeded south with a company of men and an interpreter. At the inlet Menéndez notified the Huguenots, who were stranded on the other side of the inlet, that he had taken their fort. He said he could promise nothing if they surrendered. In the end Menéndez saved ten or twelve. The rest were killed, their throats cut. (Chaplain Mendoza Grajales said 111 died and Gonzalo Solís de Merás said there were 200 killed.) Menéndez returned to St. Augustine, only to learn that another group of Frenchmen had arrived at the inlet, this time led by Jean Ribault himself. Menéndez hurried back and was met by the French leader under a flag of truce, but Menéndez would not budge from his terms that the French must yield to the Spaniards. Ribault came across the water with his captains and 70 men. Some Frenchmen retreated back toward Cape Canaveral. Five persons were spared. Ribault and the rest were killed by the inlet, ever after called Matanzas—place of slaughters.[18]

Menéndez's actions spurred the growth of the Black Legend against Spain. In France it began with the 1566 statement of Nicholas Le Challeux, a carpenter who escaped the Spanish attack on Fort Caroline. "The treason of the Spaniards against subjects of His (French) Majesty, in the year 1565. Written in truth by those who are left. A thing so lamentable to hear, that was premeditatedly and cruelly executed by the said Spaniards against the authority of our Sire, the King, to the loss and injury of all our Kingdom."[19] Michel de Montaigne applied the epithet "barbarous minds" to Spanish torturers.[20] The Black Legend survived even into modern times. In *For Whom the Bell Tolls*, Ernest Hemingway puts the following words in the mouth of Robert Jordan: "What a people they have been. What sons of bitches, from Cortez, Pizarro, Pedro Menéndez de Ávila [sic]."[21]

Within six weeks of founding St. Augustine, Pedro Menendez had eliminated the French presence in North America—a turning point in history of the Americas and of Europe. French ships would

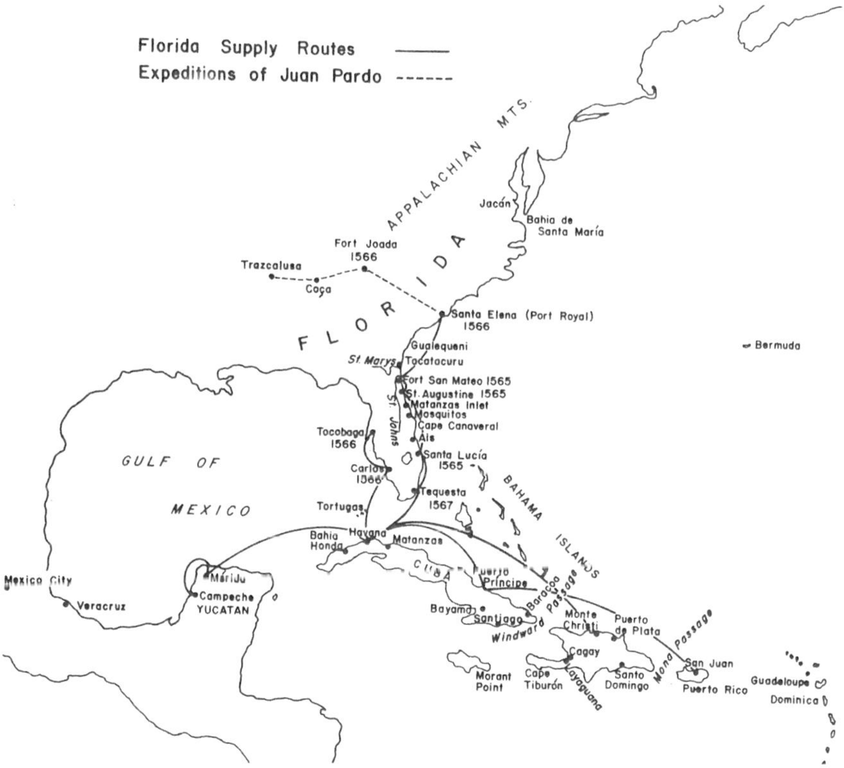

La Florida and the Caribbean c. 1565. Reprinted from Eugene Lyon, *The Enterprise of Florida: Pedro Menéndez de Avilés and the Spanish Conquest of 1565-1568* (Gainesville: University Presses of Florida, 1990), 254.

land along the coast of La Florida to trade with the Indians, but the French would make no attempts to settle in La Florida for a century to come.

With the French expelled from Florida, the adelantado advised King Philip of his next plans, which included a settlement at Santa Elena (at today's Parris Island, South Carolina). Then he sailed onward to Chesapeake Bay to seek out the key to the continent–waterways which he believed led to the Mexican mines and to the wide Pacific. Menéndez believed his mission to be to "fix our frontier lines here, gain the waterway of the Bahamas, and work the mines of New Spain."[22]

Learning that there were still a few escaped Frenchmen in Florida, Pedro Menéndez led troops by land and sea south to the French-built fort near Cape Canaveral, and promised the French their lives if they surrendered. They gave no trouble. There Pedro Menéndez met the cacique of the Ais Indians. But he found no trace of his son Juan despite the tantalizing testimony by the captured Frenchman. Leaving Captain Juan Vélez de Medrano with 200 Spaniards and 50 French prisoners behind to establish an outpost at Ais,[23] Pedro Menéndez sailed to Cuba, seeking supplies for his Florida garrisons.

Shortly after his departure half of the soldiers at Ais mutinied over lack of food and Indian hostilities. The outpost was abandoned, and a new fort was established some 45 miles south, named Santa Lucía for the saint's day on which it was founded. There too Indian attacks and starvation troubled the garrison. Artilleryman Diego López said that the garrison resorted to cannibalism, killing and eating many French prisoners.[24]

Although the adelantado learned that King Philip was sending a large reinforcement fleet to Florida,[25] until that happened, providing supplies was a major concern. Once in Cuba, Menéndez sold prize vessels for cash to send material relief to Florida. He sent a captured French small boat loaded with supplies to soldiers and French prisoners left at Ais, not knowing that the colony left at Ais had been abandoned. He also leased a Portuguese caravel and sent it to Yucatán, where corn was cheap and available, and sent two small supply vessels on to Florida.

Menéndez believed that the St. Johns River emptied into the Gulf of Mexico, thus giving free passage through the peninsula to Mexico through that route. Seeking the west end of that waterway, he sailed in February 1566 to Florida's southwest coast, passing between Half-Moon Shoals and the Dry Tortugas (islands). This route is named the Cuchiaga Passage for the nearby Indians and it became the standard route for New Spain ships sailing from Vera Cruz to Havana. The adelantado stopped at the main town of the Calusa Indians and persuaded the Calusa's main cacique to release eighteen Spanish captives, including the captive, Hernando Escalante Fontaneda, who had been imprisoned twenty years.[26] Menéndez also accepted the gift of the Indian leader's sister as a wife. The adelantado had the woman christened Doña Antonia, and

Fragments of enameled glass found at Menendez's first settlement at St. Augustine (today Fountain of Youth Park). Courtesy of Florida Museum of Natural History.

felt it politic to consummate the "marriage." Pedro Menéndez then sailed back toward St. Augustine.

On his return voyage to St. Augustine, Menéndez learned the fate of the people left at Ais, and at last, on March 19, 1566, he rescued the survivors at Santa Lucía and returned with them to St. Augustine. There he found more trouble. Mutineers, led by Sebastián de Lezcano had seized the St. Augustine fort and locked Pedro de Valdés and others inside it. The spirit of mutiny spread to Fort San Mateo. Resourceful Valdés escaped and retook the fort and city, and had Lezcano hanged.[27] Menéndez also learned that many soldiers had deserted St. Augustine and San Mateo. Menéndez was infuriated to find that "such great mutinies, disgraceful insubordinations and . . . treason" had occurred among his garrisons.[28]

After reinforcing his forces with more than 200 men from Cuba, Menéndez began an exploratory trip north. Juan López de Velasco, Royal Geographer, described the land northward as: "From the river of San Mateo the coast runs to the northeast to Santa Elena. The coast is made up entirely of great and small islands, which create many bars and inlets, so that, although it seems to be a mainland, it is not.[29] The adelantado discovered a route along the sea-islands. As he encountered Native American groups he strived to acquaint them with basic Catholic beliefs and to seek peace in the name of his King. He developed the tactic of mutually exchanging hostages. The Guale Indians, whom he met on his northward journey, were so impressed by Menéndez's devotion to Christianity that they named him "Mico Santamaría" (Holy Mary's Chief of Chiefs)[30]

Soon the Spaniards approached the point of land now called Hilton Head, but long known to them as Santa Elena, the finest harbor in La Florida, near Ribault's former fort at Port Royal. They took possession of the land for Spain. He left orders to build Fort San Salvador, promising to send supplies to his latest garrison.[31] But when he returned to St. Augustine, Menéndez found that Indian attacks and fire had destroyed the storehouse of his fort there.

Menéndez and his captains decided to move the town and fort across the river to Anastasia Island.[32] Then, while Menéndez was gone on yet another voyage to Havana, the promised Royal reinforcement fleet under Sancho de Archiniega finally arrived at St. Augustine with men and supplies. When Menéndez returned, the two leaders agreed on a division of the soldiery. The recently arrived Captain Juan Pardo was sent to Santa Elena with a company of men to strengthen that settlement, and also to undertake exploratory journeys into the interior.

Menéndez's settlers built a town at the new island site of St. Augustine with a customhouse and storehouse,[33] and a new fort.[34] The Spaniards also built a stronghouse on the western shore of the Matanzas River and another two leagues south on the eastern shore that they named San Julián.[35] In August of 1566, just four months after the move to the island, another mutiny erupted among the

Spanish garrison, also scotched by Pedro de Valdés, who hanged three of the guilty parties. Indian warfare also broke out near St. Augustine.[36] Menéndez, tired of the many mutinies in his Florida garrisons, established seventeen severe and harsh ordinances for the provinces he controlled.[37] In each fort, the city council or *cabildo* met twice a week on local government matters and to issue land grants.

Pedro Menéndez could spend little time in St. Augustine. He was continually attempting to provide adequate supplies for his outposts, explore the La Florida territory, expand settlement, and bring Christianity to the Native Americans. Menéndez planned to equip his soldiers with *escupiles*, the padded cotton armor used in New Spain and Yucatán, which were the best protection against Indian arrows. He also decided to acquire crossbows, to give his men more and faster shooting power. In late summer of 1566, Philip II sent another Florida supply shipment on the ship (urca) *Pantecras,* which carried Pedro de Bustinçury, the former shipwreck victim rescued by Laudonniere, and three Jesuits.[38] This was the beginning of the Jesuit mission to Florida.[39] He dispatched Francisco de Reinoso to Calusa territory to build a fort and mission there at Carlos.[40] The settlement at Carlos was known as San Antón de Padua, but Father Rogel, the Jesuit missionary assigned there, could accomplish little among the Calusa.

On October 20, 1566, Menéndez left on a lengthy voyage to fortify the defenses of the Spanish Caribbean.[41] He would not return to St. Augustine until May 1567. Upon his return to the continent, Menéndez travelled to Santa Elena, where he called upon Captain Juan Pardo to report on his first journey westward to the interior. Pardo had left December 1, 1566, and travelled more than 500 miles, traversing the Piedmont, to reach the Appalachian Mountains. At the foot of the Blue Ridge near present-day Morganton, North Carolina, he built Fort Joara and left a garrison. The land, reported Pardo, was rich with red clay soils and was "good for bread, wine and all kinds of livestock."[42] The adelantado prepared to continue his continental plan. First he wrote the head of the Jesuit Order, stating his (mistaken) belief that it was just 500 leagues (about 1200 miles) from Santa Elena to the Mexican mines. He vowed to build two towns along the way for forts and mission centers.[43] Then he asked the king for another license and contract to control in the area of Pánuco, north of Tampico in Mexico. He also filed a claim to his sovereign, seeking reimbursement for his heavy costs and losses in his Florida enterprise.[44] The claim was honored, and on October 24, 1567, the King named Menéndez Governor of Cuba[45] and Captain-General of a new armada for the Caribbean.[46]

Now Menéndez could proceed with more settlements in La Florida. He contracted with farmers from the province of Toledo, who each would receive passage, land-grants, twelve cows, a bull, two oxen, two mares, a dozen sheep, chickens, hogs, and goats. He agreed to furnish shoots for vineyards, a house for each family and to provide one shepherd-boy and one male and one female slave.[47] On October 7, 1568, the caravels *Nuestra Señora de la Vitoria* and *Nuestra Señora de la Concepción* sailed from Cádiz with 225 emigrants for La Florida, mostly small farmers, with wives and children, committed to remaining for two years.[48] For the most part the settlers were to go to Santa Elena, and by August 1, 1569, 193 settlers had arrived there. Soon they had built 40 houses. One house held five bachelors who had come on the same ship. Another was home to Diego Hernández, a leader among the immigrants, his wife Juana, and their eight children. A tailor, Alonso de Olmos, his wife and mother-in-law were crowded in with six children. Another house held people a cut above the others—the well-educated Dr. Juan de la Rosa, his wife Doña Antonia, three children, a nephew, and three servants. By the end of October, there were 327 people in the town of Santa Elena.[49]

Meanwhile, there were disturbances elsewhere. In the north Florida peninsula, Timucuan Indians were displaying open hostility to the Spaniards. Captain Pedro de Andrada and his 80-man company were ambushed at Potano, near present-day Gainesville, and decimated. Other Timucuans allied with the Frenchman Dominique de Gourges, who led a French expedition to Florida seeking revenge for the 1565 massacre at Ft. Caroline. On Good Friday of 1568 they attacked the blockhouses at Fort San Mateo (formerly Fort Caroline) and then burned the fort itself, hanging two Spaniards. Many of the Spanish garrison at San Mateo escaped to St. Augustine.[50] The Spaniards then determined to build a new fort-mission on Cumberland Island, to guard better the route from St. Augustine to Santa Elena. The old fort San Mateo could be abandoned.

In South Florida, the missions at Tequesta, Tocobaga, and Carlos were also abandoned around this time, and the Jesuit effort shifted north, near Santa Elena. Meanwhile, Captain Pardo had made a second expedition to the north, but by June of 1568 news came of the abandonment and death of soldiers in Pardo's inland forts.[51] Captain Pardo had renewed his garrisons at Joara and Guatari, the latter near present-day Hickory, North Carolina, and had reached Trascaluza (near present day Montgomery, Alabama), which marked for him the western boundary of the adelantado's jurisdiction. From there, he mistakenly believed, it was only nine to eleven days' travel to New Spain. Actually, it was more than a thousand miles from Trascaluza to the nearest point in New Spain. This was Menéndez's worst geographic foreshortening of continental distances.

Father Juan Rogel could see the obstacles to the success of the Florida enterprise: Spanish soldiers had treated the Indians badly, demanding their food and abusing their women. But the Jesuit failed to understand that exclusive acceptance of Christianity implied a complete change in Indian life, totally altering their culture. At last, Father Rogel realized that his mission had failed and he moved into Santa Elena.[52] In August of 1570, Jesuit Father Juan Bautista de Segura led an eight-man mission to the Chesapeake, probably near present-day Yorktown, Virginia, guided by Don Luis de Velasco, a Christianized Indian who had been taken to Spain and returned with the Jesuits. But Velasco deserted the Spaniards and led his own people in a massacre of the Jesuits–only one boy escaped. After this, the Florida Jesuit mission ended, citing Indian hostility, the Indians' reluctance to settle in Christian communities, and the greed and cruelty of Spanish soldiers.

In 1571 Phillip II made a decision that would impact Spanish Florida and St. Augustine until 1821. The king agreed to provide a royal subsidy (situado) to maintain the royal troops. He acknowledged the difficulties in Florida and that Menendez had expended his own funds to maintain the troops.[53] Shortly after that, Pedro Menéndez moved to his capital, Santa Elena, with his wife, Doña María de Solís, his two daughters and their families, along with their servants and luxurious household goods.[54]

For a few years the importance of Santa Elena would eclipse St. Augustine. From Santa Elena sarsaparilla root gathered with Indian labor was shipped to Spain.[55] Oak and cedar were also exported, and the southeastern fur trade took root for a while at Santa Elena in the sixteenth century. Bartolomé Martín, said "in Santa Elena, I have planted with my own hands grapevines, pomegranates, orange trees and figs, wheat, barley, onions, garlic and...many vegetables."[56]

The residents in St. Augustine and Santa Elena took part in the regular worship, feast days and processions of the Tridentine Roman Catholic Church. The church in both towns was a plain enough structure. The church at Santa Elena had rich furnishings: a painted retable displaying a gilded crucified Christ, the image of Santa Clara, an embossed leather canopy and frontal, fine linen altar-cloths, altarware and costly vestments. The Confraternity of the True Cross comforted the sick and buried the dead.[57]

Things did not go well in either town. In 1571, an English raider, Sir William Winter, attacked St. Augustine but was driven off.[58] Sometime in the year 1572, St. Augustine was moved from Anastasia Island to the mainland. The new mainland location of the city was laid out according to royal regulations. The oldest part of St. Augustine, just south of the plaza (town square), still reflects the street grid established in the late 1500s.[59]

Santa Elena's glory days would be short-lived. In 1573, settlers at Santa Elena complained that Indian hostilities prevented them from expanding their planting and livestock. Indian dissatisfaction plagued Spanish settlements. Pedro Menéndez traveled to Madrid to complain of warlike acts of the Florida Indians all the way from the Florida Keys to Santa Elena. He asked the Crown for the right to capture those enemy Indians and sell them as slaves to the Caribbean Islands. The King refused the petition. It was an important decision. Future kings of Spain would maintain the same position against enslaving Indians in Florida.[60]

King Philip called Pedro Menéndez de Avilés to greater service. In 1574, he was sent to Santander to prepare a large armada of 150 ships and 12,000 men to serve in the English Channel and Flanders. About that time, the Florida adelantado wrote a poignant letter to his nephew, Pedro Menéndez Marquez, in which he recounted his urgent wish to return to Florida and the King's approval to do so in the spring. He then stated that, after the salvation of his soul, he had no greater wish than to end his days in Florida saving (Indian) souls.[61] Then tragically, the typhus running rampant through his ships struck its leader and on September 17, he died.

He left a truly entangled inheritance. The adelantado's only son Juan had died at sea and his favorite daughter Ana was murdered in Asturias in 1568. Another daughter María, a professed nun in Avilés, had renounced her family inheritance. Thus his heirs were his two daughters, Catalina and an illegitimate daughter María. Both were married to noblemen. Like Henry VIII of England, Pedro Menéndez was obsessed with the continuation of his family name and legacy. To ensure that, he signed dower contracts with his two sons-in-law, obligating them to serve in Florida.[62]

Menéndez's sons-in-law would vie for control of La Florida. The two men and their respective supporters levied charges to discredit the other.[63] Catalina's husband, Hernando de Miranda, was quick to claim the top Florida offices and moved there after the death of his father-in-law. This put him in direct competition with María's husband, Diego de Velasco, who had been in charge until then. Although Menéndez had favored Velasco over Miranda, Velasco was a man of temper and pride and had treated the people of Santa Elena harshly. He ordered the tailor Alonso de Olmos and the *cabildo* (city council) secretary Francisco Ruiz to work with other men to rebuild the fort, which had burned. When they refused, he ordered them hung, but the priest intervened and the men worked on the fort in chains, instead.[64]

Another incident involving Governor Velasco disclosed much about the social structure of the Spanish colony. Upon leaving church at Santa Elena on May 8, 1576, the Velasco party met Olmos' daughter, whom the Governor felt was putting herself above her station by intruding into the procession. He called her a "proven bitch," and called out to Olmos with religious insults, "See the Lutheran going to the synagogue!" The tailor sued the Governor for slander.[65] But at least Velasco had followed Pedro Menéndez's lead. He had given gifts to the Native Americans in Orista and Guale.

When Hernando de Miranda arrived and took over the governorship, he indicted and jailed Diego de Velasco. He allied himself with Pedro Menéndez the Younger, the adelantado's nephew and the colony's Treasurer, with a view to mutual profit. Miranda also neglected to provide regular gifts to the Indians, and condoned their mistreatment by soldiers. The Guale, Orista and Escamazu tribes joined in confederation against the Spaniards.[66] Consequently, 1576 became a year of continual stress. First, an expedition commanded by Sergeant Hernando de Moyano went to Escamazu seeking food, and the natives wiped out all but one man. Then, in Guale, all three finance ministers, including Treasurer Pedro Menéndez the Younger, and an interpreter were killed by Indians. Finally, the Indians moved onto the island of Santa Elena itself.[67] As the Indians surrounded the town and fort, they set fire to Santa Elena. The Spanish women, many of whom were recent widows, forced Hernando de Miranda to take two small boats and evacuate to St. Augustine. St. Augustine again became the capital of La Florida.

From St. Augustine, the royal inspector notified the king that Hernando de Miranda had deserted his post.[68] The king resolved the situation with a momentous decision. A royal order named Pedro Menéndez Marquez to be Governor of Florida, but not adelantado. Menéndez's proprietary government of Florida ended on March 22, 1577.

French and English ships landed along La Florida's Atlantic coast, violating Spanish territorial claims. In December 1576, Nicolas Strozzi, cousin to the French Queen Mother, brought his ship *Le Prince* to the Santa Elena harbor entrance. Indians in the area welcomed the French. When Governor Menéndez Marquez learned of this, he mounted retaliatory expeditions in Guale and Santa Elena, attacking and burning the Indian towns that had collaborated with the French. He captured Captain Strozzi and took him to St. Augustine for execution.[69] Menéndez Marquéz decided to rebuild the burnt fort and town of Santa Elena. The town soon had a church and more than thirty houses.[70]

In April 1584, Walter Raleigh's advance fleet departed England for the West Indies and left a colony on Roanoke Island, North Carolina. The disappearance of those colonists still puzzles. Englishman Sir Francis Drake, having sacked Spanish Santo Domingo (Dominican Republic), headed for Florida. He arrived at St. Augustine June 6, 1586, with 41 ships and put 2,000 men ashore. At this, the St. Augustinians retreated into the woods while the English captured the fort and sacked and burned the town. But Drake departed and St. Augustine remained Spanish. The impact of Drake's Caribbean sweep and his burning of St. Augustine led to the second and final abandonment of Santa Elena on August 16, 1587.[71]

Baptista Boazio, *Augustini: pars est terra Florida, sub latitudine 30 grad, ora vero maritima humilior est, lancinata et insulosa,* 1589. Hans and Hanni Kraus Sir Francis Drake Collection, Library of Congress, https://www.loc.gov/maps/?fa=contributor%3Aboazio%2C+baptista.

With the death of Pedro Menéndez Marquez in 1594, the Menéndez family no longer controlled the governorship of Florida. Domingo Martínez de Avendaño succeeded him, but died in office on November 25, 1595. The new governor, Gonzalo Méndez Canzo, appointed on March 22, 1596, was born in Tapia de Casariego on the Asturian border with Galicia. On his way to his post he had a friendly meeting with the cacique of the Ais. But, when Canzo sent soldier Juan Ramírez Contreras to Ais on a peace mission, the Indians killed him. His tearful widow asserted that "they drink from his skull."[72]

Méndez Canzo had a vision to expand Spanish Florida to the northwest to an area in to present-day Georgia. But a rebellion, fostered in Guale by an Indian leader named Juanillo, upset the Governor's plan. Five missionaries were killed in a rebel attack on Franciscan missions. The Governor reacted vigorously, quelling the insurrection, and many native leaders came to St. Augustine to swear allegiance to the King. But the ongoing problems and disputes over Florida had now led to a full-blown investigation into the colony's viability. Testimony, at times quite heated, was heard in St. Augustine in 1602.[73]

In the end, however, St. Augustine survived. Forty-four years after the founding of St. Augustine, the Spanish established Santa Fe (New Mexico); forty-two years after the founding of St. Augustine, English colonists settled Jamestown (Virginia); fifty-five years after the founding of St. Augustine, the Plymouth colony (Massachusetts) was settled. Today St. Augustine, established in 1565, still remains a living and vibrant city.

NOTES

1 The close-knit band of Asturian families, which governed Spanish Florida, is described in Lyon, "The Control Structure of Spanish Florida," unpublished paper (St. Augustine Restoration Foundation, 1979).

2 A signed copy of the contract for Florida is found in Archivo General de Indias (hereafter AGI), *Escribanía de Cámara* (hereafter EC) 1024-A. Many other copies exist in Spanish archives. See Roscoe R. Hill, "The Office of Adelantado," *Political Science Quarterly* 28, No. 4 (December 1913): 645-68.

See Eugene Lyon, *he Enterprise of Florida: Pedro Menéndez de Avilés and the Spanish Conquest of 1565-1568 (Gainesville: University Presses of Florida, 1974), 213-219, for a translation of the contract.*

[3] See "Report on the French who went to populate Florida," Governor to Crown, Havana, July 9, 1564, AGI *Santo Domingo* (hereafter SD) 99.

[4] Pedro Menéndez to a Jesuit friend at Cádiz, St. Augustine, October 15, 1566, from Eugenio Ruidiaz y Caravía, *La Florida: Su conquista y colonización por Pedro Menéndez de Avilés* (Madrid: Imprenta de los hijos de J.A. García, 1893-94) 2: 155-156.

[5] See "Información of Governor Blas de Merlo," AGI *Justicia* (hereafter JU) 212

[6] See AGI *Patronato* (hereafter PAT) 19, No.1, *ramo* 14

[7] House of Trade to Crown, Seville, March 26, 1565, in AGI *Contratación* (hereafter CT) 5167, Book III.

[8] Crown to Pedro Menéndez, Madrid, March 30, 1565, AGI EC 1024-A.

[9] This key report has been printed in full by Antonio Tibesar, ed., "A Spy's Report on the Expedition of Jean Ribault to Florida, 1565.' It comes from the archives of the Real Academia de la Historia (Madrid), No. 9-30-3:6271. See also Eugene Lyon, "Les armes secrètes de Pedro Menéndez," *Floride, un rêve français ((1562-1565)*; eds. Mikaël Aueron, John DeBry, and Annick Notter (La Rochelle: Musée du Monde Nouvelle, 2012).

[10] "Supplies, arms, artillery and munitions that the said Adelantado Pedro Menéndez carries for account of that which he is obligated. . . " AGI EC 1024-A, fol. 23-24,

[11] Menéndez claimed that he had brought his fleet back to Cádiz, anchored offshore and ferried out many additional men. See "Información ante Alcalde deste Corte," Madrid, October 16, 1567, in AGI EC 1024-A

[12] It is now generally accepted that the landing-place of Pedro Menéndez in 1565 was on the property now occupied by the Fountain of Youth attraction. See Kathleen Deagan, "2008 Fifty Years of Archaeology at the Fountain of Youth Park site (8-SJ-31). St. Augustine," *Florida Museum of Natural History Miscellaneous Project Reports in Archaeology* # 59 (Gainesville: University of Florida, 2008). http://www.flmnh.ufl.edu/histarch/foy_site_reports.htm.

[13] Pedro Menéndez said as much in his letter to his King written from St.

Augustine on October 15, 1565, from AGI SD 231. Moreover, it had taken him two days to march from St. Augustine to Fort Caroline through a continual storm of wind and rain, while the French ships further south, were also in a storm This sounds more like a northeaster than a hurricane.

[14] See "La Florida," *Envío* 25-H, No. 162, Archivo del Instituto de Don Juan (Madrid). In this, Philip II describes the finding of the strongbox to Guzmán de Silva, his Ambassador to London. His letter is from Archivo General de Simancas *Estado* (hereafter ES) 819. All these things are lost to modern times.

[15] See Pedro Menéndez to Crown, St. Augustine, trans. Edward W. Lawson (St. Augustine, 1955), typescript, 223-224. See also Eugene Lyon, "Captives of Florida" *Florida Historical Quarterly* 50, No. 1(July, 1971) 1-24.

[16] "Lettres et papiers d'estat de Fourquevaux," in Paul Gaffarel, *Histoire de la Floride Française* (Paris: Firmin-Didot et Cie, 1875), p.445.

[17] See Ambassador Fourquevaulx, "Lettres et papiers d'état de Fourquevaulx" in Gaffarel, *Histoire de la Floride Française*, 417, 421. See also AGI *Contaduría* (hereafter CD) 941, "*Los Viejos*."

[18] See Pedro Menéndez to Crown, St. Augustine, October 15, 1565, from AGI SD 231. Menéndez held three captured French noblemen for ransom.

[19] Nicholas Le Challeux, *Discourse de l'histoire de la Floride* (Dieppe, 1566)

[20] *Montaigne's Essays: John Florio's Translation,* ed., J.I.M. Stewart (London, 1921) 2:317.

[21] Ernest Hemingway, *For Whom the Bell Tolls (*New York: Charles Scribner & Sons, 1940), 354.

[22] See Pedro Menéndez to Crown, October 15, 1565. Menéndez had no way of knowing that his ship *San Pelayo*, sent away for safety during the first days of arrival at St. Augustine, had been hijacked by English "heretics," sailed to the English Channel, and lost on the coast of Denmark. See "Ship Losses of the Adelantado," AGI EC 1024-A.

[23] See "Testimonio de los documentos de Capt. Juan Vélez de Medrano," from Archivo Histórico de Protocolos de Madrid (hereafter AHP), Protocolo 646, fol. 256-59.

[24] Captain Vélez's recollections are found in "Testimonies," St. Augustine, May 15, 1566, from AGI JU 999. See also "Méritos y Servicios de Diego López," St. Augustine, December 16, 1569, from the Woodbury Lowery Collection

(microfilm, P.K. Yonge Library, University of Florida) 1: 2: 414:265-290. López stated that the fort was in "Xega."

[25] See Pedro Menéndez to Crown, Matanzas, Cuba, December 5, 1565, AGI SD 115. On September 4, 1565, House of Trade officials had reported to the King that cannon, gunpowder, matchcord and lead were being gathered in the Seville warehouses for the reinforcement. See Casa to Crown, Seville, AGI CT 5,167, Book 2. Although they were still trying to gather ships, the King advised that he had sent to Vizcaya for 1,000 arquebuses and helmets. See Crown to Casa, Bosque de Segovia, September 6, 1565, AGI CT 5012.

[26] It is generally agreed that the Calusa capital was on Mound Key in Estero Bay. Escalante and Bustinçury both appear in AGI CD 901, ration list for 1566-57, fol. 9 and 10. See also Hernando d'Escalante, *Memoir of Hernando d'Escalante Fontaneda*, trans. Buckingham Smith, ed. David O. True (Coral Gables, Florida: University of Miami Press, 1944). (The original dates from ca. 1575.)

[27] See "Order to have Sebastián de Lezcano hanged," St. Augustine, March 13, 1566, from "El Fiscal de su Magestad con el Capitán Pedro de Redrobán," AGI JU 999.

[28] See Eugene Lyon, "The Florida Mutineers," *Tequesta* 44 (1984): 44-61

[29] López de Velasco, *Geografía universal de las Indias, 1571-1571*(Madrid: D. Justo Zaragoza, 1894), 168

[30] See Bartolomé Martín, "Martirio de los Padres," in Felix Zubillaga, *Monumenta Antiquae Floridae* (Rome: Monumenta Historica Societatis Jesu, 1946), 586-588, and AGI EC 1564-A, fol. 1067-1068.

[31] See the records of shipments from Cuba and Yucatán in AGI CD 1174 and in "Despachos que se hicieron," in AGI EC 1024-A.

[32] For a more detailed account of the city on Anastasia Island, see Eugene Lyon, "The First Three Wooden Forts," *El Escribano* 24 (1997): 130-147. Note 14 notes that this is in disagreement with Jeannette Thurber Conner in "The Nine Old Wooden Forts of St. Augustine,"*Florida Historical Quarterly* 4 (1925-26): 103-111, 171-180, in which she expresses the view that the first St. Augustine was built on the island.

[33] AGI CT 2932, ramo 2, no. 3.

[34] Testimony of October 26, AGI EC 154-A, fol. 1359vo.

[35] See AGI CD 941, "Accounting of pikes, arquebus balls, lead and matchcord." See also John Griffin, "An Archaeological and Historical Survey of the Griffin Point Development, St. Johns County, Florida," unpublished report, 1989. San Julian Creek still appears on maps.

[36] See Pedro de Valdés to Crown, St. Augustine, Sept. 12, 1566, AGI SD 168.

[37] "Ordinances which the very illustrious Señor Pedro Menéndez, Governor and Captain-General of the land and coast of these Provinces of Florida for His Majesty and Adelantado of them provided and instituted in these said Provinces" (n.d., September, 1566) from AGI JU 999.

[38] See AGI CD 294, No. 2b, 304, no.1, 102:4-103- 1; 306, no.2, 1, 24:1. 306, no. 2, 2. The author is indebted to Dr. Paul E. Hoffman for these citations. An *urca* was a large capacious vessel with fairly flat-bottom contours, valuable for carrying freight across shallow bars.

[39] The Jesuit mission began with a letter from Pedro Menéndez to Francisco de Borja (Borgia) sent from Madrid in March, 1565. Borja replied favorably from Rome on May 12, 1565, in Zubillaga, *Monumenta*, 6-9. Royal approval of the mission was given by Philip II in a letter sent to Diego Carrillo, Provincial of the Order from Ucles on April 9, 1565, *Monumenta,* 42-44.

[40] The Gayón mission is described in "Provanza hecha a pedimento de Gonzalo de Gayón" AGI SD 11, and authorization of Reinoso's mission in Menéndez to Crown, St. Augustine, October 15, 1566, AGI SD 115.

[41] An excellent account of the Windward Islands expedition of 1566-67 has been given by Paul E. Hoffman in "The Background and Development of Pedro Menéndez' contribution to the Defense of the Spanish Indies"(MA thesis, University of Florida, 1965)

[42] The Pardo reports are found in Eugenio Ruidíaz y Caravía, II, 474-480, and in AGI CT 58 and in AGI EC 154-A, fol. 16vo.

[43] Pedro Menéndez to Francisco Borgia, Madrid, January 18, 1569, from Zubillaga, *Monumenta*, 228-234.

[44] This case is in a single *legajo* (bundle), AGI EC 1024-A. Only nine pieces are in the bundle, and the lawsuit continues until 1633. See Lyle McAlister's cogent summary of parallels between this rich material and the Solís de Merás and the Barrientos narratives in Gonzalo Solís de Merás, *Pedro Menendez de Aviles: memorial,* trans. Jeannette Thurber Connor, facsimile reproduction with introduction by Lyle N. McAlister (1964), xxi-xxii.

45 AGI SD 115.

46 The Armada appointment is in AGI CD 454, No. 3. Shortly afterwards, he received an *encomienda* (a grant of the profits and proceeds) of the town of Santa Cruz de la Zarza, a property of the Order of Santiago at Campos, near Palencia, Spain. See the dower agreement dated at Avilés March 27, 1574, AGI EC 153-A.

47 See Menéndez to the Crown, St. Augustine, October 20, 1566, from AGI SD 115.

48 The list of settlers is found in AGI PAT 19, No. 1. ramo 15. Other settler data is filed with an order dated July 26, 1568 and an agreement with Dr. Zayas, from AGI JU 980, no. 2.

49 See certification of Pedro Menéndez Marquez, AGI JU 980, No. 3, ramo 2.

50 See "La Reprinse de la Floride par le captaine Gourgues," published in translation by Jeannette Thurber Connor and reprinted in Charles E. Bennett, comp., *Settlement of Florida* (Gainesville: University of Florida Press, 1964), 202-226.

51 The deaths of soldiers in the inland forts is mentioned in the 1566-67 ration lists in AGI CD 941, fol. 5-9.

52 See Juan Rogel to Pedro Menéndez, Havana, December 9, 1570, in Zubillaga, *Monumenta*, 471-479.

53 See Crown decree, Segovia, November 15, AGI SD 235, also November 15, 1570, from AGI SD 2325.

54 See AGI JU 817, No. 5, piece 6.

55 An early illegal shipment of sarsaparilla was made on one of the Royal Armada ships; see AGI JU 892, No. 3. Six such shipments are described in AGI CD 1089, no 2, ramos 1 and 2. See protocol of Martín Calvo de la Puerta, *Archivo de Protocolos de la Havana.*

56 See Martínez to Crown, Havana, February 17, 1577, AGI SD 125,

57 The contents of the church and the records of the confraternity were examined by Visitor Castillo; see AGI EC 154-A, fol. 370vo. The image of Santa Clara and perhaps the gilded cross were likely gifts of Doña María, wife of the Adelantado. See AGI JU 817, No. 5, piece 1. See also "Statement of Gómez," in AGI CD 454.

58 See Irene Aloha Wright, *Documents Concerning English Voyages to the*

Spanish Main, 1569-1580 (London: Hakluyt Society, 1932) xxxvi-xxxvii, 37-39.

[59] See Alonso de las Alas to Crown, St. Augustine, January 12, 1600, from AGI SD 229.

[60] See "Daños de los Indios de la Florida," Madrid, AGI PAT 257, No.3, ramo 20.

[61] Pedro Menéndez de Avilés to Pedro Menéndez Marquez, Santander, September 8, 1574 , from Eugenio Ruidíaz y Caravía, *La Florida,* 2: 288-292.

[62] The Miranda, dated 1574, is in AGI EC 1024-A, piece 4; that of Velasco in 1573, AGI EC 153-A, fol. 72vo. and also in AGI JU 928, no. 9, fol. 23vo-31vo.

[63] Castillo y Ahedo's report is found in "Probanza de las cosas de la Florida," or "visita" for short, in AGI EC 154-A .

[64] See visita, fol. 1054.

[65] The Lara-Olmos case is in visita, fols. 457-505.

[66] See Baltasar de Sigüenza, visita, fol. 340.

[67] The Moyano episode is described in "Petition of Doña Isabel de Quiñones," Havana, 1602, AGI SD 129. The deaths in Guale are described in "Testimony of Juan López de Avilés, Havana, August 14, 1602, from 16-2, AGI SD 2533. The loss of the Solís contingent is narrated in AGI EC 154-A, fol. 1066vo- 1067.

[68] See Castillo to Crown, Havana, January 18, 1577.

[69] See Menéndez Marquez to Crown, April 2, 1579, from AGI SD 168.

[70] See Quirós' description of his activities in AGI SD 125.

[71] See "Services of Gutierre de Miranda," St. Augustine, 1588. 131 pages, AGI SD 231.

[72] Payment to María de Junco, AGI CD 948, October 20, 1598.

[73] See Charles W. Arnade, *Florida on Trial* (Coral Gables: University of Miami Press, 1959).

L

3

The Noble and Loyal City

1600 - 1668

Amy Turner Bushnell

St. Augustine, naval base and mission center, spent the first two thirds of the seventeenth century in relative obscurity, experiencing wartime disruptions in its finances, supply lines, and manpower, as Spain made war on the English, the French, the Dutch, and, during the Thirty Years War, a series of Protestant coalitions, not to mention revolts in Portugal and Catalonia. On the margins of empire, information could be difficult to obtain and to transmit. Between 1605 and 1655, Florida's documentary record is particularly uneven: sometimes it overflows with *legajos* (bundles) full of reports on rebellions, pirates, and official misbehavior; other times, the cupboard is so bare that the only evidence for a critical campaign may be a single "merits and services" petition submitted to the Crown years later.

During the years of royal inattention, the colony made strides toward economic self-sufficiency. Not by chance, it simultaneously acquired a hinterland of mission provinces, and with them food security, a labor supply, and access to marketable "fruits of the land." When the provinces reached their territorial apogee in the mid 1650s, however, their populations were already in decline, for

Left. By 1600 St. Augustine's residents had rebuilt several times after attacks, fires, and storms and replaced the structures shown in this map. The street grid remained. This map of St. Augustine in 1586 is the earliest view of a city in the United States (see page 41).
S. Augustini: pars est terra Florida, sub latitudine 30 grad, ora vero maritima humilior est, lancinata et insulosa. Drawn by Baptista Boazio to illustrate Walter Bigges, Summarie and True Discourse of Sir Frances Drake's West Indian Voyage, published 1589. Library of Congress Rare Book and Special Collections Division.

the Indians lacked immunity to the pathogens that came as part of the Spanish baggage. In Florida, as in other mission fields, there were years when the Franciscans were forced to content themselves with harvests of souls baptized *in extremis* (at the point of death).

St. Augustine entered the seventeenth century as one of two remote outposts on Spain's North American frontier, and although scholars have long lumped Florida and New Mexico together as the earliest "Spanish Borderlands," they differed in significant respects. Santa Fe, founded in 1609, two years after Jamestown, was forty-four younger than St. Augustine, yet New Mexican settlers were dependent on the medieval system of the *encomienda*, which gave Spanish settlers control over the native population, while Florida settlers relied on the early modern solution of the *situado*, a subvention from the royal treasury to a frontier garrison. Unlike Santa Fe, a landlocked settlement 7,000 feet above sea level, St. Augustine faced the sea, guarding the return route of the *Carrera de Indias* that kept the silver of Mexico and Peru flowing to Spain's bankers and, in the process, acquiring a cosmopolitan cast and a distinct set of dangers and opportunities.[1]

Without someone of Pedro Menéndez's stature and means in Spain to recruit colonists, the sea no longer brought the colony families of settlers, only bachelor soldiers and sailors who lived in mess groups of four or five–not in the better houses of vertical boards roofed with wooden shingles, but in wattle and daub huts with roofs of palmetto thatch.[2] If Florida was ever to be populated, these men would have to settle down and raise families, for there was no one else. With rare exceptions, the few Spanish women who arrived were either already married or "of quality," putting them out of a soldier's reach. In 1600, when St. Augustine's population was approximately five hundred, all of the married officers had Spanish wives, but if one included the rank and file, only one man in five possessed a wife, and half of those wives were Indian. Native cookware and cooking methods predominated in an outwardly Spanish town. By the time births brought the sex ratio nearer to equilibrium, many *floridanos* were part Indian, a fact that they kept to themselves.[3]

Other ethnic elements existed in the presidio. Since 1580, black "slaves of the king" had maintained the fortifications. Well-to-do residents owned a few slaves, some of them Indians enslaved in the "just wars" of other frontiers.[4] St. Augustine also contained a variety of Europeans, for in the Spanish empire, one's orthodoxy mattered more than one's origins. Many of the skippers and pilots in town were Portuguese, at least twice the resident surgeon was French, and in 1598, a single ship introduced an Irish priest, six German artillerists, and an English fifer.[5]

In the late 1590s the price of imported foodstuffs soared. The friars, who like the Indians were paid in goods rather than money, were fortunate that the king's alms for such things as habits and footwear, wax, and wine kept pace with the cost of living. But the soldiers, whose daily ration was limited to what two and a half *reales* would buy and whose wages were rigidly fixed by the Crown, became increasingly dependent upon local foods to feed their families. A soldier's portion of bread, eaten with vinegar, olive oil, and vegetables, like a salad, and his ration of salt meat and wine, may have been bartered for family necessities, being too expensive for everyday consumption. A soldier's family ate maize, beans, and pumpkins, seasoned with garlic and hot peppers and stewed with whatever protein was available: fish, shellfish, or the flesh of nocturnal garden raiders. Their drink, like the Indians', was the caffeine-rich cassina tea, with a lower bacterial count than straight well water. For treats they had the oranges, peaches, pomegranates, mulberries, grapes, and figs that grew in their fenced yards. Only a royal official or a merchant could afford imported delicacies like quince paste, hazelnuts, or chocolate.[6]

Stationed beside the Gulf Stream, St. Augustine repeatedly demonstrated its value to the Fleet of the Indies and other Spanish shipping. But even a maritime presidio needed a hinterland to guard its land approaches, keep it in local provisions, and function as a labor reserve. The *adelantado* had promised to found a colony based upon Indian converts as well as Spanish settlers, and it was always Spain's intention to strengthen its foothold on the Atlantic coast with Indian alliances. The mechanism was contractual. In the four-part chiefdom-presidio compact, the "lords of the land" agreed to recognize the overlordship of the king of Spain, to receive missionaries, to trade only with Spaniards, and to stand beside them in times of war. The chiefs' motives were straightforward. Of all the Europeans who courted their friendship, the Spanish were the worthiest on four counts: they were tough fighters with superior weapons, their magic was strong, they had goods to trade, and they understood the meaning of gifts.[7] According to the Spanish plan, if all went well, the towns that accepted Christianity would develop into an ecumene of language-based mission provinces--a collective Republic of Indians to go with the Republic of Spaniards. If a hitch developed in the process, the towns that withdrew their consent could be charged with rebellion and attached by conquest, for the chiefdom-presidio compact was irrevocable.[8]

The natives nearest to St. Augustine--the eastern Timucuans, with their "freshwater" and "tidewater" districts--were the first to accept Christianity and to demonstrate their loyalty. When five galleons of the treasure fleet wrecked on the Florida coast in 1588 and hundreds of castaways took shelter in St. Augustine, doña María Meléndez, *cacica* (chief) of the nearby town of Nombre de Dios, relieved the food shortage with maize from her people's reserves, for which the Council of the Indies thanked her with 300 ducats worth of axes and hoes, wheat flour, and clothing, in two installments. The people of Guale, on the coast of present Georgia, grew less maize, but their land produced sassafras, a medicinal root highly valued in Europe, bringing corsair traders into their harbors. After the loss of Santa Elena in 1587, the Spanish launched a campaign to bring the Guales into the Spanish orbit and secure the northern border. The number of Franciscans in Florida rose rapidly, many of them assigned to Guale.[9]

In 1596 Florida received another strong governor trained in the Menéndez armada, Gonzalo Méndez Canzo. On his way north from Havana, the governor visited and made peace with the non-agricultural Ais on the coast below St. Augustine, where corsairs liked to stop for wood and water and trade for sassafras and ambergris. The coastal Indians must have reconsidered the idea of allying themselves with Spaniards, for they drowned the interpreter that the governor sent them. He retaliated by killing 60 men and enslaving 54 women and children from the town of Surruque on the border--a "just war" sentence that the king reversed four years later. No sooner were the Ais dealt with than a more serious rebellion broke out. The Guale Uprising of 1597, which lasted for six years, would be especially well documented, thanks to its five Franciscan martyrs.[10]

In 1599, the Spaniards' own city was devastated. First a fire swept through the Franciscan convent, the granary, and fourteen houses, then the sea rose during a hurricane and carried away more structures. In that storm, most of the Indians of a nearby village drowned, a sheltering island disappeared, and a sandbar shifted, making the inlet even shallower. Until the days of modern dredging, the harbor would be closed to vessels of over 90 tuns, except for the flat-bottomed flyboats designed to haul cargo in Dutch canals.[11]

The compounded disasters gave Governor Méndez Canzo an opportunity to rebuild St. Augustine his way. South of town he laid out more lots. North of town he marked out a plaza large enough for a parade ground and around it built a guardhouse, a warehouse-treasury, and a governor's house. Perhaps it was his wife, doña Magdalena Luaces Estoa y Miranda, whose travel papers described her as having a "good figure and large eyes," who suggested that he open a public market and install an animal-powered mill to relieve the women of St. Augustine of the task of grinding maize for the day's ashcakes and thickened stews. In order to finance his ambitious program, the governor drew upon the "goods of the deceased," or the back salaries of soldiers who died intestate, and exacted contributions from the *vecinos* whose homes were still standing. For loggers and sawyers, he used the 56 slaves of the Crown, the 250 *gente de guerra* and *gente de mar* (fighting men and sea men) on the payroll, an unknown number of *forzados* (prisoners) serving sentences at the presidio, and extra shifts of Indians.[12] Philip III responded to the multiple disasters with an assortment of alms: 2,400 ducats from the city's tithes to rebuild the main church, 1,100 ducats from the Mexico City treasury to rebuild the Franciscan complex, and a 500-ducat grant to the hospital.[13]

To add to the cultivable land, Méndez Canzo drained the swamp called *El Gran Mosquitero*. He asked the Christian chiefs for laborers in order to grow maize in the presidio environs and, over the objections of the treasury officials, paid them in trade goods: red cloth, iron knives, and fat glass beads. As he surely knew, this labor levy was an extension of the native *sabana* system of public finance, in which the common people of a town worked a number of communal fields and used the produce to support their chiefs and healers, provide for widows and orphans, and guard against famine.[14]

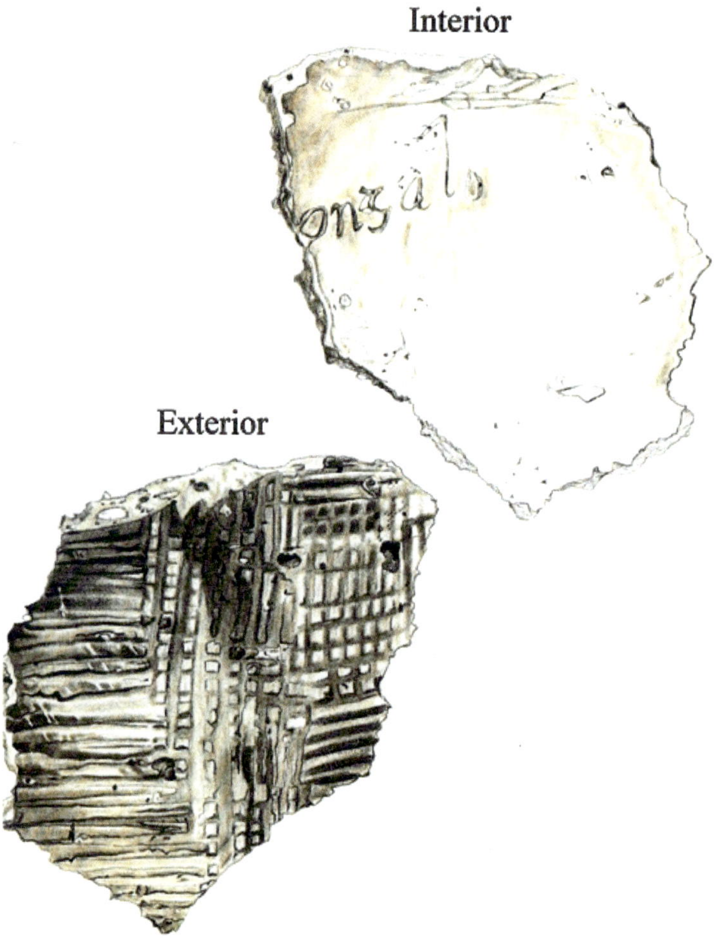

Drawing of Native American jar fragment with European name incised in vessel's interior. Writing suggests the name "Gonzalo," "Gonzales", or "Gonzals". Found during archaeological excavation of 17th-century well about 500 feet north of Franciscan monastery. Courtesy of Carl Halbirt, City of St. Augustine Archaeology Program.

The "noble and loyal city," as St. Augustine came to call itself on formal occasions, was becoming a place of some standing, as colonial places went. In 1603, there were eighty-some families there, Méndez Canzo said, and each family owned from two to ten cows.[15] The Crown might soon look for tax revenues from the colony, he thought, for the original royal treasury officials, drawn from the Menéndez family *comuño*, had been replaced, and the treasury's longstanding idiosyncrasies were being tempered by the visit of a royal auditor, Pedro Redondo Villegas.[16]

Meanwhile, reports to the Council of the Indies of rebellions and natural disasters in Florida had reopened an old discussion about whether it would be better to move the garrison to another spot or to abandon the colony entirely. Cuban governor Pedro de Valdés, ordered to give his opinion, sent his son Fernando to Florida to take the testimony of veteran soldiers, officers, and friars. Redondo Villegas, meanwhile, was seeing ineptitude on all sides, although he could only take accounts back to 1586, "the year the books were burned." Investigations in Florida were likely to drag on until a new threat to Spain's ports and possessions arose, when an appointee on the margins of empire could find himself suddenly back in royal favor.[17]

The death of Philip II's nemesis, England's Elizabeth I, in 1603 gave Spain a respite from Anglo-Spanish wars in Europe, but in the Americas, unemployed soldiers and seamen only turned to piracy, making any voyage an adventure. Pedro de Ybarra, a Basque officer on his way to take up his post as governor of Florida, was pursued by several English vessels in the Caribbean. Escaping in the ship's launch, he tossed about on the open sea for five days, only to be robbed by the same pirates when he reached shore. Dropped off at a deserted Cuban cove, the resourceful Ybarra, living on crabs, snails, and wild fruit, walked to Havana, borrowed a shirt and a frigate from Governor Valdés, and resumed his interrupted journey.[18]

Ybarra's determination to fix a personal monopoly on the ambergris and sassafras trade brought him into conflict with royal officials, Franciscans, Cuban traders, and French corsairs, who, since their country was at peace with Spain and no privateers were being licensed, found themselves reclassified as pirates. A St. Augustine skipper on a routine run trapped a French vessel trading with the natives at the Savannah River. Ybarra awarded himself 1500 ducats prize money for the ship and distributed the 21 prisoners among his Indian allies. The standing order was to hang all pirates, but Ybarra hoped that the Crown would relent and allow these unfortunates to raise a ransom or change sides. Also, St. Augustine was expecting its first episcopal visit, and he counted on the mighty arguments of the bishop to restore the heretics to the bosom of the Church and save their souls.[19] Ybarra had long been urging the Crown to arrange this episcopal visit in order to bring the independent Franciscans into line, for some of them were openly defying his authority. Fray Gerónimo de Celaya's inflammatory preaching was provoking the Indians to rebellion and the soldiers to mutiny, and it did not help matters for Ybarra's own confessor, Father Alonso de Peñaranda, to be circulating the rumor that the governor was a defrocked friar.[20]

Bishop Juan de las Cabezas Altamirano arrived in Florida in 1606, having survived several pirate scares and a hurricane that carried his ship far into the Cuban mangroves. What may have been the same storm had flattened and flooded much of St. Augustine, where the bishop set an example of charity by signing over his half of the parish tithes to the rebuilding and upkeep of the parish church. In St. Augustine and Nombre de Dios he confirmed 370 floridanos and 273 Indians, and in the reestablished missions of Guale, 756. The other pressing business was to deal with the pirates, whose executions had been put on hold. Bishop Altamirano, with the aid of a special Inquisition examiner and the French-speaking Ybarra, labored earnestly for the Huguenots' souls, and all but the great corsair Beltran Rogue from St. Malo, worth 200,000 ducats in ransom, returned to the Church to die as Catholics. The event was edifying, as seventeenth-century spectacles went, with the town's confraternities turning out for the funeral processions and burials.[21]

St. Augustine experienced a religious revival, and some enthusiasts campaigned for a local branch of the Holy Office to deal with other schismatics, but the bishop discouraged this as an unnecessary luxury in so small a place, and Ybarra dismissed it as a Franciscan scheme to introduce contraband. In other parts of the Indies, friars claiming to represent the Inquisition reportedly boarded incoming vessels and sealed boxes of imported goods under the pretext that they contained prohibited literature, when their contents were actually expensive clothing, a portable form of property.[22]

The founding of Jamestown in 1607 put a quietus on talk of abandoning St. Augustine, as Spain waited to see whether England's latest settlement would survive. Hard pressed by Dutch rebels in the Spanish Netherlands, the mother country was undergoing a period of xenophobia that would culminate in the expulsion of the Moriscos, industrious people of Moorish descent. In the Americas, the Crown ordered *audiencias* and governors to report all aliens on the payroll, even the Portuguese, who since 1580 had shared the same royal house. Governor Ybarra dutifully reported 32 Portuguese residents, three Frenchmen, five Germans, and two Flemings.[23] Florida competed for emigrants with the rich kingdoms of New Spain and Peru. As a presidio on a maritime periphery, it could not afford to be choosy, if it wanted its population to grow and its garrison to be at full strength.

Juan Fernández de Olivera, who arrived to be governor in 1610, reported that the country overflowed with deer, wildfowl, fish, fruits, and garden produce and that the inhabitants lived comfortably. "The only bad thing about this land," he declared, "is the bad name it has been given!"[24] St. Augustine had the reputation of a place of exile for unruly officers and trouble-making friars. It was also something of a penal colony, with condemned criminals in evidence, rowing galleys and hauling firewood. Many of the soldiers also had records, for in order to fill the roster of the garrison, the Crown often swept its peninsular prisons clean of debtors and petty thieves, while the Viceroy of New Spain supplied vagrants and rioters of mixed blood and reputedly low character.[25]

Fernández de Olivera had missed the colony's first 45 years, when Florida was truly a land of living war. It had not been an easy mission field, the Franciscans wrote to the Crown in 1612. From the first, the Indians had hated the Spaniards and mocked the true religion. They had exterminated good livestock as though it were vermin and rooted up unfamiliar trees and plants, "wishing to leave no trace nor smell of us." Foreign heretics interested only in trade had been welcomed more warmly than the missionaries sacrificing to save their souls.[26] Things had finally begun to change, however. On Cumberland Island and the Guale coast, missions were rooted as firmly as in the Timucuan villages near St. Augustine. In them the Indians learned to read and write and attended prayers and singing school. On the other side of the peninsula, a gunboat campaign against the warlike Indians of the Gulf coast had stopped their raiding of river towns and made it possible to found missions among the Timucuans of central Florida. In some places, the friars admitted, they had been unable to advance without military reinforcement, but as soon as the governor had soldiers to spare, they intended to extend conversions into the rich region of Apalache, even farther from their headquarters in St. Augustine, and some of them had already begun to learn the Apalache language. In recognition of the mounting numbers of baptisms, the Franciscan leadership combined the custodies of Florida and Cuba in 1609 and elevated them to the Province of Santa Elena three years later.[27]

Members of the St. Augustine garrison were frequently detached to mission stations as bodyguards for the friars. They also did terms of duty on board ship, making the frequent trips to Havana and Vera Cruz for supplies, to Spain with dispatches, or to show the flag and trade along Florida's miles of coastline. After a storm, presidio boats scoured the coast for the survivors of shipwreck and, with equal diligence, for salvageable cargoes and ships' artillery. It was in this sense that St. Augustine was essential to the yearly fleet that sailed majestically up the Gulf Stream well out of sight, sixty miles off shore. The town's little harbor functioned as a station of the Spanish coastguard, the only one along six hundred miles of strategic sea lane.[28]

Ensign Juan Rodríguez de Cartaya was carrying messages to Spain in 1613 in the St. Augustine-built frigate *San Juan Bautista*, when his men sighted a huge Portuguese *não* listing to her side, sails lowered. She was a dreaded plague ship. Over 200 of her crew had died and been thrown overboard; the others, too weak to man the pumps or raise the sails, had let the ship drift out of the East Indian trade route around Africa and into the return route from the West Indies. Rodríguez and his crew, at the risk of their lives, climbed the steep ladder, put the não in order, and sailed her to Sagres in Portugal, their little frigate bobbing like a pull-toy behind them. Philip III, king of Spain and Portugal, rewarded their heroism as was fitting.[29] In the Southeast what may have been the same plague was beginning to spread, perhaps carried ashore by the rats that lived on sea-going ships by the thousand.[30] In the next four years half of the 16,000 converted Indians in Florida and uncounted numbers of unconverted natives died of this unidentified form of plague. Friars hurrying with the Viaticum from one deathbed to another urged that the survivors be gathered into fewer towns, closer together. This scourge, Spaniards did not escape. Franciscans died, and soldiers' and seamen's places were filled with family men or Indians, for anyone else would desert at the first foreign port.[31] The beautiful land of Florida seemed accursed.

Ironically, the floridanos who survived this demographic disaster found it possible for the first time to raise cattle, on the savannah-like old fields of deserted villages.[32] The ranch products of hides, tallow, and dried meat went mostly to Havana, but floridanos also managed to get the cargo value of St. Augustine's yearly ship-of-permission raised from two to three thousand ducats' worth of fruits of the land in the form of cured cowhides.[33] Houses in the small town still looked little like the plastered shellstone that we now associate with colonial structures, but people's building materials were gradually moving from the quickly rotting rough boards to *tapia*, a mixture of burned lime, sand, water, and shell aggregate, poured into board forms around vertical poles.

In the 1620s, while Pilgrims struggled with the rocky soils of New England and Virginians with the unhealthy site of Jamestown, floridanos were combating pirates and hurricanes. The great storm of 1622 was responsible for the loss of many ships between the Keys and Bermuda. For years afterward the Spanish salvaged bullion from the wreck sites. Dutch and English corsairs, aware of their operations, hung about Cape Canaveral like sharks, waiting to chase returning frigates onto the shoals. Indians of the coast below St. Augustine welcomed and traded with these interlopers as they came ashore for wood and water. No help could be expected from the Crown, embroiled in the Dutch wars. Instead, St. Augustine found its reinforcements and war matériel diverted to other garrisons. Its subsidy, cut to the bone, fell years behind. It was a time of short rations and withheld wages. More than one supply ship trying to escape pursuit ran aground on the St. Augustine sandbar. The low point was reached in 1628, when the Dutch admiral Piet Heyn, coursing along the coast of Cuba, captured the Fleet of the Indies with the subsidies for all the Caribbean presidios, and there was no money to replace them.[34]

Harassed from the sea, the Spaniards in Florida turned their energies inland. The Franciscans made dramatic, unapproved entrances into new territory with banners flying and escorts of arquebus-armed Indians. There was a resurgence of exploration. During the term of Governor Luis de Rojas y Borja alone, three successive parties of Spaniards and Indians were sent to check out old tales of silver and gold mines, hills with diamonds, and lagoons of freshwater pearls. The third expedition relocated fabled Cofitachequi, looted by Hernando de Soto 82 years earlier.[35] But the 1620s were a period of contraction, not expansion, in the New World, and the Crown refused the governor permission to extend the Florida conquest 200 leagues northward into the land of pearls.

Governor Andrés Rodríguez de Villegas, who arrived in 1630, reported that the fort was little more than a stockade, with walls so dry that discharging one of the guns would have set them on fire. In times of danger the women and children had to take refuge among the Indians. Those natives, he argued, were the ones most to be envied in the New World, since in Florida there were no workhouses or mines and no labor service other than a little in the soldiers' fields, for which they were paid. They owed no tribute; instead, the king spent thousands of ducats a year on gifts for them, while the friars cared lovingly for their souls. Yet, unaccountably, the Indians of Florida were dying like Indians elsewhere.[36]

In truth, the Indians near St. Augustine were beginning to find the Spanish presence a problem that increased as their numbers declined. Because Florida had few beasts of burden, Indian commoners were drafted three times a year to supply the friars stationed in ever longer strings of *doctrinas*, and every expedition or campaign meant another call for baggage carriers and auxiliary warriors. Uprisings continued to be put down harshly. The people of Tolomato, whose fathers had been implicated in the Guale rebellion, remained in exile in a service town, digging a canal to open an inland waterway north from St. Augustine. In 1629, the cacica of the ferry town of San Juan del Puerto, near the old site of Fort Caroline, freed her brother from a Spanish detail, then fled into hiding. Governor Rojas y Borja tracked her down, brought her to the presidio for trial, and hanged her, sentencing her supporters to labor on the fortifications of Havana, with their ears docked.[37]

The depopulation and decline of the missions near St. Augustine was offset in 1633 when Governor Luis de Horruytiner approved the evangelization of Apalache, a land both populous and fertile. Its port, he promised, would provide the Fleet of the Indies with a refuge in the northern Gulf from storms and corsairs and would serve as a supply depôt for the distant Timucuan missions. The food supply for St. Augustine's five hundred some inhabitants would be assured. Boatloads of maize would leave the Apalache port, be rowed up the San Martín River (the Suwannee and its Santa Fe tributary) to a point near present Gainesville, and from there be carried overland to the capital.

What Governor Horruytiner did not mention was the growing market of Havana, a short week's sail from Apalache's port. In the advance of Christianity and the extension of the king's domains, Horruytiner had scented personal profit and he was not wrong. His descendants, allied to the important floridano family of the Florencias, would be prominent in Florida for the next 130 years, thanks in part to the lucrative Gulf trade. The officials of the royal treasury, similarly well connected, neglected their account books and applied themselves to ranching and trade. The Franciscans, frequently in debt for the travel expenses of new missionaries, saw in Apalache a way to solve their financial difficulties. Their efforts to keep soldiers out of the new province were only partly inspired by a desire to protect their converts from exploitation and bad examples. The friars also wanted their syndic to handle the province's agricultural surplus and direct the profits to their own worthy needs and projects. This objective would bring them into conflict with each governor in turn and last as long as the missions themselves.[38]

Horruytiner's last year in office, 1638, was notable for two disasters: the worst storm to hit St. Augustine in thirty years, and the sequestering of the Florida subsidy by none less than the king. Philip IV, whose involvement in the Thirty Years War had brought him to desperate financial straits, ordered the captain general of the fleet carrying the Caribbean subsidies to bring them to him in Spain and to give the waiting garrison agents promissory notes instead of money to cover their payrolls and satisfy their creditors.[39]

The result in Florida was financial chaos. For the next 30 years there was almost no circulation of money. Merchants in Havana raised their prices to Florida buyers and supplied them with inferior goods. Speculators bought up, for as little as a third of face value, the certificates that the soldiers received in lieu of wages. The soldiers of the presidio and all of the tradesmen who depended on their business fell deeply in debt. When currency again became available, Florida's wary *situadores*, or subsidy agents, spent it in New Spain in order to forestall a second sequestration, while Florida's skippers tried to avoid Havana, where the presidio's creditors waited at the docks, armed with writs to impound their cargoes.[40]

The government in Madrid had little time for the problems of Florida. Iberia itself was splitting apart in 1640, with both Portugal and Catalonia in rebellion; small, deficit-running colonies would have to shift for themselves. In St. Augustine there followed years of famine when the maize harvests failed and no ship brought relief. The wooden fort rotted, artillery rusted, and the soldiers went wrapped in blankets for lack of coats.

When their regular gifts from the Crown failed to appear, the Guales, always inclined to practice seasonal mobility, began drifting off to their winter hunting grounds in the interior. Bands of Chiscas wandered into Spanish territory. Governor Damián de Vega Castro y Pardo hoped to attach these newcomers by inviting them to track down fugitives from the missions.[41] Instead, in 1647 the Chiscas and a faction of unconverted Apalaches murdered three friars, the deputy governor, and his wife and three daughters. With the help of Timucuan chiefs and warriors, suspended governor Benito Ruiz de Salazar y Vallecilla and co-governors Francisco Menéndez Marquez and Pedro Benedit Horruytiner "pacified" the province and obligated the Apalaches, Christian and non-Christian alike, to the labor levy, because, as they explained, the "presidio could not be conserved without the service of these natives."[42]

With this conquest of Apalache the Florida provinces reached their fullest extent. Later attempts to expand the borders by placing missionaries south in Mayaca and Jororo, northwest in Apalachicola, or southwest in Calusa territory, would be unsuccessful.[43] Christianity was a religion of fixed settlements and taxable surpluses--then, as now, the gauges of civilization--and the kingdom of God was unable to incorporate a society that would not reduce itself to farming and herding.[44] Only Guale, Timucua, and Apalache achieved administrative maturity within the Spanish system. Each of the three provinces consisted of a loose federation of Indian towns, whose chiefs met on occasion to deliberate on common problems. The Franciscan friars lived by twos in the larger towns and visited the smaller ones. They too had a council, convening every three years in St. Augustine.[45]

After the Apalache rebellion, secondary garrisons were stationed in every province, allowing deputy governors and chiefs to coordinate military campaigns and labor levies, to accumulate maize and other provisions for shipment to St. Augustine, and, over the friars' protests, to represent the governor's interests in the growing trade with the provinces' non-Christian neighbors. A small settlement of floridanos grew up around the detachment in Apalache. In central and western Timucua, floridanos leased Indian lands and ranched, bred mules, or planted crops.[46] This spreading out of the Spanish-speaking population has been under-reported since, wherever a floridano lived, he was a parishioner of St. Augustine, the only town of Spaniards east of Santa Fe.

Someone who spent more time on his estates in the provinces than on the job in St. Augustine was Governor Ruiz de Salazar y Vallecilla. He had earned the governorship of Florida by contracting to build a 500-tun galleon for the Crown, and he hoped

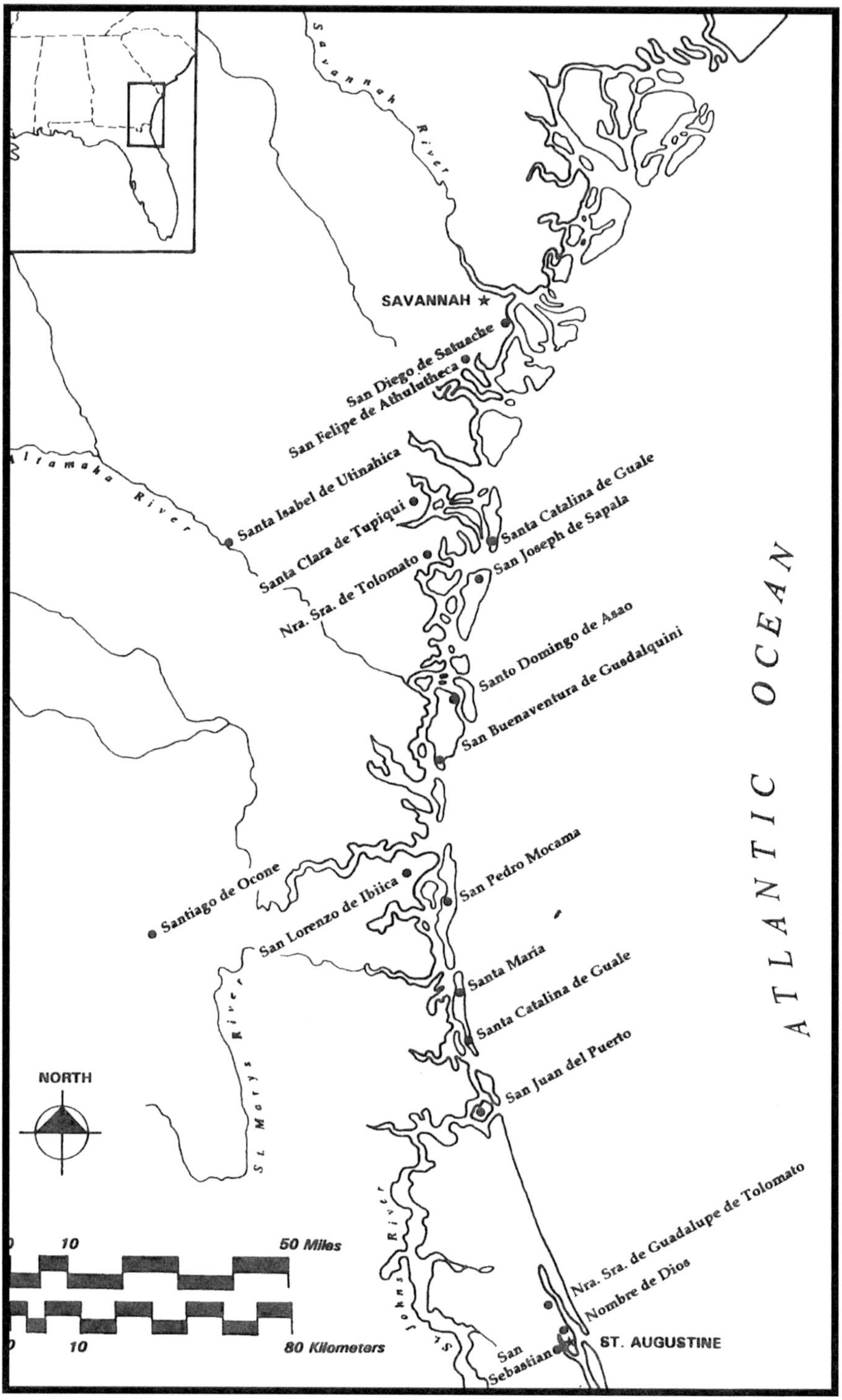

Left: Missions East; Right: Missions West.
Michael Gannon, ed., *The New History of Florida.* Gainesville: University of Florida Press, 1996, with permission.

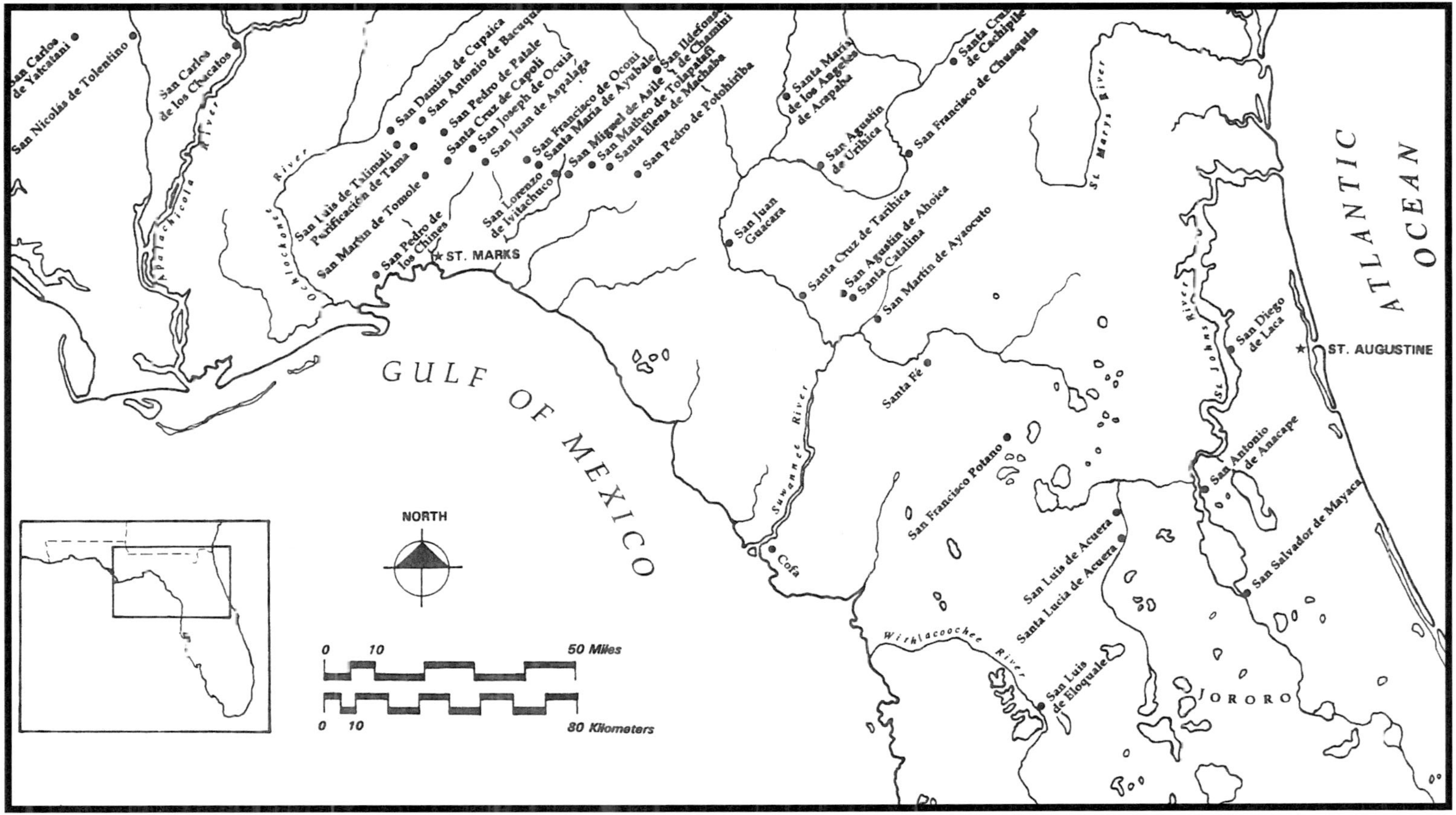

ATLANTIC OCEAN
GULF OF MEXICO
ST. AUGUSTINE
ST. MARKS
San Carlos de Yatcatani
San Nicolás de Tolentino
San Carlos de los Chacatos
Apalachicola River
Ochlockonee River
San Luis de Talimali
Perificación de Tama
San Martín de Tomole
San Pedro de los Chines
San Damián de Cupaica
San Antonio de Bacuqua
San Pedro de Patale
Santa Cruz de Capoli
San Joseph de Ocuia
San Juan de Aspalaga
San Lorenzo de Ivitachuco
San Francisco de Oconi
Santa María de Ayubale
San Miguel de Asile
San Matheo de Tolapatafi
Santa Elena de Machaba
San Ildefonso de Chamini
San Pedro de Potohiriba
Santa María de los Angeles de Arapaha
San Agustín de Urihica
Santa Cruz de Cachipile
San Francisco de Chuaquia
San Juan Guacara
Santa Cruz de Tarihica
San Agustín de Ahoica
Santa Catalina
San Martín de Ayaocuto
Santa Fé
Suwannee River
St Marys River
St Johns River
San Diego de Laca
San Antonio de Anacape
San Salvador de Mayaca
San Francisco Potano
Cofa
San Luis de Acuera
Santa Lucia de Acuera
Withlacoochee River
San Luis de Eloquale
JORORO
NORTH
0 10 50 Miles
0 10 80 Kilometers

to recoup his costs by large-scale agricultural production on the Gulf coast, as near as possible to Havana. As one of his ventures he started a wheat farm beside the Aucilla River and sent to the Canaries for millstones and a miller. The tithes from farms like this, he boasted, would soon be enough to support an abbot.[47]

The governor would learn that economic enterprise in Florida was at the mercy of war, weather, and disease. The fleet that left Vera Cruz for Cuba in the spring of 1649 carried an unidentified "plague" whose symptoms suggest either typhus or yellow fever. After killing a third of the inhabitants of Havana, the "black vomit" moved north. Unlike earlier diseases, which had concentrated on the native population, this one bore down on the Republic of Spaniards. In Florida, many, perhaps most, of the friars died, as did the two company captains, the two treasury officials, the sergeant major, and the governor.[48]

At the presidio, where central authority had all but disappeared, the interim officers, all floridanos, met and elected one of their own, Pedro Benedit Horruytiner, who repaid them with 55 officers' patents, including 23 for captain. When Horruytiner left the city so much as to inspect his plantings, the fort banner dipped in salute and a salvo was fired.[49] At the request of the Franciscans, Horruytiner dismantled Governor Ruiz de Salazar y Vallecilla's farms, selling slaves, horses, oxen, and tools for half their value.[50] He also withdrew the garrison detachment from Apalache, leaving the friars and chiefs free to trade with the Dutch and the English. The next royal governor, Diego de Rebolledo, put the garrison back, assuring the Crown that without a military presence in that place, foreigners would soon take over the commerce in the Gulf as they had in the Caribbean.

In Florida, the "plague" was followed by an epidemic of smallpox in which every one of the royal slaves died. Fray Gómez Engraba claimed that, of 200 Timucuans dispatched to St. Augustine to labor in the soldiers' fields, only ten survived to return home.[51] As if this were not sufficient disaster, a windstorm at the wrong time beat down the ripening maize and caused a famine. Taking stock in 1655, the Franciscans of Florida reported barely 26,000 Christian Indians in all three provinces.[52]

In that year, 1655, Oliver Cromwell's forces captured Jamaica, sending a shudder of fear through the Spanish Caribbean. Even if the English remained content with one island, there would now be no rest from their privateering.[53] No help could be expected from the king, who had again kept back part of Florida's money. To strengthen the defenses of St. Augustine, Governor Rebolledo called up 500 warriors from Apalache and Timucua together and an unspecified number from Guale. The Guales arrived without provisions and were rationed on hardtack. The Timucuans, ordered to bring 75 pounds of maize apiece on their backs, objected on principle. Their chiefs and principal men were exempt from manual labor, a status that they could lose only by committing a crime. Disregarding the Franciscans' warnings, Rebolledo repeated his order with threats.[54] The chiefs of Timucua rose in rebellion, killing seven persons. Unwilling to be sent against them, the Guales announced that the biscuits were making them sick and went home--without their firearms, which the governor seized to equip his soldiers. The rebellion spread, with the tacit support of many friars. Throughout Timucua Province, towns were deserted and bands of hungry people wandered about, sacking mission buildings and rustling cattle. Although Rebolledo captured and executed eleven ringleaders, it was the combination of disease, starvation, and out-migration that brought the "Great Rebellion" to a close. As usual, the friars had the last word. In response to a barrage of letters, the Crown ordered the arrest and prosecution of the governor of Florida for provoking the lords of the land to rebellion and cruelly hanging them. Rebolledo escaped punishment only by dying before the royal order arrived.[55]

In the year 1659 an epidemic of measles visited Florida and, by one estimate, 10,000 Indians died of that disease alone. The survivors in central Timucua were congregated into towns along the trans-peninsular road to operate the ferries and maintain the overland link with Apalache.[56] That province's produce was more essential than ever to St. Augustine, from which, like a colony, it was trying to break away.[57] A band of Chichimecos went on a rampage in Guale, burning churches and killing Christians. They had been set in motion by white settlement to the north and were one of many such shock waves to strike the Spanish provinces.[58] There was little to deter them. After the midcentury rebellions, Florida was a hollow peninsula, virtually deserted between St. Augustine and Apalache, apart from cattle ranches and service towns. North of St. Augustine, the Guales had commenced the slow withdrawal that, despite an influx of Yamasee refugees, would turn the sea islands into a "debatable land" by 1685.[59]

The population of St. Augustine, by contrast, recovered and began to grow. In 1659, the city had a population of 700, of whom 300 were on the garrison payroll. Only 130 of the 300 were common soldiers, for included in the payroll were the mariners, the officers, the treasurer and accountant, a surgeon, barber, and apothecary, a smith, an armorer, and a locksmith, the rations notary, the slave overseer, the chaplain, the parish priest and his assistants, and 43 of Florida's seventy friars.[60] The English were making contacts among the Indians of the Southeast to prepare the way for the colony of "Carolana," a grant made by Charles II to English proprietors, who planned to settle it with the surplus population of Barbados. One of the proprietors' scouts was the physician John Henry Woodward, who spent more than a year among the Indians, learning their languages, before petitioning the Spanish governor in Latin for religious asylum. Parish priest Francisco de Sotolongo, with a degree from the University of Mexico, invited the learned doctor to be his guest while he was prepared for baptism.[61]

There was another foreign doctor in town, the French surgeon Pierre Piquet. After war was declared between France and Spain in 1667, Piquet fell under suspicion and took passage on a supply ship. When privateers out of Jamaica seized the ship off the coast of Cuba, Piquet gave them some interesting information. Marcos Luzio, a military engineer salvaging the wreck of the Almiranta with native divers, had recovered a number of silver bars and deposited them for safekeeping in the king's coffer in St. Augustine. The privateers headed for Florida.[62]

Led by their captain, Robert Searles, they sailed the presidio's vessel up to the bar at St. Augustine as if returning with supplies.

RIGHT: St. Augustine resident Isabel de los Ríos, a free woman of color, baked and sold pastries. Her basket holds *rosquetes*, spiral-shaped sweetcakes, which are still popular in Spain. Florida Museum of Natural History, with permission.

Isavel de Los Rios

When the launch came out with the harbor pilot, they kicked pilot and crew below deck. In the dead of night, a hundred cutthroats landed on the wharf below the plaza. Before the town was awake they had seized the guardhouse, the armory containing the soldiers" firearms, and the counting house, along with 138 marks of silver. Sergeant Major Nicolás Ponce de León II fled to the woods with most of the 120 weaponless soldiers, while the privateers killed 60 persons in the streets, including Ponce's baby daughter. Governor Francisco de la Guerra y de la Vega slipped out a side door of his house and ran to the fort with the enemy at his heels. For what it was worth, the wooden fort was held, but the rest of the town was sacked. Captain Searles allowed the principal citizens to retrieve their wives and daughters before paying their ransoms, after the parish priest offered to take their place and preserve their honor, but he adamantly refused to release his Indian, African, mestizo, or mulatto captives, even those with Spanish fathers, saying that his license from the governor of Jamaica permitted him to sell anyone who was not a Spaniard. Searles did not burn St. Augustine, which to the inhabitants meant only one thing: the English would be back to occupy it. Dr. Woodward departed with the privateers.[63] Parish priest Sotolongo laid the blame for the disaster squarely on Governor de la Guerra y de la Vega, who without fear of God had openly had a mistress for the last three years. Because St. Augustine had tolerated this public sin, said the priest, God had visited the town with a drought, a storm, two ships lost, and this pirate attack, all in one year.[64] A royal governor was forbidden to ally himself with local families during his term, but this had not kept don Francisco from falling in love. His mistress, doña Lorenza de Soto y Aspiolea, a niece of the priest's, bore three children during the governor's five-year term, each one adopted by the couple as a "child of parents unknown." Six days after his successor took office, don Francisco and doña Lorenza were married, securing their children's legitimacy.[65] Unions between local women and outsiders were in the St. Augustine tradition. Between 1658 and 1670, 86 percent of the women whose marriages were recorded in the parish register were native born, but only a third of the men were, the others being about equally drawn from Spain's poorer regions, mainly Andalusia, and her overseas kingdoms, mainly New Spain.[66] The Searles raid of 1668, followed in 1670 by the colonization of Carolina, persuaded the Council of the Indies to grant Florida a larger share of the defense budget. A masonry fort for St. Augustine was something that had been proposed for 70 years; funds had even been allocated for the purpose, only to be diverted to more urgent needs as fast as they arrived. This time, the Council resolved not only to approve the money for construction, but to increase the situado by another 50 *plazas* and to pay the 43 friars from other sources, in effect adding 93 soldiers to the garrison.[67] Heralding a new era, these orders-in-council would find their way through mazes of clientage and thickets of red tape and emerge at last, translated into real money, live troops, and a day of groundbreaking for a new stone fort.[68]

NOTES

[1] Amy Turner Bushnell, "Borderland or Border-sea? Placing Early Florida," review essay in the *William and Mary Quarterly*, 3d ser., 59:3 (July 2003), 643-653; David J. Weber, *The Spanish Frontier in North America* (New Haven: Yale University Press, 1992), 87-91, 122-133.

[2] Paul E. Hoffman, *Florida's Frontiers* (Bloomington: Indiana University Press, 2002).

[3] Hoffman, *Florida's Frontiers*, 75-76; Kathleen Deagan, "Accommodation and Resistance: The Process and Impact of Spanish Colonization in the Southeast," in David Hurst Thomas, ed., *Columbian Consequences*, Vol. 2: *Archaeological and Historical Perspectives on the Spanish Borderland East* (Washington, D.C.: Smithsonian Institution Press, 1990), 297-314; Deagan, "Mestizaje in Colonial St. Augustine," *Ethnohistory* 20 (1973): 55-65.

[4] Amy Turner Bushnell, *Situado and Sabana: Spain's Support System for the Presidio and Mission Provinces of Florida*. American Museum of Natural History, Anthropological Papers, No. 74 (Washington, D.C.: Smithsonian Institution Press, 1994), 33, 118-119, 139; Bushnell, *The King's Coffer: Proprietors of the Spanish Florida Treasury, 1565-1702* (Gainesville: University Presses of Florida, 1981), 31-33.

[5] Bartolomé de Argüelles to the Crown, 8-3-1598 and 10-31-1598, *Archivo General de Indias, ramo Gobierno: Santo Domingo, legajo* 229, *documentos* 24 and 25. Hereinafter, SD 229/24 and 25.

[6] Bushnell, *The King's Coffer*, 24-26, 38-39.

[7] Amy Turner Bushnell, "Spain's Conquest by Contract: Pacification and the Mission System in Eastern North America," in Michael V. Kennedy and William G. Shade, eds., *The World Turned Upside Down: The State of Eighteenth-Century American Studies at the Beginning of the Twenty-First Century* (Bethlehem, Penn.: Lehigh University Press, 2001), 289-320; Bushnell, "'Gastos de Indios': The Crown and the Chiefdom-Presidio Compact in Florida," in Salvador Bernabéu Albert, coord., *El Gran Norte Mexicano: Indios, misioneros y pobladores entre el mito y la historia* (Sevilla: Consejo Superior de Investigaciones Científicas, 2009), 137-163.

[8] Amy Turner Bushnell, "Ruling the Republic of Indians in Seventeenth-Century Florida," in Gregory A. Waselkov, Peter H. Wood, and Tom Hatley, eds., *Powhatan's Mantle: Indians in the Colonial Southeast* (Lincoln: University of Nebraska Press, 2006), 195-213.

[9] Bushnell, *Situado and Sabana*, 64-69, 120-121.

[10] Hoffman, *Florida's Frontiers*, 81-82, 87-89; J. Michael Francis and Kathleen M. Kole, *Murder and Martyrdom in Spanish Florida: Don Juan and the Guale Uprising of 1597*. Anthropological Papers of the American Museum of Natural History, No. 95 (Washington, D.C.: Smithsonian Institution Press, 2011).

[11] Bushnell, *The King's Coffer*, 85; Hoffman, *Florida's Frontiers*, 75; Charles W. Arnade, *Florida on Trial, 1593-1602* (Coral Gables: University of Miami Press, 1959), 16-18.

[12] Arnade, *Florida on Trial*, 8-9.

[13] Bushnell, *Situado and Sabana*, 87-88.

[14] Gov. Gonzalo Méndez Canzo, Report to the Crown about dismantling the presidio, St. Augustine, 9-22-1602, SD 224; Bushnell, *Situado and Sabana*, 111-112.

[15] Juan Solana, Report on the acclamation of Philip V, 1-7-1702, sent to the Crown on 3-36-1702, SD 840/45; Arnade, *Florida on Trial*, 74.

16 Bushnell, *The King's Coffer*, 125-127.

17 Arnade, *Florida on Trial*; Hoffman, *Florida's Frontiers*, 91-92.

18 Crown to royal officials in Havana, 8-16-1604, in "Registros: Reales órdenes y nombramientos dirigidos a autoridades y particulares de la Florida. Años 1570-1603" (1907 typescript at the P. K. Yonge Library of Florida History, Gainesville), 361.

19 Bushnell, *The King's Coffer*, 96; Bushnell, *Situado and Sabana*, 68-69.

20 Gov. Pedro de Ybarra to Fray Pedro Bermejo, 7-27-1605, SD 232/102; Bushnell, *The King's Coffer*, 110.

21 Diego Dávila, Report on the visita of Florida by the bishop of Cuba, don Juan de las Cabezas Altamirano, 6-26-1606, SD 235; Bushnell, *Situado and Sabana*, 52; Bushnell, *The King's Coffer*, 76-79, 83-84, 96.

22 Bushnell, *The King's Coffer*, 26-27, 89.

23 Gov. Pedro de Ybarra to the Crown, Report on the foreigners, 8-1-1607, SD 224/83. *Audiencias* were appellate courts with legislative and executive functions in addition to their judicial ones. Florida came under the jurisdiction of the Audiencia of Santo Domingo.

24 Gov. Juan Fernández de Olivera to the Crown, 12-15-1611, SD 229/67.

25 Bushnell, *Situado and Sabana*, 82, 118-119.

26 Frailes Pedro Ruiz, Pedro Bermejo, Francisco Martínez, and Esteban de San Andrés to the Crown, 10-16-1612, SD 232/61.

27 Ibid. Bushnell, *Situado and Sabana*, 50.

28 Bushnell, *The King's Coffer*, 10

29 Juan Rodríguez de Cartaya, Memorial, 5-7-1613, Indiferente General 1863.

30 Oliver Dunn, "Trouble at Sea: The Return Voyage of the Fleet of New Spain and Honduras in 1622," *Terrae Incognitae* 11 (1979): 29-41.

31 For a view of Spanish Florida as epidemiologically isolated before the advent of Carolina, see Paul Kelton, *Epidemics and Enslavement: Biological Catastrophe in the Native Southeast, 1492-1715* (Lincoln: University of Nebraska Press, 2007).

32 Amy Bushnell, "The Menéndez Marquez Barony of La Chua and the Determinants of Economic Expansion in Seventeenth-Century Florida," *Florida Historical Quarterly* 56 (April 1978): 407-431.

33 Bushnell, *The King's Coffer*, 9, 61, 71, 86, 90, 115.

34 Bushnell, *Situado and Sabana*, 45, 125-126; Hoffman, *Florida's Frontiers*, 112, 114.

35 Worth, *Timucuan Chiefdoms*, 1: 44-76; John E. Worth, "Late Spanish Military Expeditions in the Interior Southeast, 1597-1628," in Charles Hudson and Carmen Chaves Tesser, eds., *The Forgotten Centuries: Indians and Europeans in the American South, 1521-1704* (Athens: University of Georgia Press, 1994), 104-122.

36 Gov. Andrés Rodríguez de Villegas, 12-27-1630, SD 225/30. Compiler Juan Diez de la Calle, in *Memorial y noticias* (Madrid, 1646), also reported that the natives of Florida labored less and paid less tribute than was the norm for the Indies.

37 For this paragraph and the next, see Bushnell, *Situado and Sabana*, 111-116, 119, 125-127, 165.

38 Amy Turner Bushnell, "How to Fight a Pirate: Provincials, Royalists, and the Raiding of San Marcos de Apalache," in Paul A. Gilje and William Pencak, eds., *Pirates, Jack Tar, and Memory: New Directions in American Maritime History* (Mystic, Conn.: Mystic Seaport, 2007), 11-25; Bushnell, *Situado and Sabana*, 146, 148-160.

39 Pedro Beltrán de Santa Cruz to the Crown, Havana, 11-28-1645, SD 229/102.

40 Bushnell, *The King's Coffer*, 68-74.

41 Elizabeth J. Reitz, Irvy R. Quitmyer, and David Hurst Thomas, eds. and contributors, *Seasonality and Human Mobility along the Georgia Bight*. American Museum of Natural History, Anthropological Papers, No. 97 (Washington, D.C.: Smithsonian Institution Press, 2012); Gov. Damián de Vega Castro y Pardo to the Crown, 8-22-1639, SD 225.

42 John H. Hann, *Apalachee: The Land between the Rivers* (Gainesville: University Presses of Florida, 1988), 15-16, 19; John E. Worth, *Timucuan Chiefdoms of Spanish Florida, Vol. 2: Resistance and Destruction* (Gainesville: University of Florida Press, 1998), 18-21,34,35, 71.75; Bushnell, *Situado*

and Sabana, 125-129; Francisco Menéndez Marquez and Pedro Benedit Horruytiner, 7-27-1647, SD 235.

43 See John H. Hann's important series, put out by the University of Florida Presses, Gainesville: *Apalachee: The Land Between the Rivers* (1988); *Missions to the Calusa* (1991); *A History of the Timucua Indians and Missions* (1996); *Indians of Central and South Florida, 1513-1763* (2003); *The Native American World Beyond Apalachee: West Florida and the Chattahoochee Valley* (2006).

44 Amy Turner Bushnell, "The Sacramental Imperative: Catholic Ritual and Indian Sedentism in the Provinces of Florida," in Thomas, ed., *Columbian Consequences*, 2: 475-490. See also Bushnell, "'None of these wandering nations has ever been reduced to the faith': Missions and Mobility on the Spanish-American Frontier," in James Muldoon, ed., *The Spiritual Conversion of the Americas* (Gainesville: University of Florida Press, 2004), 142-168.

45 Bushnell, *Situado and Sabana*, 116, 153-155; Worth, *Timucuan Chiefdoms*, 1: 103-104.

46 Worth, *Timucuan Chiefdoms*, 1: 120-123, 198-209.

47 Ibid., 1: 203-208; Bushnell, *Situado and Sabana*, 78-79.

48 On Florida's Indian and non-Indian population, epidemics, and depopulation, see Bushnell, *Situado and Sabana*; Hoffman, *Florida's Frontiers*; Worth, *Timucuan Chiefdoms*, 2 vols.; and Theodore G. Corbett, "Population Structure in Hispanic St. Augustine, 1629-1763," *Florida Historical Quarterly* 54 (1976): 263-264.

49 Gov. Diego de Rebolledo to the Crown, 10-18-1657, SD 233/53; Bushnell, *The King's Coffer*, 104.

50 Bushnell, *The King's Coffer*, 82.

51 Fray Juan Gómez de Engraba to Fray Francisco Martínez, Havana to Seville, 4-4-1657, SD 225.

52 Worth, *Timucuan Chiefdoms*, 1: 111.

53 See Nuala Zahadieh, "'A Frugal, Prudential and Hopeful Trade': Privateering in Jamaica, 1655-89," *The Journal of Imperial and Commonwealth History* 18 (2)(May 1990), 145-168.

54 Gómez de Engraba to Martínez.

[55] Hann, *A History of the Timucua Indians and Missions*, 204-205, 213-214, 221; Worth, *Timucuan Chiefdoms of Spanish Florida*, Vol. 2: *Resistance and Destruction.*

[56] Worth, *Timucuan Chiefdoms*, 2: 97-130.

[57] Bushnell, *The King's Coffer*, 110.

[58] Hoffman, *Florida's Frontiers*, 138-139.

[59] John E. Worth, "Overview: The Retreat of Guale and Mocama, 1655-1685," in *The Struggle for the Georgia Coast: An Eighteenth-Century Spanish Retrospective on Guale and Mocama.* American Museum of Natural History, Anthropological Papers, No. 75 (Washington, D.C.: Smithsonian Institution Press, 1995), 9-55.

[60] Bushnell, *Situado and Sabana*, 43-48.

[61] Ibid., 135-136.

[62] Sgt. Major Nicolás Ponce de León II to the Crown, 8-6-1668, SD 233/73.

[63] Joseph de Prado and Juan Menéndez Marquez II to the Crown, 6-30-1668, SD 229/134; Juan Menéndez Marquez II to the Crown, 7-4-1668, SD 233; Capt. Antonio de Argüelles to the Crown, 7-6-1668, SD 223/71; Gov. Francisco de la Guerra y de la Vega to Francisco Dávila Orejón Gastón, governor of Cuba, 7-7-1668, SD 233; Ponce de León to the Crown, 8-6-1668; Bushnell, *Situado and Sabana*, 142.

[64] Lic. Francisco de Sotolongo to the Crown, 7-4-1668, SD 235.

[65] Bushnell, *The King's Coffer*, 111, 142; St. Augustine Parish Register, Births: 10-9-1666 (Joseph), 1-15-1669 (María), 2-10-1671 (Agustina); Marriages: 7-12-1671 (Governor don Francisco de la Guerra y de la Vega of Soria in Castilla to doña Lorenza de Soto y Aspiolea of this city).

[66] Hoffman, *Florida's Frontiers*, 141-142.

[67] Bushnell, *Situado and Sabana*, 45, 67, 136-140.

[68] Luis R. Arana and Albert C. Manucy, *The Building of the Castillo de San Marcos* (n.p.: Eastern National Park & Monument Association, 1977); Bushnell, *Situado and Sabana*, 136-142.

4

The Castillo Years

1668-1763

Susan Richbourg Parker

In the afternoon of October 2, 1672, Manuel de Cendoya, governor of Spanish Florida, drove the first shovel into the ground to begin construction of Castillo de San Marcos. It was a pivotal day for St. Augustine and its residents. The presence of the masonry fortification changed the international dynamics of the Southeast, of the islands of the West Indies, and of the relationship between Spain and England. That Spain's defensive improvements would challenge English plans was a goal and a logical expectation. But there were other, perhaps unintended, consequences of the construction and improved defense systems. New men arrived to build the Castillo and serve as soldiers. Experienced masons arrived from Mexico; enslaved blacks and young Indian men from Florida missions were brought in to provide labor. More money arrived to pay them and new homes were built. The placement of the fortress opened a new residential area in St. Augustine, at the very time that a growing population needed more housing.

Even before the Spanish in St. Augustine could break ground for the masonry fortification, English colonists set up the colony of South Carolina in 1670, after almost a decade of exploring the areas of Cape Fear and Port Royal (Beaufort, S.C.). For Spanish Florida officials and residents in St. Augustine, the English were now just too close. Less than 300 overland miles separated St. Augustine and Charles Towne. In 1670, only 150 overland miles lay between the Carolina settlement and the most northern Spanish enclave, the Franciscans' coastal mission of Santa Catalina (on St. Catherine's

LEFT: Castillo de San Marcos, San Pedro (southwest) bastion. FloridaHistoricCoast.com with permission.

Island, Georgia). English settlers resented the Spanish presence in the Southeast from the outset, blaming St. Augustine for making Carolina "a frontier to all the English settlements on the main."[1]

Nine wooden forts had protected St. Augustine over the century since its founding. In 1672 the local shell stone, known as coquina, served as construction material for the tenth, and what would be the last fortress. Coquina is a general term in both the English and Spanish languages for the shell stone and the little mollusk that forms the stone. The coquina stone available in St. Augustine is an accretion of small seashells bonded over millennia by pressure. It lies only a few feet below the surface of the soil in a watery environment. Although it is soft and easy to cut when quarried, it hardens in the air. Quarrymen pried the "stone" out of the ground on the barrier island directly across from St. Augustine. (Today known as Anastasia Island, it was called *Isla de la Cantera* [Island of the Quarry] at the time of the Castillo's construction.) Pedro Menéndez Marquez had seen coquina exposed on the beach and tumbling out of the sand dunes near Matanzas Inlet in 1580. Immediately, Menéndez Marquez recognized its value for

Coquina quarries on Anastasia Island, drawn in late 1800s by H. S. Wyllie for his *St. Augustine Under Three Flags in Black and White* (Record Press, 1898).

building defense works. Florida officials had requested a masonry fortification many times, but not until 1669 did the crown authorize sufficient funds to build a large and durable fortification of stone.[2]

The building of Castillo de San Marcos proceeded in the manner of so many government projects, then and now, requiring many more years to complete and at twice the original budget. Bureaucrats and bad luck delayed the project. The viceroy of New Spain was slow to send funds. In 1673, Governor Cendoya and Ignacio Daza, the military engineer for the Castillo project, died within days of each other and responsibility for the construction defaulted to persons with less knowledge and experience. A terrible storm hit St. Augustine, flooding homes and fields, and sickness followed. Still, by 1675 the north, south, and east (seaward) walls reached at least twelve feet in height, but the west wall went unbuilt until 1677.[3]

How many plots made over many years to attack St. Augustine died aborning because of the presence of the Castillo? Even as late as 1812, U.S. expeditionary forces that invaded Spanish East Florida during the Patriot War were wary of the Castillo and its guns. But the Castillo did not discourage all marauders. Spanish troops from St. Augustine and bad weather stopped pirates before they reached St. Augustine, and the Castillo itself was not tested. During the 1680s, corsairs lurked in the Gulf Stream and on Florida's west coast and found refuge with the Carolinians on barrier islands. In 1682, pirates captured a frigate from St. Augustine bound for Havana. In 1683, privateer Nicolas de Grammont landed at Matanzas Inlet and headed north for St. Augustine. The Castillo was far from completed. Spanish soldiers from St. Augustine intercepted and stopped the raiders about a mile from the capital. The freebooters retreated to their boats, sailed to the St. Augustine Inlet and anchored in plain sight of the townspeople, perhaps to taunt them. But the raiders' view was of a stalwart, if still unfinished, fortress and they did not venture ashore. In 1684, Thomas Hinckley (spelled phonetically by the Spanish as "Jingle" [Hin-glay]) set out to raid St. Augustine, but a storm scattered his ships along the coast about 24 miles north of St. Augustine. In 1686, Grammont again aimed for St. Augustine. Again Spanish forces stopped him before he reached the town and this time captured one of his boats.[4]

Spanish Florida's rival colony unwittingly provided workers for the Castillo project and new residents as well. Unfree workers (slaves and indentured laborers) ran away from Carolina soon after its founding. Blacks and whites set out for Florida "to be free--of obligations, bad treatment, and lack of food." Brian Fitzpatrick, a white indentured servant, was probably the first escapee to reach St. Augustine, in August 1672. Known as Bernardo Patricio in St. Augustine, Fitzpatrick, like so many others who bolted from the English, remained to work, marry, and become part of the St. Augustine community. Enslaved blacks soon followed what they hoped would be a route to freedom. The first blacks documented to come to Florida seeking freedom, arrived in the fall of 1687 — eight men, two women, and a baby girl. At Easter time, they were baptized at St. Augustine's Roman Catholic parish church.[5]

For enslaved blacks who arrived from Carolina, freedom or manumission in Florida might be fairly immediate or, sometimes, a long time in coming. Florida's offering of a haven to the escapees angered Carolinians. In some instances, the freedom-seeking blacks were returned to Carolinians. At other times, Florida officials discussed compensation for the loss of laborers with English claimants. Ever-changing diplomatic concerns and how loudly the Carolinians demanded satisfaction influenced the decisions of Spanish officials about freedom.

Construction of the fortress building itself was completed in the spring of 1685, although the moat and outworks still were not finished. Florida's Governor Juan Marqués Cabrera could now direct some of his energy to other matters. He was aware that Carolina Governor Joseph Morton and other officials allowed pirates to live on barrier islands and in Charles Towne, where Thomas Jingle and Captain Cahopal had "their houses and haciendas." Cahopal boasted that he "had built in San Jorge (Carolina) a white house on a bank of the great river" and that he had left in Carolina "much wealth" seized during raids in Mexico. Governor Marqués asked for help from Havana to oust the pirates from Carolina and to eliminate the settlement of Stuart's Town, established by Scots in 1684 on

Santa Elena Island and lying within territory still claimed by Spain according to the 1670 Treaty of Madrid.[6]

Two Spanish galliots (*galeotas),* commanded by seasoned pirate fighters, were dispatched from Havana. At St. Augustine, the vessel recently captured from Grammont joined the two galliots, and the three boats headed for Carolina. The fleet stopped on August 17 at a hastily abandoned Stuart's Town and set it on fire. A week later, the Spanish raiding party attacked Edisto Island and plundered plantations there, including one that belonged to Governor Morton. The Spanish found evidence that the English governor was indeed abetting pirates: a large silver candle stick stolen from a church in Campeche and other Roman Catholic religious items were in the house. The Spanish captured two white indentured servants and eleven black slaves.[7] Pirate attacks and attempted pirate raids on St. Augustine appear in histories of the city, but the 1686 retaliatory raid is often omitted. Perhaps the Spanish raid is overlooked because it did not take place in St. Augustine. Still it was an important event, demonstrating to the English that they could not raid Spanish Florida with impunity. Less exciting, but no less important was the short-term and long-term damage to the economy of Carolina; the destruction from 1686 raids from St. Augustine "scuppered plans to raise silk in that promising region."[8]

After the raids, both colonies made plans to attack each other. Charlestonians were in an uproar about the Spanish attack, but the Lords Proprietors of Carolina forbade the Carolinians to strike back at the Spanish with whom England was by then supposedly at peace.[9] Both England and Spain were ruled by a king named Charles II. The English Charles sought peace and an alliance against France with Spain's King Charles. Both Carolina and Florida were reminded that European concerns outweighed matters in the Americas.[10]

Marqués Cabrera finished the main structure of the fortress in 1685. But there was still essential work to do beyond the walls of the fortress, which would continue for another decade. Until the outworks were finished, the Castillo was vulnerable to siege guns and scaling ladders. Yet, Marqués' completion of the fortress' building and his success against Carolina were not enough to redeem his relationship with Floridians. When pirate Andrew Ranson was spared at his execution because the rope of the garrote broke, Franciscan friars proclaimed it a miracle and offered sanctuary to the lucky Ranson at their monastery. Governor Marqués did not consider it a miracle and a jurisdictional dispute ensued. The parish priest joined in the fray. Nor had Marqués endeared himself to the colony's ordinary residents. His vigorous replacement of Florida-born military men with newly arrived soldiers probably touched every family. St. Augustine's fathers, husbands, and sons lost their soldiers' salaries. Threatened with excommunication and banned from the sacraments, on April 13, 1687, Marqués sailed to Havana to worship and tell his story in person to his superior. His detractors in Florida seized the opportunity to accuse him of abandoning his post, which he denied. Marqués returned to St. Augustine in June. He was jailed first in the Castillo and then placed under house arrest.[11] There had been a strong personal element in the problems between Governor Marqués and the clergy, and the contentions continued with his successors as well. Competition escalated between parish priests and friars and eventually among the friars themselves as declining numbers of Indian worshippers lessened the number of friars needed to serve as missionaries.

With completion of the Castillo project, coquina was available for other buildings. Upgrading the governor's residence took precedence. In 1690, Governor Diego de Quiroga y Losada's new coquina executive mansion was built in 200 days. His master builder appraised the new governor's house at 6,400 pesos (a St. Augustine price), commenting that it would have been worth 10,000 to 12,000 pesos in Havana. Quiroga ordered more royal houses to be built of coquina. After completion of the fortress, coquina and trained masons were available to build private homes. Easy credit (in a seventeenth-century form) made masonry homes even more attractive. Royal policy permitted soldiers to pledge their salaries to finance new structures. Thus the soldiers drew against their pay from the crown for the coquina, which cost the crown nothing as it was merely dug from quarries on crown land. By 1702, about ten percent of the homes in St. Augustine were built of coquina, sixteen of a total of 175 homes.[12] Colonists in St. Augustine and in Carolina kept the peace, albeit grudgingly, until war in Europe provided the opportunity for Carolinians to attack La Florida. England's Queen Anne feared the power and influence that might accrue to the French royal family if Philip (Felipe) de Anjou, grandson of Louis XIV, held on to the throne of Spain after the death of childless Charles II. She declared war on France on May 15, 1702, and backed another nephew of Charles II to be king of Spain. The War of the Spanish Succession, also known as Queen Anne's War, lasted until 1713 and was fought in Europe and the Americas.

By August 1702, Carolinians had learned of the war and began to prepare an assault on their now declared enemies, the Spanish in La Florida. The invasion was a local, Carolina endeavor, not one planned from England. South Carolina Governor James Moore had been contemplating such a strike for quite awhile. The declaration of war provided him the opportunity.[13]

Carolina's plans against Florida were revealed when a Christian Choctaw woman overheard English traders in western Georgia discussing how the English would come down the Atlantic coast to attack St Augustine. She carried her information to Spanish officers in Apalache (Tallahassee area) and on October 27 a fast courier arrived in St. Augustine with news for Governor José de Zúñiga y Zerda. Zúñiga gleaned more information from English prisoners held in St. Augustine: about 1,000 troops were heading to St. Augustine, half by land and half by sea. They said Moore had captured about 40 vessels in Charleston harbor; of these he used fourteen for the invasion. The ships carried artillery guns of several sizes; round shot, chain shot, powder, and some ordinary grenades. Based on the prisoners' comments, Zúñiga concluded that his Spanish troops were too few and his weapons too unreliable for a defense against the Carolinians. The Spanish would have to wait out the siege inside the Castillo. The governor ordered St. Augustine's residents into the fortress and to bring their belongings "in carts, horses, canoes, and on their shoulders."[14]

On November 9, the Castillo's doors closed behind 1,500 persons, including two infants less than a week old. The gate would open now only for Spanish sorties or messengers. The next day English forces took over the empty town and set up headquarters in

The Castillo de San Marcos guarded St. Augustine even before it was completed in 1695. It is the oldest masonry fortification in the continental United States. The President of the United States designated the fortress a National Monument in 1924.
Image provided by FloridasHistoricCoast.com.

the St. Francis monastery (St. Francis Street) almost out of range of the fort's cannon. Spanish soldiers destroyed buildings within a musket shot of the fortress (750 feet) to deprive English snipers of cover. On November 25, the English set fire to the monastery and buildings near it, sparing the church, which headquartered Governor Moore.[15]

Inside the Castillo the circle of life went on. On November 15, two babies were born inside the fort--Francisco, son of Marta María, a Guale wage worker (*naboría*) married to a slave, and Maria, daughter of a soldier from Spain and his St. Augustine wife. A third infant, baby Josefa had to come into the fort four days after her birth and thus before there was time to baptize her. At five weeks of age and probably near death, she was baptized "in necessity" inside the fort.[16]

Both the English and the Spanish looked toward the Caribbean for help. The English dug trenches to place their artillery and waited for bombs to arrive from Jamaica. Inside the Castillo, the Spanish hoped and prayed for a relief force from Havana. By December 19, Carolinian troops were poised within a pistol shot of the Castillo. A week later four Spanish warships from Havana arrived at St. Augustine and the English retreated, setting fire to the town's remaining buildings as they left. Between 20 and 30

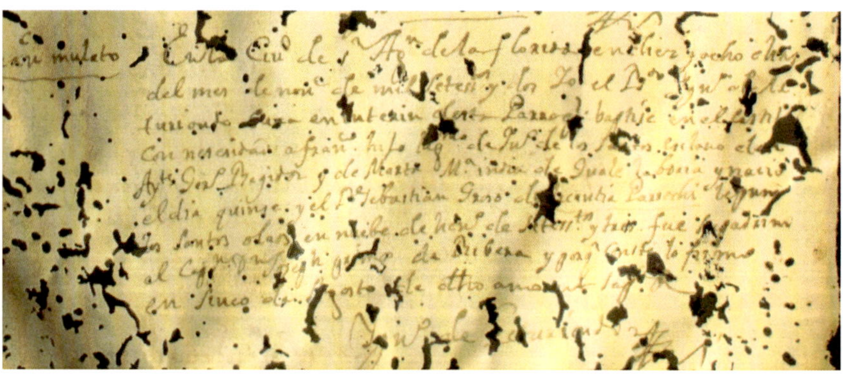

"Francisco, mulato,"(written in margin) was born November 15, 1702, inside the Castillo during the siege. This baptismal entry records that his mother was a Native American and his father a black slave. Cathedral Parish Records, Book of Baptisms, entry dated August 5, 1703. Image from http://www.vanderbilt.edu/esss/index.php.

structures survived. On December 30, St. Augustinians emerged to a town in ashes.[17]

The 1702 siege of St. Augustine was a major event in St. Augustine's history, in the history of the North American mainland, and the Atlantic world. For six weeks control of the North America's coast hung in the balance. Failure of the siege maintained the political *status quo ante bellum*. How different would history be if the English had gained control of the Atlantic coastline in 1702 rather than after 1763? Although counterfactual, the question points out the importance of the siege and the endurance of Spanish control. For St. Augustine itself, the invasion brought almost total physical destruction. Immediately after the siege it was almost as if the town had stepped back more than 135 years to the day that Pedro Menéndez and his settlers stepped ashore.

The siege received little attention in early histories of St. Augustine. George R. Fairbanks (1858) and W. W. Dewhurst (1881), relying on English sources, quickly passed over the siege with the comment that that "Spanish accounts of this mission are very meager." Fairbanks and Dewhurst set up a framework for St. Augustine's colonial history that was limited to assaults that involved the English. Indeed, the books clearly illustrated a perspective that nothing happened when the English were not invading. But that was not so. Charles W. Arnade read though more than 1,400 pages of Spanish reports[18] to inform *The Siege of St. Augustine of 1702*, published in 1959. Thereafter the 1702 siege became a major point in the presentation of St. Augustine's history. Claims of the ages of colonial buildings were modified, dating them no longer as 16th-century relics, but as post-siege structures, and the importance of the Castillo was heightened.

Daily life in St. Augustine in the months following the siege was harsh. The impact of inadequate shelter and food showed itself in the drastically lower birth rate for 1703. That year infant baptisms fell to one-third of the number of pre-siege christenings.[19] There are no burial records available for this time for comparison of how other residents fared under the duress.

Moore faced harsh criticism and judgments back in Carolina for the failure at St. Augustine. Yet Moore was not finished with

Spanish Florida. To redeem himself and offset financial problems, he attacked the Spanish missions west of St Augustine in 1704 and 1706 to capture Native Americans to be sold as workers to other English colonies. Some Franciscan friars and a few mission Indians made it to the safety of St Augustine. No Native American buffer zone now protected St. Augustine, and the territory open to mission friars shrank to the zone of Indian refugees closely surrounding St. Augustine.[20]

Rebuilding the homes and defenses of St. Augustine was a pressing concern after the siege. In 1703, Spain's King Felipe V, acting with unusual speed, authorized 20,000 pesos to be sent to rebuild the parish church, the St. Francis monastery, and other buildings. He decreed that an additional 6,000 pesos be sent to aid the needy of the Florida capital. Upon arrival three years later, the money went instead for food and clothing for the residents, who

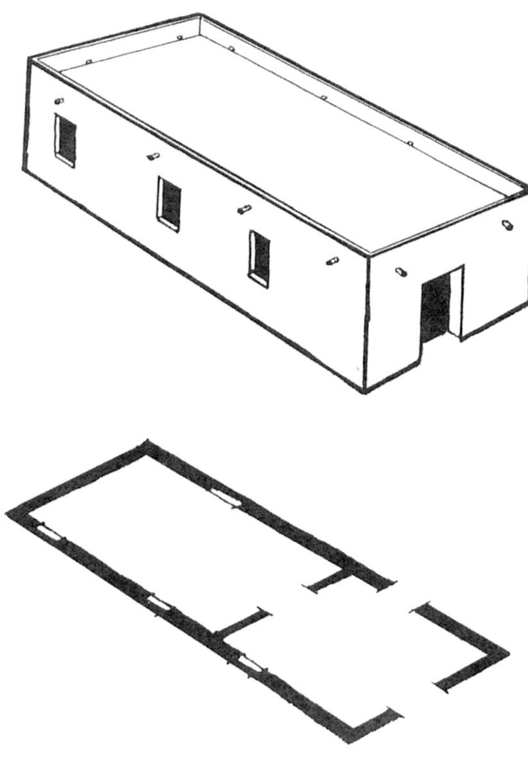

Based on archaeological records, this conjectural drawing represents the first phase of the Gonzáleź-Alvarez House (Oldest House). Drawn by Fred Amato.

at the time were suffering from losses inflicted by the hurricane of September 30, 1707. Governor Francisco de Córcoles y Martínez used the funds also for supplies for soldiers and to pay back salaries. In 1716, another allocation of 19,000 pesos arrived for rebuilding the church; again it was diverted for the needs of the residents. "Córcoles would not and could not use the money for the purposes laid down by the king," wrote historian John Jay TePaske. St. Augustinians survived because the governor misapplied the monies. Although begun, the new church building was not completed. The chapel of Nuestra Señora de la Soledad, a survivor of the siege, would continue to serve as the parish church until Spain ceded its Florida colony to Great Britain in 1763.[21]

The townspeople as well needed new buildings to replace their homes destroyed in 1702. By the middle of the 1720s some sturdy coquina homes began to line the streets, their front walls built to the edge of the streets. When Tomas González and Francisca Guevara buried their newborn child on August 14, 1727, the officiating priest inexplicably included in the burial record that the family lived in the house "near the Franciscan monastery." Thus did Father Azevedo create documentation to date the Oldest House at 14 St. Francis Street.[22]

St. Augustine's residents realized that they needed additional defenses after seeing how easily the Carolinians had entered the town in 1702. During the next two decades, strong earthworks and palisades went out from the Castillo.[23] The Cubo Line stretched from the Castillo to the San Sebastian River. The Rosario Line ran from the middle of the Cubo along the east bank of María Sánchez Creek, then made a right angle to Matanzas Bay at today's San Salvador Street to complete the enclosure of the city. The Hornabeque, another estuary-to-estuary defense line north of the Cubo Line, was created as an outer barrier, but well within the range and protection of the Castillo's cannon. The lines immediately around the city also served as social demarcations, for in the eighteenth-century Spanish world, whether one lived "inside the walls" or "outside the walls" was an important social distinction. "Outside the walls" usually implied lower cultural and spiritual development.[24]

Among those living "outside the walls" were the refugees of Carolina's Yamasee War of 1715. Indian refugees of that war sought safety with the Spanish, and the influx brought significant reorganization and expansion of the missions near St. Augustine. What a paradox! The refugees, who only a decade earlier had "played prominent roles in the destruction of the Florida missions," now ran to the Spanish for safety.[25] The villages were settled along the perimeter of St. Augustine, outside the walls. Refugees (401 of them in 1717) from several villages and language groups were mixed together within the enclaves. An Indian of lengthy association with the Spanish and a long-time Catholic usually headed the villages.

Both short-term and permanent British incursions continued to threaten Spanish Florida and St. Augustine. In 1728, Colonel John Palmer of South Carolina led a raid to within hundreds of feet of the Castillo. The walls and guns of the fortress and the city's defense walls, topped with needle- sharp Spanish bayonets (yucca), deterred his bringing an assault any closer than Mission Nombre de Dios. Palmer's raiders killed about 30 mission villagers, burned the chapel, and carried away sacred statues and altar ornaments.[26] In 1732, British colonists led by James Oglethorpe established the colony of Georgia, beginning with a settlement at Savannah. Georgians rapidly pushed ever southward. Four years later they built Fort Frederica on St. Simon's Island (Brunswick) and a fortification as close as the mouth of the St. Johns River.

Florida Governor Manuel de Montiano strengthened St. Augustine's defenses. He placed village outposts on both the north and south sides of the capital. About two miles north of St. Augustine's plaza, the governor created a village of freed blacks who had escaped from Carolina—Gracia Real Santa Teresa de Mose. To guard the southern approach, Montiano relocated Indians of Pocotalaca village to a site near Matanzas Inlet.[27] Montiano also strengthened the Castillo. To provide stone for the fort's repairs and modifications, a new quarry was opened on the barrier island, which had recently acquired the name of St. Anastasia in recognition of the chapel dedicated to her near the watchtower at the St. Augustine Inlet.[28]

Montiano said he needed "at least eight years for rehabilitation of the Castillo," but he would not have that much time. Many repairs and changes were incomplete when Great Britain declared war on Spain in 1739, invoking the insult of a Spaniard's severing the ear of British seaman Edward Jenkins as the proximate cause for the conflict. Great Britain's main target during this War of Jenkins' Ear was the Caribbean with Havana at center, and Porto Bello (Panama), Cartagena, and St. Augustine on the perimeter.[29]

British American forces commanded by James Oglethorpe, governor of Georgia, set out to take Spanish Florida. On June 13, 1740, seven British warships dropped anchor outside the St. Augustine inlet, blockading the harbor while Highlander troops and Carolina militia came over land on the north side of the city and occupied an abandoned Mose. Montiano had ordered the evacuation of the village to prevent the British from capturing Mose's residents. St. Augustine could field only a little more than half the number of the British who had arrived to fight. Yet Florida troops—Spanish soldiers, black militia, and Indian allies—made a successful attack on British-held Mose on June 26. British forces retreated from Mose; their leader John Palmer (of the 1728 raid) was killed and his head cut off. [30]

As if in revenge for the attack on Mose, British artillery began firing on St. Augustine from across the Matanzas estuary. The bombardment would last 27 days. At times, the residents sought shelter in the woods and in the covered way of the Castillo. How many children listened to their parents and grandparents tell "war stories" of their childhood, reminiscing about the siege of 1702? The guns of the Castillo and the fast little Spanish galliots in the harbor held back the British, who remained at artillery emplacements on Anastasia Island and at Point Cartel on the north side of St. Augustine's inlet. But Governor Montiano was as much concerned about the food supply as the ordnance, fretting on July 6 that "if we get none [supplies], there is no doubt that we shall die of hunger."[31]

Spanish supplies were landed at a harbor south of Matanzas Inlet and shallow-draft boats from St. Augustine were able to retrieve provisions and bring them to hungry St. Augustinians.

At the same time, Oglethorpe's naval commander, Commodore Pearse, in fear of hurricane season, refused to remain in Florida in order to support a British assault on the Castillo. Oglethorpe knew he was beaten and withdrew on July 6. St. Augustine's residents had been able to "live relatively unmolested in the city's houses," unlike the siege of 1702. As with the aftermath of the 1702 siege, the British expeditionary forces faced opprobrium back home for their failure; cooperation between Georgia and South Carolina had been shattered.[32]

To retaliate for the 1740 attack on Florida, Cuban governor Juan de Güemes y Horcasitas began assembling a powerful Spanish force to destroy "all the towns, posts, plantations and settlements of the enemy" up to Port Royal. He chose Governor Montiano to lead the expedition. On July 4, 1742, a Spanish force four times larger than any in Georgia, appeared off St. Simon's Island. Overwhelmed, Oglethorpe decided to ambush the Spanish in a low area of tangled oaks and moss. Georgians routed the Spanish advance guard at the "Battle of Bloody Marsh" and the rest of the Spanish force never attacked. Between the time of the 1740 assault on St. Augustine and the Battle of Bloody Marsh, Spanish workers had begun building a small coquina fort at Matanzas Inlet. Since 1569, wooden watchtowers had guarded the southern entrance to Matanzas River. The new fortification proved its worth in September 1742, when its guns fired on British ships lingering near Matanzas Inlet. Seven months later a minor expedition, with Oglethorpe aboard one of five ships, tried to negotiate both the St. Augustine and Matanzas inlets. This time weather was the biggest defender of St. Augustine as "Sea Mountains ran high on the shore." The little fleet turned back without firing a shot. The Carolinians, now hostile toward the Georgians, levied charges against Oglethorpe of misusing army funds. Oglethorpe went to London to clear his name. He never saw Georgia (or Florida) again. The British did not make another attempt against Spanish Florida until the 1756 outbreak of the Seven YearsWar (French and Indian War). Indian allies of the British raided the outskirts of St. Augustine, although there was no declaration of war between Spain and Great Britain until 1762.[33]

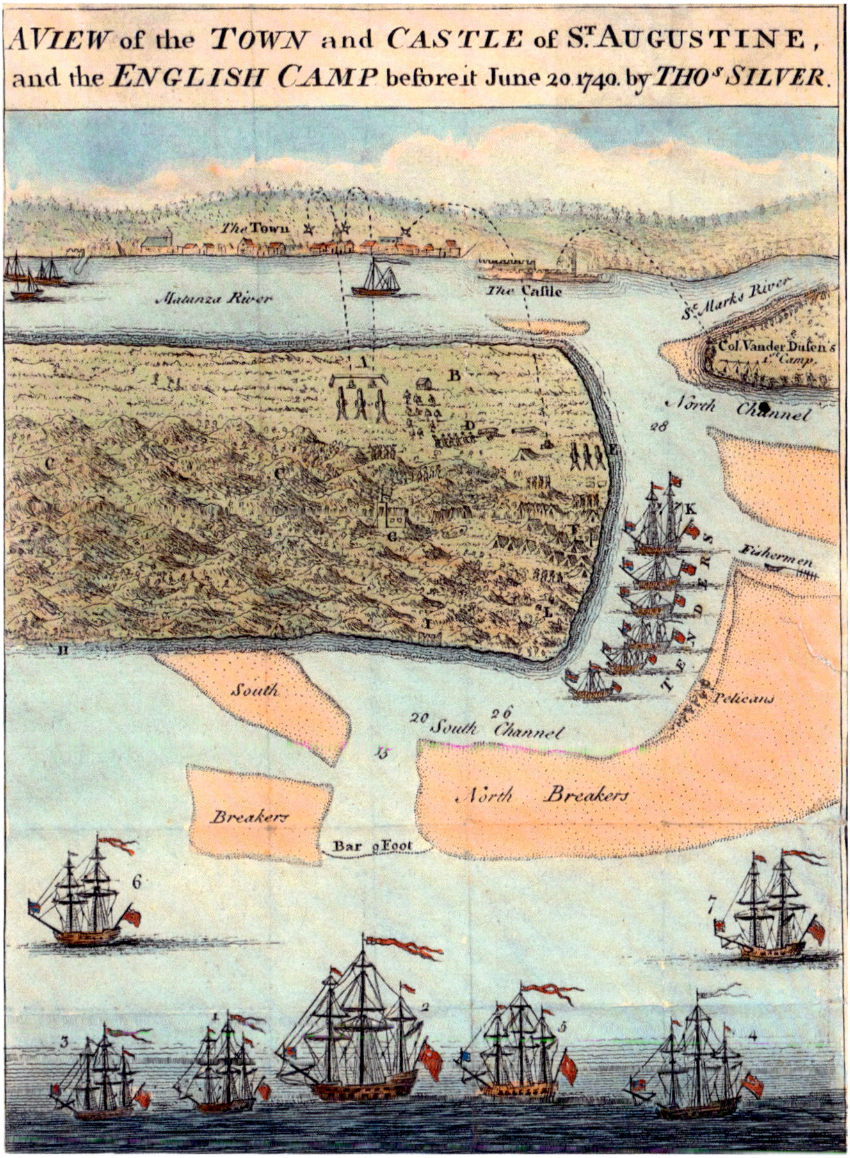

Thomas Silver's map of the 1740 siege of St. Augustine by British General James Oglethorpe. The general's main force is shown in the center on Anastasia Island, firing at Castillo de San Marcos. A secondary force under Colonel Alexander Vander Dussen is north of the inlet at the top right. The map first appeared in *Gentleman's Magazine* (London) in 1740.

For the twenty years following the Battle of Bloody Marsh, hostilities abated between Spanish Florida and the nearby British colonies. No enemy convoys or troops arrived in Florida; still, intermittent assaults by British-allied Indians in the countryside beyond St. Augustine took a few lives with each incident. Burial records noted repeatedly the St. Augustine residents who were "killed in the woods by Indians." Indians at St. Augustine took advantage of the manpower needs of the military to move into the mainstream economy, into mainstream society, and into homes in the town-- to live "inside the walls." Some Indian men originally from the missions enlisted in the Spanish army in St. Augustine. Others held support positions for the presidio, such as harbor pilot. Indian women who were midwives probably contributed income to the household. With economic and social integration, former mission villagers, by now *vecinos* or householders, changed their identity in the records from listing an "Indian" identity to an occupational identity, sometimes with no racial category, the latter category implying "white." They were members of the parish church, not of the mission churches, and protested when friars attempted to include them with the mission residents. Pedro Tomás de Ribera, previously of the Tolomato mission village and by 1745 a *vecino*, complained that his inclusion with the mission Indians was "against my wishes." Mission villages continued to encircle St. Augustine, but there were ever fewer enclaves and residents. Death from sickness depleted the villages and villagers married into the St. Augustine community and left the village for homes along St. Augustine's streets. [34]

The relative peace between 1743 and 1763 meant more to buy in St. Augustine shops. During peaceful times, imported items cost less and more merchandise arrived. As the world of available goods grew throughout the Atlantic, so did the offerings in St. Augustine's stores. In the early 1740s, shoppers could find shops offering "rum, wine, vinegar, sugar, tobacco, spices, lard, soap, tallow candles, and other provisions with a few kinds of silk, wool, linen goods, ribbons, and other trifles." British-owned shops sold manufactured items while shops with goods from Spanish lands carried sugar, alcoholic spirits, and nails.[35]

St. Augustine's residents must have been stunned when, in 1763, they learned that Florida would be transferred to Great Britain. After withstanding attacks and raids by British colonists and Indians, St. Augustine was to become a British town without a single cannon shot fired in or at the city. Ink, not artillery, brought the change of flags. Signatures on the Treaty of Paris to end the Seven Years War authorized the transfer. Spain agreed to give up its Florida colony to ransom Havana from British occupation. St. Augustine's residents prepared to relocate.

Between April 12, 1763, and January 21, 1764, about 3,100 persons sailed from St. Augustine—39 headed to Campeche, the other three thousand plus to Havana. Stories like that of Juana Navarro were repeated many times at dockside. In October 1763, Juana, with a five-week-old baby in her arms, six other children, and her husband, Salvador de Porras, boarded the brigantine *San Antonio* for Havana. Their furniture, chests, and strong boxes holding personal records went with them. Notary records, lawsuits, and all sorts of other private legal documents sailed away to Havana. Their location is not known, or whether they even survived the two and a half centuries of ordinary deterioration and political upheavals in Cuba. Departing ships also carried military matériel and the possessions of St. Augustine's churches and religious confraternities to Havana. St. Augustine's records of baptisms, marriages and burials left St. Augustine for storage in the parish church (later cathedral) of Havana along with the religious paraphernalia. The records would return to St. Augustine in 1906, worse for the years in a tropical climate. With the oldest entry dated January 24, 1594, they are the oldest records of American origin in the United States.[36] The removal of the documents in 1763 has left a fragmentary base for examining life in St. Augustine.

On January 22, 1764, the day after the last evacuee left for Cuba, Juan José Elixio de la Puente completed his map of property ownership in St. Augustine. His drawing is the first map or plan that is known to detail civilian housing and buildings of St. Augustine. Elixio de la Puente was concerned with selling the evacuees' land, and the list of property owners actually surrounds the map and creates a visual frame. Elixio's drawing was schematic,

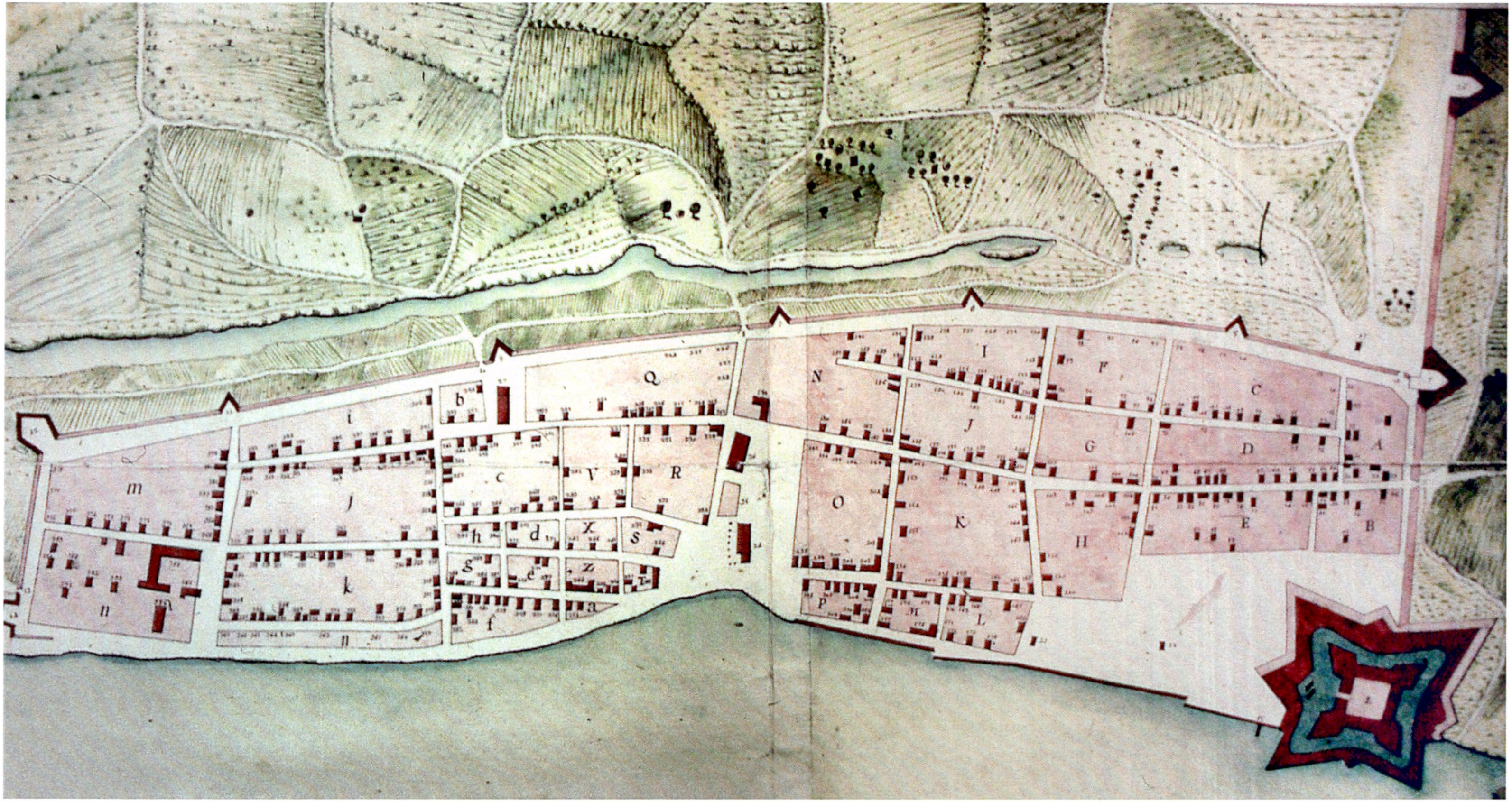

Juan Joseph Elixio de la Puente, Plan of the Royal Fort, Bastion, (Defensive) Line of the Town of St. Augustine of Florida with its Main Parish Church, Monastery and Church of St. Francis: Houses and Lots of the Residents; and other Works and the Gardens Beyond the Town Walls, all according to and in the form that it exists today 22 January1764. Original in Museo Naval in Madrid, Spain.

including only main structures in a representational manner and succinct lengths and widths of lots, without the irregularities that had evolved over years of human use and disagreement. Pablo Castelló had drawn St. Augustine in June of 1763. With his engineer's eye for detail, Castelló portrayed irregular lot lines and numerous outbuildings, but there is no surviving key to Castelló's map to indicate ownership.[37] Together these two maps provide an invaluable picture of St. Augustine and its residents at the time the Spanish departed.

The evacuating residents were listed in a chart made in April 1764 by sex, race, free or slave with the respective ships that transported them from Florida. Five years earlier, in 1759, Father Juan José Solana had described St Augustine's population as "composed of Spaniards, Indians, Negroes and Mulattos." In December of 1765 British visitor John Bartram repeated the Spanish priest's observation, noting that "the [inhabitants] of St. Augustine were of all colours at the time of the evacuation...." The last ship carrying evacuees to Havana had embarked almost two years before Bartram arrived in St. Augustine, so he was not an eyewitness. The tableau of departing residents must have so impressed British observers of the evacuation that they relayed to Bartram their recollections of the "whites, negroes, mulattoes, Indians, etc." who had peopled St. Augustine.[38]

NOTES

1 Robert M. Weir, *Colonial South Carolina: A History* (Columbia: University of South Carolina Press, 1997), 47-59 for English explorations, territorial claims and settlement attempts before 1670. Quote by South Carolina Governor Nathaniel Johnson, 1709 in *The Colonial South Carolina Scene, Contemporary Views,1697-1774*, E. Roy Merrens, ed. (Columbia: University of South Carolina Press, 1977), 47.

2 Pedro Menéndez Marquez to Crown, 27 December 1583, Archives of the Indies, Sevilla, Spain (AGI), Stetson Collection microfilm, University of Florida (SC) 54-5-9/18.

[3] Luis Rafael Arana and Albert Manucy, *The Building of Castillo de San Marcos* (n.p.: Eastern National Park and Monument Association, 1977), 25-27.

[4] Luis R. Arana, "Pirates March on St. Augustine, 1683," and "Grammont's Landing at Little Matanzas Inlet, 1686," both in *El Escribano* 9 (1972), (2): 51-62 and (3) 107-113 respectively. Arana and Manucy, *Building of Castillo,* 30; John E. Worth, *The Struggle for the Georgia Coast* (Tuscaloosa: University of Alabama Press, 2007), 40, 146-147; James G. Cusick, *The Other War of 1812: The Patriot War and the American Invasion of Spanish East Florida* (Gainesville: University Press of Florida, 2003), 144-152. The Patriots encamped north of St Augustine, staying beyond the range of the cannon on the fortress' gun deck, thus never taking possession of the capital city.

[5] Statements of Diego Flamenco, Thomas Vide, Jugo Jordan and Carlos Miller enclosed in Nicolás Ponce de León, 8 May 1674, AGI SC 58-1-35/16; Baptisms, April-June 1688, Cathedral Parish Records (hereafter CPR), Diocese of St. Augustine Archives. The St. Augustine parish church was not a cathedral until 1870, but the parish records (1594-present) are known collectively as Cathedral Parish Records.

[6] Weir comments that Carolina settlers refused to establish themselves in compact townships but spread out in isolated plantations along the rivers. *Colonial South Carolina*, 61. The Spanish on the other hand were urban oriented.

[7] Arana and Manucy, *Building of Castillo,* 30; testimonies by several witnesses in Worth, *Georgia Coast,* 150-160. An inscription on the candlestick indicated it had been donated in 1676 to the Church of Santo Cristo de San Román in Campeche.

[8] Ben Marsh, "Silk Hopes in Colonial South Carolina," *Journal of Southern History* 78 (2012): 816 n. 29.

[9] Timothy Paul Grady, *Anglo-Spanish Rivalry in Colonial South-East America, 1650-1725* (London: Pickering & Chatto, 2010), 64; Weir, *Colonial South Carolina,* 66.

[10] J. Leitch Wright, Jr., *Anglo-Spanish Rivalry in North America* (Athens: University of Georgia Press, 1971), 58

[11] Arana and Manucy, *Building of Castillo,* 32, 35; Robert L Kapitzke, *Religion, Power and Politics in Colonial St. Augustine* (Gainesville: University Press of Florida, 2001,) 48, 52-58, 63

[12] Appraisal by Juan Marqués de Molina, master builder, 21 March 1691, 54-5-13/19; Quiroga to Crown, 8 June 1690, 54-5-12/02; 20 March 1691, 54-5-

13/19; 20 April 1691, 54-5-15/114; 12 December 1691, 54-5-13/27; Joaquín de Florencia, 14 May 1691, 54-5-13/19, all in AGI SC. Luis R. and Eugenia B. Arana, "Private Coquina Construction in St. Augustine, 1689-1702," *El Escribano* 6 (3) (1969): 28-31.

13 Weir, *Colonial South Carolina,* 76. Moore had been making war plans even before the outbreak of hostilities.

14 Charles W. Arnade, *The Siege of St. Augustine of 1702* (Gainesville: University of Florida Press, 1959), 30, 36.

15 Arnade, *Siege*, 43; Baptism of Juana, 8 January 1703, born 7 November 1702, Cathedral Parish Records (CPR).

16 Baptisms, dated November 1702-April 1703, CPR.

17 Arnade, *Siege*, 57-58; Baptism of Francisco, mulatto son of Juan de los Gasdos, slave of Adjutant Gerónimo Regidor, and Marta María, 18 November 1702, recorded 5 August 1703, CPR.

18 Arnade noted that the "two principal *legajos"* or bundles that chronicled the siege in Spanish archives contained 849 pages and 598 pages. *Siege,* 63.

19 Baptisms, 1698-1706, CPR.

20 Kapitzke, *Religion Power and Politics,* 150.

21 Ibid., 148-150; Charles W. Arnade, "The Architecture of Spanish St. Augustine," *The Americas* 18 (1961):152; John Jay TePaske, *The Governorship of Spanish Florida, 1700-1763* (Durham: Duke University Press, 1964), 91-92.

22 Burials, CPR.

23 Arana and Manucy, *Building of Castillo*, 42.

24 Jane Landers, "Gracia Real de Santa Teresa de Mose: A Free Black Town in Spanish Colonial Florida," *American Historical Review* 95 (1990): 28-29; Arana and Manucy, *Building of Castillo*, map on inside back cover.

25 John H. Hann "St. Augustine's Fallout from the Yamassee War," *Florida Historical Quarterly* 68 (1989): 182-200; quote on 180.

26 TePaske, *Governorship*, 130-131

[27] Letter book of Florida Governor Manuel de Montiano, 3 January 1739, no. 13 and 31 January 1740, no.180, Bundle 37 East Florida Papers, Library of Congress Manuscript Collection (microfilm copies at St. Augustine Historical Society).

[28] Montiano Letter book, 7 April 1739, no. 145; Antonio de Arredondo to Governor of Havana, 24 November 1736, AGI SC 87-1-1/59.

[29] Arana and Manucy, *Castillo*, 46.

[30] Edward Kimber, *A Relation or Journal of a Late Expedition to the Gates of St. Augustine on Florida / conducted by the Hon. General James Oglethorpe with a Detachment of his Regiment, etc. from Georgia* (London, 1744, reprint, 1935) 89.

[31] Arana and Manucy, *Building of Castillo*, 47-50; Montiano Letter book, 6 July 1740, no. 203.

[32] Wright, Jr., *Anglo-Spanish Rivalry in North America*, 92.

[33] Luis R Arana, "The Fort at Matanzas Inlet, 1740-1821," *El Escribano* 17 (1980): 3, 7-8.

[34] Burials 1740-1763; Marriages, books of white and books of non-whites, CPR. Statement of Pedro Tomás de Ribera, 9 February 1745, AGI Santo Domingo 846.

[35] Warfare limited availability of British and Spanish goods and drove up prices on all freight because of the increased costs of doing business. Conversely, peace brought lower prices. Carl E. Swanson, *Predators and Prizes: American Privateering and Imperial Warfare, 1739-1748* (Columbia: University of South Carolina Press, 1991), 187. Quote in Michael Scardaville and Jesús María Belmonte, eds. and trans., "Florida in the Late First Spanish Period: The 1756 Griñán Report," *El Escribano* 16 (1979): 10.

[36] Inventory of the Ornaments, Altars, Images, Bells, and Sacred Vessels belonging to the Parochial Church and the Religious Brotherhoods of the Garrison Town of St. Augustine, Florida, 5 November 1764, AGI Cuba 372 (typescript at St. Augustine Historical Society in MC-63, Furnishings and Inventories file); Michael V. Gannon, *The Cross in the Sand: The Early Catholic Church in Florida, 1513-1870* (Gainesville: University of Florida Press, 1965), 191.

[37] Claim of Juana Navarro, Bundle 320, Claim no.15, Claims for Town Lots, Spanish Land Grant manuscripts, Florida Division of Historical Resources, Tallahassee (microfilm copies at St. Augustine Historical Society). Juan José

Elixio de la Puente, "Plan of the Royal Fort, Bastion, (Defensive) Line of the Town of St. Augustine of Florida with its Main Parish Church, Monastery and Church of St. Francis: Houses and Lots of the Residents; and other Works and the Gardens Beyond the Town Walls, all according to and in the form that it exists today 22 January1764." There are many copies at the St. Augustine Historical Research Library and other repositories, of this map, made with ever-changing technology since the 1850s. The original is in the Museo Naval in Madrid. Pablo Castelló, "Map of the Presidio of St. Augustin' . . . . [1764]," original in Spanish Ministry of War.

[38] Juan José Solana, 22 April 1759, enclosed in Solana to Julián de Arriaga, 9 April 1760 AGI SC 87-6-21/41, SD 2584; William Stork, *An Account of East Florida with Journal Kept by John Bartram of Philadelphia, Botanist to His Majesty for the Floridas; Upon a Journey from St. Augustine up the River St. John's* . . . (London: W. Nicoll, 1769), Ch. 1, p. 8.

5

"Not So Gay A Town as This"

1763 - 1784

Daniel L. Schafer

On July 20, 1763, a British ship carrying Captain John Hedges and four companies of the First (Royal) Regiment of Foot was anchored off St. Augustine. The regiment had previously been in Havana, part of the last major campaign of the Seven Years War (French and Indian War in North America). To regain control of Cuba, Spain ceded Florida to Britain under terms of the Peace of Paris. British officials and the king declared that the Florida territory would be two separate governments: West and East Florida, with St. Augustine as the capital of the latter.[1]

Ten days later, Major Francis Ogilvie of the Ninth Regiment replaced Hedges. For the next thirteen months, until a British governor arrived, Major Ogilvie directed both military and civil affairs in East Florida. He quartered troops at Fort St. Mark or at the unfinished house of the Bishop of Cuba at the southwest corner of the parade ground. Officers were assigned rooms in private homes, a move that aroused the ire of Spanish residents. Lieutenant Colonel James Robertson, deputy quartermaster general for North America, informed Major General Jeffery Amherst that the Spaniards so disliked having "strangers in their familys" that they abandoned their houses.[2]

Spanish Governor Melchor Feliú sympathized with the residents and blamed the British soldiers for demolishing houses and "plundering whatever they could find in them easy to carry,

Left: Governor's (Government) House, 1764, portrayed at the time when Spain ceded Florida to Great Britain following the Seven Years War. The original watercolor is preserved by the British Library. Post card courtesy of Henry E. Hird, III

and all combustible material on account of their scarcity of fire wood." Despite these tensions, interactions between the two commanders were generally cordial, yet Ogilvie was relieved when "all the Spaniards inhabiting this town sail'd from this place on 21st [January] 1764." Ogilvie thought the Spaniards were "the least Industrious of any People I ever saw, having depended entirely on our Colonies in America for supplies of Provisions." Colonel Robertson agreed, informing General Amherst that East Florida was "capable of producing everything [yet] affords nothing at present but fish, not an herb, not a cabbage, all is overgrown with weeds."[3]

Governor James Grant arrived at St. Augustine on August 29, 1764. Born at Ballindalloch Castle in the Highlands of Scotland, Grant held an officer's commission in the British army for more than a half-century. During the Seven Years War, he saw action against the French and Indians in the Ohio country and in Canada. In 1760, Grant commanded a highly successful campaign against the Cherokee in South Carolina. He was next sent to Cuba to serve briefly as lieutenant governor of Havana following the British capture of that port. He was appointed governor of East Florida on November 23, 1763.[4]

At St. Augustine, Grant found a nearly abandoned town and a garrison of only 197 men. After touring the hinterland, he described East Florida as being "in a State of Nature...not an acre of land planted...and nobody to work or at work." He wrote urgent letters to James Box of Georgia and James Moultrie of South Carolina, newly appointed as attorney general and chief justice respectively, demanding that they come to Florida immediately. To Moultrie, Grant wrote: "I cannot proceed to one act of government until you are on the Spot." Consequently, inauguration ceremonies were delayed until October 31, 1764, when the Royal Council members were in St. Augustine.[5]

Grant encouraged Royal Council member John Moultrie, an experienced South Carolina planter and medical doctor, to "prevail with some of your friends to come and live amongst us, tis a better climate, better soil, and better everything than in Carolina." Grant's friendship with the Moultrie brothers and other prominent leaders of colonial South Carolina and Georgia had been established during the Cherokee campaign.[6]

In the absence of municipal institutions, St. Augustine was governed by Grant, the Royal Council, and the courts of the province. An annual parliamentary appropriation of £5,700 funded salaries and expenses of government, one-half of which paid the salaries of the governor, council members, clergy, teachers, provost marshal, harbor pilot, and other minor officials. A bonus fund of £500 was set aside to encourage cultivation of needed agricultural products, and the remaining £2,250 was to be used to pay for unexpected expenses and to buy gifts for Native American leaders.[7]

Governor Grant's authority was limited to the "civil establishment." Largely a garrison town in the beginning, St. Augustine served as brigade headquarters for Brigadier General Frederick Haldimand for one year, and also accommodated the Fourteenth Regiment. Grant's cordial relationship with the military was enhanced by his weekly practice of hosting the entire officers' corps for dinner and drinks.

The early settlers in St. Augustine found one man in control of nearly two hundred buildings and lots, approximately one-half of the entire housing stock of the town. The departing Spaniards had not been able to sell their property before the British arrived and had reached a confidential agreement with Jesse Fish, agent for a New York merchant. A resident of the town since age thirteen, Fish promised to sell the properties after real estate prices recovered and submit the proceeds to Havana through a trusted intermediary, Juan Josef Elixio de la Puente, a Royal Engineer, surveyor and cartographer, who moved from East Florida to Cuba with the Spanish evacuees in 1764.[8]

Fish explained that the precipitous order to embark for Havana prompted him to act on behalf of his Spanish friends by assuming their debts to his employer, William Walton and Company, in exchange for titles to 187 houses and lots. His job soon terminated, however, leaving him in debt to Walton for "a considerable sum … "and the interest running on." According to Puente, the agreement was to prevent confiscation of the properties by the British.

Fish's troubles began shortly after the British soldiers arrived and vandalized the houses, causing resale prices to plummet. He was also hindered by Puente's refusal to provide authenticating documents. Puente acknowledged that he "always ignored his [Fish's] letters" because the agreement violated terms of the Spanish-British treaty. Fish was also the victim of embezzlement by friends and relatives who betrayed his trust. Luciano de Herrera helped to untangle the confusion and transmit funds to Havana that satisfied most of the former owners, but Fish remained mired in debt until the end of his life.

Puente arranged a second agreement that Governor Grant viewed as a potential roadblock to development of the colony. Charleston merchant John Gordon, Jesse Fish, and Lieutenant Colonel James Robertson formed a partnership to purchase ten million acres of land from the departing Spaniards. Fish and Gordon insisted that the land titles were "executed in the most formal and solemn manner, according to the laws of Spain" but Grant, with authorization from the Board of Trade, disavowed the legality of the transactions.[9]

Grant faced a further challenge with the need to establish peaceful relations with the Creek Indians located at villages in Alachua and near Tallahassee. Grant advocated just treatment of Indians and honest negotiations rather than going to war. He also believed in generous distribution of presents and strict regulation of the British traders to prevent them from fomenting trouble in Indian villages. On November 15, 1765, Grant and John Stuart, Superintendant of Indian Affairs in the Southern Colonies, met with chiefs of the Lower Creek villages at Fort Picolata on the St. Johns River. The Creek leaders agreed to cede the coastal lands east of the St. Johns and as far south and west of the river as the tidal waters flowed.[10]

A few days later, the Cowkeeper, headman of the Alachua Creek (soon to be known as the Seminole), brought 60 warriors to St. Augustine to parlay with the governor. To win their friendship, Grant entertained his guests lavishly and proclaimed the Cowkeeper a Great Medal Chief. For the next twenty years the presence of Seminole men and women in St. Augustine's markets and stores was a common occurrence. They brought cattle, hides, and furs to sell to town merchants. Their presence was not without peril, as disputes with residents could explode into violent episodes. To head off retaliatory violence when an Indian boy was killed in December 1768, Grant had two white hunters arrested and brought the father of the murdered boy into the governor's residence while the accused men were tried in court, convicted, and executed.[11]

The satisfactory conclusion of the November 1765 Picolata conference permitted Governor Grant to concentrate on development of the vast unpopulated hinterland of East Florida. Soon after arriving at St. Augustine, Grant wrote to John Perceval, the second Earl of Egmont: "I consider the whole [province] as a great plantation put under my care, and in fact I am anxious about the success of every individual." He avidly promoted plantation development, writing to influential grantees to encourage them to invest heavily during the startup phases of their estates. Substantial initial sums were needed to acquire a labor force to clear the virgin lands, dam and dike the marsh land for rice fields, and cut timber and construct shelters, but once established the harvests would return annual profits.[12]

Each grantee was warned that white settlers became lazy or debilitated by the high temperatures. He advised one grantee: "Settlements in this warm climate must be formed by Negroes, our indented white people can hardly be prevailed upon to work for their own subsistence." Even indented Germans, so prized in the northern colonies, "won't do here" Grant advised: "Upon their landing they are immediately seized with the pride which every man is possessed of who wears a white face in America and they say they won't be slaves and so they make their escape."[13]

In 1765, Grant established his own experimental farm at a 300-acre tract north of the city gate. In addition, he established Grant's Villa six miles north of St. Augustine at the merger of the North and Guana rivers, which became a highly successful indigo plantation worked by enslaved Africans. After only four years, the profits from indigo exports repaid all of the startup expenses, including the cost of seventy-eight slaves.[14]

British period residents Joseph and Mary Peavett added the wooden second floor to the coquina house at 14 St. Francis Street, abandoned by the Tomás González family. Today it is known popularly as "The Oldest House" and formally as the González-Álvarez House National Historic Landmark. The Peavetts opened an inn, store, and tavern in their home.

Residents of St. Augustine acquired farms and plantations west of the town and along the St. Johns River, and north along the North, Guana, and Pablo rivers. Carpenter George Grassell owned four farms. Merchant Spencer Mann hired an overseer to supervise 60 slaves at nine rural properties. Cartographer, engineer, and provincial surveyor J. William Gerard de Brahm acquired a dwelling across the lane and north of the governor's residence. Francis Philip Fatio and Francis Levett had houses in St. Augustine as well as 10,000-acre estates on the east bank of the St. Johns River. South of St. Augustine, John Moultrie, Robert Bissett, and other St. Augustine residents established coastal estates. Denys Rolle and his wife resided briefly in St. Augustine. The eccentric Member of Parliament from Barnstaple and one of the wealthiest men in Britain, owned approximately 80,000 acres at three sites along the St. Johns River.[15]

Dr. Andrew Turnbull built a residence north of St. Augustine and rented a dwelling on St. George Street. Turnbull recruited 1,403 laborers from Italy, Greece, and Minorca on indenture contracts and transported them to work at Smyrnea Plantation, two adjoining 20,000-acre tracts seventy miles south of St. Augustine at Mosquito Inlet. Turnbull's partners were William Duncan, physician to King George III, and George Grenville, former prime minister of Great Britain. The immense scale of development at Smyrnea was unmatched in the British North American colonies. Sickness and agonizingly high death rates, drought, hurricanes, funding and food shortages, labor unrest, rebellion, and charges of oppressive labor conditions led to the collapse of the settlement in 1777 and 1778. The surviving laborers settled in the northwest section of St. Augustine that became known as the "Minorcan Quarter." They rented vacant farmland near the town, and became fishermen, laborers, and merchants.[16]

By 1771, the number of plantations in East Florida had increased significantly. Cultivated fields, slave quarters, and the dwellings of planters or their agents and overseers could be found on the banks of most of the province's waterways. Coasting vessels from Charleston and Savannah supplied over two dozen merchants in St. Augustine, who met the needs of the planters and laborers at the provincial farms and plantations, as well as the town's innkeepers, shipbuilders, ship carpenters, and laborers.

There were no local newspapers, but official notices were posted at Robert Payne's Corner, a retail store. On more than one occasion, broadsides critical of the government were posted alongside official notices. News and gossip could be heard at the taverns, the town market, the public slaughter pen at the town gate, and the public bathhouse.

An important feature of life in St. Augustine was the existence of publicly supported education. Parliament provided an annual subsidy that included a salary for two teachers. The first was Enoch Hawksworth, who arrived in 1765, and was followed by Jones Reed, the Reverend John Leadbetter, and the Reverend John Kennedy. Wealthy merchants and planters hired private tutors to educate their children

Originally a drab barracks town, St. Augustine became the unlikely seat of a lively social life, at least for the elite residents. For the more prominent men, Grant founded a Masonic Lodge and became its first Grand Master. The gourmet bachelor governor entertained often and lavishly, believing that social functions were necessary to counter the disadvantages of life in an under-populated frontier town. On the king's birthday and other holidays, Grant hosted dinner parties for the town's leaders. Deference to rank was insisted upon, to the extent that he blocked Martin Jollie from a rightful seat on the Royal Council because he came from a low social rank: his father had been a tailor in Scotland. Jollie was the agent for Lord Egmont's plantations in East Florida.[17]

The frequency of the governor's social events can be gauged by "The State of the Governor's Cellars," monthly inventories he maintained. During his first year in office, items "drunk from the Governor's Cellars" tallied 86 gallons of Jamaican rum, 150 gallons of common rum, 140 gallons of Madeira wine, 76 gallons of Tenerife wine, 1,200 bottles of claret, 519 bottles of port, and similar amounts of champagne, sweet wine, porter, beer, ale, cider, arrack, and "old hock." The governor and his guests also consumed four barrels of beef, two barrels of pork, four barrels of rice, twelve barrels of flour, prodigious amounts of fresh lamb, turtle, fish, venison, oyster, turkey, chicken, duck, capon, and hams and bacon. Three women in the town each made daily deliveries of eggs and milk.[18]

Overconsumption may have contributed to the painful gout condition and other health problems Grant suffered during his years in St. Augustine. He was determined, however, to remain in East Florida until a stable government was in place and the farms and plantations were established and successful. When his ailments worsened in May of 1771, he returned to England for medical treatment, appointing John Moultrie as interim governor.

Back in London, Grant actively supported East Florida enterprises. He wrote to Moultrie often with detailed directions for managing the province, renovating public buildings, and completing a north-south network of roads. Work on these projects had been delayed until sufficient funds could be saved from the annual budgets to pay for construction. In April 1772, Grant directed Moultrie to act with urgency to convert the old Spanish hospital to a jail and transform the Spanish Bishop's house into a Town House containing Council chambers, an assembly room, and offices for customs, the land surveyor, secretary, register, and naval affairs.[19]

Work on the Town House began in October. Moultrie predicted it would be the least expensive public building constructed in the American colonies. After Grant informed Moultrie that church bells and a town clock had been acquired, Moultrie responded: "I see you begin to think of serving yourself a seat in Heaven." He promptly ordered a wooden spire constructed at Parson Forbes' Church of St. Peter's, which became the home for the clock and church bells.[20]

Road construction was well under way by late June 1772, when the route south to Matanzas Swamp was completed. "In the wettest season," Moultrie said, "a wagon or coach and six may go full trot over it to the end." Captain Robert Bisset agreed to construct the road ninety miles south of St. Augustine, to Stob's Farm, owned by London merchant William Elliot. When completed, Reverend Forbes reported: "Captain Bisset's road really may with propriety be called the King's Highway: it forms a wide beautiful avenue, not a stump of a tree to be found." John Fairlamb contracted with Moultrie to build a 35-mile segment of road from St. Augustine north to the ferry at Cowford on the St. Johns (today's downtown Jacksonville). The remaining 36-mile portion of the road, north from the Cowford to the St. Marys River, was constructed by Charles and Jermyn Wright and completed in 1774.[21]

James Grant never returned to East Florida to view the completed public works. In April 1773 he became a Member of Parliament and resigned as governor. He hired overseers and agents to direct his planting interests and supervise his slaves, and depended on letters from his close friends, John Forbes, John Moultrie, Frederick George Mulcaster, and David Yeats for news of life in St. Augustine.

Until Grant's replacement was named, John Moultrie continued to preside over the province. During Moultrie's time in office, a serious spirit of discord surfaced in St. Augustine. A leader of the dissenting faction was Chief Justice William Drayton. A scion of a prominent South Carolina family trained in the law in London, Drayton had informed Grant as early as 1768 that proclamations of the Royal Council were potential violations of English law until an elected House of Commons was established in East Florida. Grant and Drayton developed a harmonious relationship.

Harmonious is not a word that described the relationship between Drayton and Moultrie. Records emphasize the haughty and vindictive behavior that characterized their public clashes, but significant issues were involved. Drayton and his compatriots, Andrew Turnbull and planter-merchant James Penman, were principled advocates of the rights of Englishmen in the colonies, and believed those rights were being violated as long as East Florida was without an elected House of Assembly.

Reverend Forbes forecast the trouble ahead in a letter to James Grant. "We were uninterruptedly quiet and happy under your guidance, at a time all America was in a blaze," but after recent unsettling changes former friends "can scarce bear to look at one another." By acting "dogmatically, improperly and unpopularly, Moultrie was partly to blame," Forbes thought, but Drayton was being "disruptive, conceited and irascible."[22]

Frederick Mulcaster, a Royal Engineer and the provincial surveyor, was shocked when Drayton announced that East Florida's black slaves might be freed as a result of a judicial decision known as the "Somerset Affair" that abolished slavery in Great Britain. "I suppose he will say as the laws of Great Britain are to be enforced in the colonies—he will therefore execute his duty by doing it effectually and therefore enfranchise the whole negro tribe! Don't you think he is mad? Don't you think he is paving the way for his own and his family's destruction?"[23]

After a dispute with Moultrie over the right of the Council to examine and censure contingent fund expenditures, Drayton resigned from the Council in October 1771. Officials in London reinstated him, and confrontations continued. In August 1773, Moultrie suspended Drayton from the Council, but as he was still Chief Justice he continued to criticize the interim governor. Moultrie accused Drayton of being "a man destitute of worth, self-conceited, proud and envious." Drayton asked former governor Grant to intercede, arguing that the controversy was the result of Moultrie's efforts to suppress examinations of expenditures on public works:

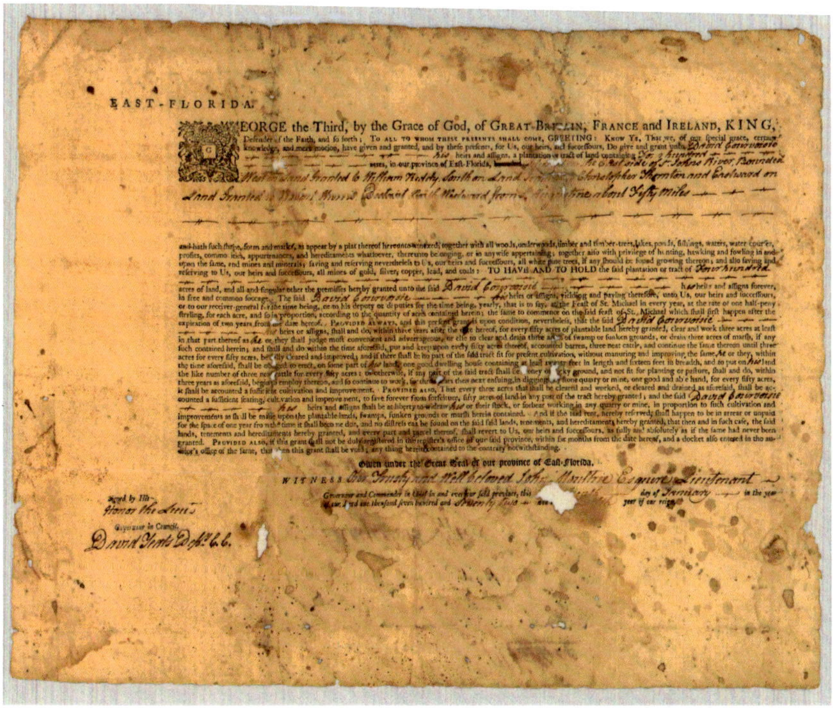
EAST-FLORIDA.

GEORGE the Third, by the Grace of God, of GREAT-BRITAIN, FRANCE and IRELAND, KING,

Given under the Great Seal of our province of East-Florida.

Land grant to David Courvoisie for 400 acres on St. Johns River, signed by Lt. Governor John Moultrie on January 10, 1772. Claim of F. J. Fatio et al., Confirmed grant F 12, Spanish Land Grants, State Library and Archives of Florida.

"Every matter relative to [government] may be supposed to partake of the general ferment which now unhappily prevails over this continent."[24]

This contentious atmosphere marked the arrival of the second governor of East Florida, Lieutenant Colonel Patrick Tonyn. Tonyn, age 49 and a veteran of combat in Germany during the Seven Years War, was the owner of an East Florida plantation on the St. Johns River and Black Creek established in the 1760s. His arrival in March 1774 had been keenly anticipated in hopes he would restore the tranquility and gaiety of earlier days. Upon hearing of the appointment, James Grant predicted Tonyn would "bring all into good humour and drown animosity in a Bottle of Claret."[25]

It soon became apparent to Grant's close friends that Tonyn would accentuate rather than diminish the spirit of discord. Initial criticism of the new governor was sometimes petty, as in Mulcaster's gossipy comment that the new governor failed to entertain the local dignitaries until six weeks after he arrived in St. Augustine, and then he served "bad port, bad Madeira, bad sherry...a very bad dinner and a tawdry dessert." Reminding Grant of his prediction that Tonyn would restore tranquility, Mulcaster wrote: "You are quite mistaken in your man – he neither drinks nor gives Claret–he has no wine of any kind, at least that is good for anything, and he... hangs at home miserably, no method, bad servants and a dirty table cloth..."[26]

In November, Parson Forbes commented that "hopes have failed with Tonyn," he is "not very alert at his pen" and "not very wise," although "a good-meaning man," he "will never bring fire to the pan." David Yeats, secretary of the province and agent for Governor Grant's plantation and business affairs, complained that Tonyn refused to pay for furniture he agreed to buy from the former governor. After six years and repeated requests for payment, the debt was finally settled."[27]

The bitterest denunciations of Tonyn concerned treatment of three enslaved domestic servants, Alexander, Peg, and Sue, whom Tonyn rented from Grant. Late in 1775, Yeats complained that Tonyn had not paid "a shilling" of the agreed upon rental fee and that the servants were "greatly complaining about bad usage." He blamed Mrs. Tonyn, saying "she appears to be of a cruel hard-headed disposition, at least to the servants."[28]

Reverend Forbes sent a dire warning to Grant: "It will be cruel to sell your Negroes to Governor Tonyn. They plead hard and the town says they have got Iron Caps...Alexander complains that Madam is the devil, he told me the governor is well enough, but since I saw him he has had the cap above mentioned and been flogged." Two days later, Forbes sent another urgent letter: "Your Negroes, from the mismanagement of a capricious cruelty of a fine lady, are considered as being in a state of the most abject slavery. Alexander has got an iron cap with which he walks the streets."[29]

This news infuriated Grant. He sent an unequivocal order to Yeats: "If Alexander and Peg are still in the woods [they had run away], which I wish them to be, you are publicly to make it known that Governor Tonyn has nothing to do with them, that they have nothing to fear, and are to live in the future at Grant's Villa."[30]

Discord persisted throughout Tonyn's tenure as governor, although the repercussions diminished as the war for independence engulfed the American colonies. Whatever his shortcomings in the social expectations of his office, Tonyn became an adept military governor, especially when dealing with the provincial militia, shoring up defenses, and maintaining alliances with the Seminole and Creek.[31]

A portent of troubles ahead came in August 1775, when the *Betsy*, under Captain Lofthouse, was attacked off St. Augustine by a rebel vessel out of South Carolina. Loaded with gunpowder, the ship was anchored overnight to await favorable winds and tide before entering the harbor. Sailing north from Matanzas Inlet at daybreak, a rebel privateer surprised and sacked the *Betsy* without a shot fired in defense.

Governor Tonyn's review of the town's military preparedness revealed that little had been done to maintain the decades-old defense lines surrounding St. Augustine. The supposedly impregnable Fort St. Marks and its system of trenches and redoubts were in serious disrepair. The governor ordered drafts of plantation slaves to repair and strengthen the defense lines under supervision of military engineers.

With fewer than 200 men of the Fourteenth Regiment on station at the beginning of the war, Tonyn ordered a census of white inhabitants fit to bear arms, and of the enslaved men who could be trusted with weapons. Seven white and four black militia companies were formed to augment the troops assigned to St. Augustine. Thomas Brown, a refugee who had been tarred and feathered in Georgia for his loyalist beliefs, was given command of the East Florida Rangers.[32]

Tonyn negotiated a military alliance with the Creek and Seminole. In concert with John Stuart, the governor arranged a December 1775 congress at the Cowford ferry landing on the south

Within a year of British arrival Thomas Jeffreys produced a map of St. Augustine based on one by the Spaniard Juan de Solís, but with English identifications. Original in Public Records Office, Kew, England.

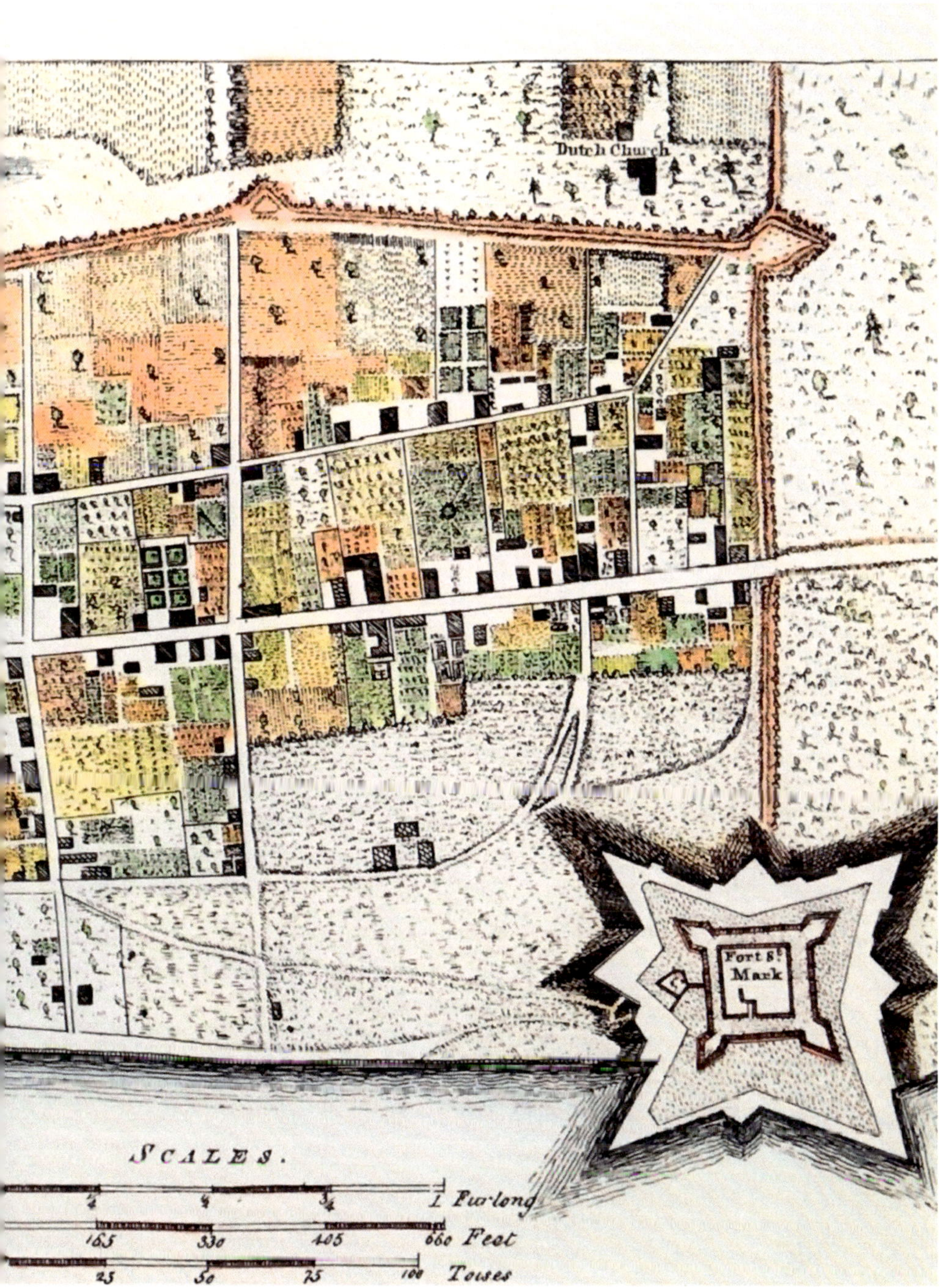
Dutch Church
Fort St. Mark
SCALES.
1/4 1/2 3/4 1 Furlong
165 330 495 660 Feet
25 50 75 100 Toises

side of the St. Johns River in today's Jacksonville. Anticipating the need for well-armed Indian allies to repel invaders from Georgia, Tonyn supplied the Creek and Seminole with weapons and gunpowder in return for future support as scouts and skirmishers.[33]

In February 1776, convinced that William Drayton's political principles were in agreement with the "factious leaders" in the northern colonies, Tonyn suspended the chief justice. Andrew Turnbull and other long-time members of the province defended Drayton, but David Yeats felt that Drayton "drew it upon himself." Yeats worried about repercussions, since "this town may literally be said to be divided against itself."[34]

The town was indeed divided. At Wood's Tavern, Drayton's supporters held a meeting chaired by Turnbull. Prominent planters and merchants, including the unquestionably loyal Francis Philip Fatio, Spencer Mann, and James Penman, signed a petition to the Crown. Tonyn refused to forward the petition.

Drayton traveled to London to plead his case before the Board of Trade. He was reinstated and returned to St. Augustine, only to be suspended again in December 1777. He journeyed again to London but decided to resign from office before a second plea was considered.

Partisan discord and tense personal animosities were commonplace in St. Augustine, but Parson Forbes retained an optimistic and opportunistic outlook. He was rewarded with appointments to the Royal Council, Court of Vice Admiralty, and Court of Common Law. Always anxious to increase his income, Forbes asked James Grant to support his quest to replace William Drayton as chief justice, saying "the study of divinity is laying a good foundation for law." Grant was unwilling to make the recommendation.[35]

As the Revolution intensified in the north, John Moultrie was appointed to command a militia regiment that mustered 300 men. He noted a paradox that would continue throughout the war: St. Augustine remained safe from attack, even flourished in trade and population, while the northern portion of the colony, between the St. Johns and St. Marys rivers, became a frontier battle zone of raids and counter raids for plunder of cattle and slaves and incendiary attacks on the rural settlements. "This town is full of people who have fled for safety, our planting thrives finely, good indigo, plenty of provisions; every plantation has enough and some to spare…." Each year, dozens of vessels carried loads of lumber away from the port. With exports of forest products from North Carolina and New England blocked by the Royal Navy, cargoes of timber, pitch, tar, and turpentine from East Florida sold in the British West Indies for abnormally high prices.[36]

Away from the town, rebel attacks destroyed several plantations north of the St. Johns River. The Reverend Forbes feared property beyond the St. Johns could not be protected from the "lawless banditti…. We have been pestered here by the Rebels from Georgia driving away our cattle and stealing our Negroes. They have lately carried away between thirty and forty Negroes on the west side of the St. Johns River." Wealthy planters considered dismantling their estates and moving their slaves closer to St. Augustine.[37]

With a border war raging, Reverend Forbes condoned the plunder raids into Georgia by East Florida militia. In one action, "70 men and 25 crackers" backed by Chief Cowkeeper and his Seminole warriors raided Georgia farms and plantations and drove captured cattle to St. Augustine to feed the growing population. Forbes thought the Seminole "will be the best guard to the settlements" and was pleased that Lieutenant Colonel Thomas Brown was appointed to command the East Florida Rangers. Taking his sermon from the Old Testament, Reverend Forbes predicted that Brown "will seek revenge."[38]

The East Florida Rangers were a lively and colorful presence in the crowded streets and markets of wartime St. Augustine. Dressed in leather hunting shirts, breeches and leggings, apparel appropriate for border marauders, the Rangers were a mixed militia corps of white and black men. The markets became even more crowded when the Swiss and German recruits of the Sixtieth Regiment arrived in St. Augustine to train under the command of General Augustine Prevost.

A Spanish resident who stayed in town under the British carefully observed the increased military activity. Luciano de

Herrera gathered news from sailors, refugees, and travelers that was secretly dispatched to Juan de la Puente in Havana. Herrera's dispatches were not detected until late in the war.[39]

In February 1777, East Florida forces captured Fort McIntosh on the Satilla River in Georgia, and returned to St. Augustine with 68 prisoners and 2,000 head of cattle. In May, a Georgia invasion force retaliated, but was turned back at Thomas Creek, a tributary of the Nassau River. Captain John Mowbray, a former Royal Naval officer who returned to duty, leased his sloop *Rebecca* to Governor Tonyn. With fifteen sailors and thirty-five marines aboard, Mowbray turned back an attempt by an American naval force to invade East Florida.

In March 1778, the East Florida Rangers again crossed the Georgia border to capture and burn Fort Barrington on the Altamaha River. Three thousand Americans counterattacked in June, captured Fort Tonyn on the St. Marys River, and moved south toward St. Augustine. The rebel force was finally turned back at the Alligator Creek Bridge on the Nassau River, ending what was to be the last attempt to invade East Florida.

Reinforcements, eventually 2,000 strong, began arriving at St. Augustine late in the summer of 1778 to prepare for a major invasion of Georgia. In November and December, British forces under General Prevost pushed north all the way to Savannah. The northern frontier of East Florida was thereby secured from further invasion.

"Sometimes alarmed, never much afraid and not hurt," was John Moultrie's memory of St. Augustine in 1777 and 1778. Moultrie boasted that the East Florida economy had been stimulated by the war. His one complaint was the shortage of fresh meat at the market: "the Georgia stocks of cattle lately have supplied us well, they now fail us, the large stocks of their frontier pretty well expended."[40]

Moultrie's own plantations south of St. Augustine had escaped rebel raids and were prospering. The province's growing population led to higher prices for plantation produce, prompting Moultrie to advise a friend: "I plant nothing but what goes in the mouth." He also anticipated the completion of his "handsome stone house at Bella Vista, near finished, which I shall retire to....It will last forever, a good country house with ten rooms, plows and carts going in the fields since March, more rice than I can beat out....A fine stock of cattle and hogs and plenty of beef, fish, butter and cream cheese, everything."[41]

Moultrie was also proud of his contributions to the defense of East Florida. "I have become a prodigious manufacturer of gallies," he boasted, "my *Thunder* gally with two 24 pounders draws only 18 inches water and has done more than all the fleet at Savannah. She took the famous rebel gally, the *Congress*, besides several other vessels.... We have four [gallies] for the defense of the St. Johns, St. Augustine, and Mosquito inlets. Nothing can oppose them, their metal so heavy and their draw of water so small."[42]

David Yeats' enthusiasm was tempered with concern that the prices for supplies and slave clothing was six times higher in St. Augustine stores than in London. Many of the sick and destitute refugees flocking to St. Augustine were unable to pay the £7 to £9 price demanded for a barrel of flour, causing Yeats to worry about future public health crises. His fear of a possible smallpox epidemic prompted him to initiate an inoculation program for sickly incoming refugees.[43]

The influx of soldiers, sailors, and loyalist refugees meant unprecedented opportunities for work and profit for the town's artisans and merchants. Crews worked overtime equipping and feeding the soldiers and repairing ships of the Royal Navy. Carpenters and stonemasons worked feverishly to house the burgeoning population.

Among the refugees seeking shelter in 1777 were 600 Minorcan, Greek, and Italian laborers who walked to St. Augustine from Dr. Andrew Turnbull's colony at New Smyrna. After complaining to Governor Tonyn of cruel treatment, they were released from their indenture contracts by Turnbull's attorneys. Accompanied by their parish priest, Father Pedro Camps, they re-established the Church of San Pedro on St. George Street, and joined the town's labor force.[44]

Late in 1780, 63 rebels captured in Carolina were transported to St. Augustine to be held as prisoners of war. Tonyn paroled those who pledged not to attempt escape and permitted them to move freely about the town. Only Christopher Gadsden refused parole and chose confinement in Fort St. Marks. Alexander Moultrie, the younger brother of the lieutenant governor, was paroled with his family to his brother's country estate, Bella Vista. The other prisoners rented rooms and houses in the town.[45]

"The malignant spirit has almost subsided," Governor Tonyn declared in 1779, signaling that it was time to satisfy the pent-up demand to elect representatives to a House of Assembly. Tonyn had opposed an assembly for years, but the thousands of refugees who settled in East Florida after 1776 included Henry Yonge, William Panton, Jermyn and Charles Wright, James Hume, and Thomas Brown, men of distinction and proven loyalty whose presence convinced Tonyn that an elected assembly could prove beneficial to governing the colony. The governor nevertheless delayed the elections until February 1781.[46]

In March 1781, two legislative bodies met in chambers at the Town House. Moultrie presided over the Royal Council, and Colonel William Brown was elected Speaker of the Assembly. Legislation passed included a police act that established standards of sanitation, building codes, fire prevention, and uniform weights and measures at the town market. The Assembly and the Council now regulated municipal matters, which had previously been controlled exclusively by the governor's pronouncements.[47]

In May 1781, news reached St. Augustine that British West Florida had fallen to Spanish troops. Spain was a late combatant in the war against Britain, and posed a threat to St. Augustine and the isolated rural settlements along the Atlantic coast. In October the news was even more distressing. Lord Charles Cornwallis surrendered his entire 7,000-man army to General George Washington at Yorktown, Virginia. St. Augustine residents again lived in fear of an attack.

Even more demoralizing news arrived in May 1782: British commander Sir Guy Carleton ordered the evacuation of Savannah and St. Augustine. After years of struggle the province had finally become prosperous, and residents who had sacrificed and remained steadfast in their loyalty to the Crown felt betrayed. Dr. Yeats, thrown into "utmost consternation" by the news, felt "totally ruined" and could envision "nothing but want and misery" in his future.[48]

A reprieve came in late July. Carleton designated East Florida a haven for Loyalists from Savannah and Charleston, a decision that brought more than 7,500 refugees to East Florida in 1782, boosting the population to more than 17,000. Yeats noted in September that many of the refugees were "sick and destitute." Tonyn supervised distribution of tools and rations and confiscated land from uncultivated tracts titled to absentee owners in Britain to redistribute among incoming Loyalists. St. Johns Town, a new settlement near the entrance to the St. Johns River, grew to more than 300 houses in only a few months. The town of Hillsborough was developed on the St. Marys River in response to an upsurge in exports of lumber and naval stores.[49]

The influx of Loyalists also brought changes to St. Augustine. On February 1, 1783, the town's first newspaper, *The East-Florida Gazette*, was printed. Charles Wright was the printer for John Wells, Jr., a refugee editor from Charleston. On March 3, 1783, the town's first theater opened with a performance at the State House; proceeds from the performance were pledged to assist needy refugees.[50]

This hopeful spirit vanished in April, when Governor Tonyn received a copy of the Preliminary Articles of the Peace of Paris and learned that the province had been returned to Spain. John Moultrie informed James Grant: "I may probably once more join company with you. We have often parted without a prospect of meeting again but the chapter of accidents has brought us together; tis the only good chapter." After finally achieving a life of "real plenty, ease and elegance," Moultrie dreaded being "turned adrift, [to] again seek a resting place." For his slaves, many of whom had been employed by in the Moultrie family for generations, the resting place would be Long Island in the Bahamas. "England … will bring me up," Moultrie declared. "My feelings, principles, everything prevents me … [from] remaining in America."[51]

The chaotic two years during which the Loyalists prepared to depart, was marred by cruel raids by "lawless banditti" left

VOL. I. THE No. 16.

East-Florida GAZETTE.

NULLIUS ADDICTUS JURARE IN VERBA MAGISTRI. Hor.

From SATURDAY, MAY 10, to SATURDAY, MAY 17, 1783.

ST. AUGUSTINE, May 17.

ON Sunday laſt arrived off our Bar, after a tedious paſſage from New-York, his Majeſty's ſhips Narciſſus and Beliſarius, having under convoy four veſſels laden with proviſions for this province. Three other victuallers had ſailed in company, alſo for this place, but ſeparated by ſome accident on the paſſage.

EAST-FLORIDA.

By his Excellency PATRICK TONYN, *Eſquire, Captain General, Governour and Commander in chief in and over his Majeſty's Province of Eaſt-Florida, Chancellor and Vice Admiral of the ſame.*

A PROCLAMATION.

WHEREAS his Excellency Sir GUY CARLETON, Commanding in chief his Majeſty's forces in North America, hath informed me that proviſions to the 1ſt of October next, have been ſent to this province, for the ſupport of his Majeſty's good and faithful ſubjects, who have been under the neceſſity of leaving the provinces of South Carolina and Georgia: And whereas his Excellency the Hon. ROBERT DIGBY Eſquire, commanding his Majeſty's naval forces in North America, from his tender and compaſſionate regard for the ſufferings of his Majeſty's loyal ſubjects, and anxious to lighten their diſtreſſes by every means in his power, hath given me the ſtrongeſt aſſurances of every aſſiſtance being afforded the inhabitants of this province for their removal; that the commanding officer of his Majeſty's ſhips of war on this ſtation has his directions to conſult the convenience of the inhabitants; and that tranſports may be had for ſuch of them as wiſh to proceed to England or the Weſt-Indies, or any other part of his Majeſty's dominions, previous to the evacuation of the ſaid province, which probably will not be effected during the courſe of this ſummer, as there are no accounts of the definitive treaty of peace being ſigned. I have therefore thought fit by and with the advice of his Majeſty's Honourable Council, to notify and make publick, and I do hereby notify and make publick ſuch information and aſſurances to all his Majeſty's good and faithful ſubjects of this his Majeſty's faithful province of Eaſt-Florida; and that ſuch of the ſaid inhabitants, who may not be employed in agriculture, and are deſirous of taking the earlieſt opportunity of departing, do forthwith give in their names, numbers, and deſtination, to the Secretary's Office, that they may be properly accomodated, hereby offering every aſſiſtance and ſupport in my power; and I do earneſtly recommend and require all his Majeſty's ſaid ſubjects who may be employed in agriculture, to be attentive in raiſing their crops of proviſions now in the ground for their future ſubſiſtance.

PATRICK TONYN.

Given under my Hand, and the Great Seal of his Majeſty's ſaid Province, in the Council Chamber, at St. Auguſtine, the twenty-ninth day of April, one thouſand ſeven hundred and eighty three, and in the twenty-third year of his Majeſty's Reign.

God ſave the King!

By his Excellency's command,
David Yeates, Secretary.

ALL perſons who have any demands againſt the eſtate of the late JOHN RAND deceaſed, are required to bring in their accounts properly atteſted, and all thoſe any ways indebted to the ſaid eſtate, are required to make payment immediately to DONALD M'CALPIN & WILLIAM BENNIE. } Adms.

St. Auguſtine, April 22, 1783.

(BY PERMISSION.)
On TUESDAY Evening, the 20th of May,
WILL BE PRESENTED,
At the THEATRE,
In the STATE-HOUSE,
DOUGLAS,
A TRAGEDY,
To which will be added,
The ENTERTAINMENT of
BARNABY BRITTLE;
The Characters by Gentlemen, for the benefit of the diſtreſſed *Refugees.*

Doors to be opened at SIX o'Clock; Performance to commence at SEVEN; no money taken at the door, nor any perſon admitted behind the Scenes.

Tickets to be had at Mr. JOHNSTON'S ſtore, formerly Mr. Payne's.

PITT, 5s. 9d. *GALLERY,* 4s. 9d.

PUBLICK AUCTION.
On THURSDAY next, the 22d inſt.
At ELEVEN o'Clock,
WILL BE SOLD,
(Without reſerve)
At Major MANSON's quarters, new Barracks,

A MAHOGANY Bed-ſtead with elegant Furniture, and Window Curtains
A good eight-day Clock
A double Cheſt of Drawers
A Book Caſe
A Deſk and other Drawers
Chairs and a Sopha
Pier, Chimney and dreſſing Glaſſes
Carpets
Braſs and other Doggs
Tea and Table China
Glaſſes and Glaſs
Shades
A well toned Guittar
Some Plate, &c. &c.

JOHN CHAMPNEYS.

ANY perſon having the following NEGROES, good property, which they wiſh to diſpoſe of, may hear of a purchaſer, who will pay down the caſh, by applying to the Printer.

A good Carpenter, two Bricklayers, a Black-Smith and a good Cardener.

TEN DOLLARS REWARD.

STOLEN or ſtrayed out of my yard, on the night of Tueſday laſt, a bright bay Horſe, upwards of fourteen hands high, about eight years old, paces, trots, and canters; lately branded on the mounting ſhoulder, M.S. with a ſlit in his left ear. The above reward will be given to any perſon that will deliver the ſaid Horſe to the ſubſcriber in St. Auguſtine, *Captain Cameron* at Pacolato, or to *Mr. Sutherland* at Heſter's Bluff.

JAMES SEYMOUR.

NOTARY PUBLIC.
JOHN MILLS,
For the conveniency of Captains of Veſſels, Merchants and others,
HEREBY GIVES NOTICE,
That he keeps his *Notary-Office*
At his Houſe the North end of *Charlotte-ſtreet*, near the houſe of Mr. ROBERT MILLS, Houſe Carpenter.
All ſorts of LAW PRECEDENTS done with care and expedition.

FROM THE ORIGINAL IN THE PUBLIC RECORD OFFICE, LONDON

FIRST NEWSPAPER PRINTED IN FLORIDA

The East-Florida Gazette, St. Augustine, May 10-17, 1783. First newspaper printed in Florida.

over from the war. The raiders were a mixed group of refugees and Florida residents, veterans of the cattle and slave raids that had traumatized both sides of the Florida-Georgia border during the war. Daniel McGirtt, a former East Florida Ranger, led the "banditti," raiding plantations north of St. Augustine for cattle, horses and slaves, paying little attention to whether their victims were rebels or loyalists. They robbed and kidnapped travelers on the King's Road and ambushed troops sent against them.[52]

Like Moultrie, Yeats decided to leave rather than live under Spanish rule. "The idea of keeping possession of Estates in this Province, under the Spanish government is now I suppose vanished." British residents who wished to remain were required to "publickly profess the Catholic religion or absolutely quit their Estates." He was relieved when the marauding bandits tormenting rural settlements were subdued in July, permitting him to keep slaves working at Grant's Mount Pleasant Plantation, rice and provisions tract near the headwaters of the Guana River. Within six weeks he expected to harvest a corn crop and pack it in barrels to carry to an estate in the Bahama Islands with Grant's slaves.[53]

On June 27, Spanish Governor Vicente Manuel de Zéspedes y Velasco arrived in St. Augustine with a 500-man garrison. The Spanish flag flying above Fort St. Mark was a distressing sight for the British Loyalists, although they found the governor to be "a polite, well bred gentleman [who] shows every disposition to make matters as easy and agreeable to the British inhabitants as possible." Governor Tonyn did not agree. He and Zéspedes quarreled for months.[54]

One problem that neither governor could solve was the depressed market for houses in St. Augustine, which had plummeted to approximately ten percent of construction costs. The market for country plantations was even further depressed, without "the smallest prospect of a shilling being offered for them," Yeats lamented. "In a few months we must abandon our property without money and without price to His Catholic Majesty's subjects…."[55]

On June 1, 1785, Yeats accompanied Tonyn from St. Augustine to the St. Marys River, where planters were living alongside slaves in a tent city waiting for transports to carry them to other British colonies. Tonyn informed Governor John E. Powell of the Bahama Islands that the "frames of the Pews of the church of St. Augustine" had been sent to New Providence Island, where Loyalists intended to build a church. "By another opportunity," Tonyn wrote, "I shall send likewise the Bells of this City, and the fire Engine..." Five months later, the governor departed for England, accompanied by Yeats and Chief Justice James Hume. They arrived at Portsmouth, England on January 11, 1785.[56]

For the second time in only twenty years, East Florida experienced a mass exodus of its resident population. In 1786, 469 Mediterranean migrants, survivors of Turnbull's Smyrnea Plantation, were living in St. Augustine. Other families from the Smyrnea settlement were living at nearby rural properties. Thomas and Honoria Clarke, their six children, and a small number of other British planters and overseers also remained after the change of flags. Francis Philip Fatio had a town house as well as a family residence at his rural estate. Jesse Fish, a British colonial who had resided in St. Augustine since his early teen years, remained at his plantation at nearby Fish Island. The families of Luciano de Herrera, Francisco Xávier Sánchez, and Manuel Solana, Spaniards who had remained in St. Augustine throughout St. Augustine's British years, rejoiced at the return of Spanish rule.[57]

Returning Spanish residents found much to remind them of the city they had formerly called home, but they also discovered changes. Dozens of new dwellings had been constructed, and numerous one-story, flat-roofed Spanish dwellings now supported second stories, brick chimneys, fireplaces, pitched roofs, and glazed sash windows that faced the narrow streets of the town. At the Plaza, a new two-story structure measuring 51 by 21 feet was standing at the corner of Hospital Street (Aviles now). The unfinished house built for the Bishop of Cuba at the southwest corner of the Plaza had been transformed twice: in 1764 it became a troop barrack; in 1772-1773 it was converted to the nine-room British Statehouse with a second floor, upper verandas, pitched roof, cupola, and a welcoming entrance piazza facing the Plaza adorned by grand neoclassical columns. When completed, John Moultrie had proudly proclaimed the renovated public building "an Ornament to this Young Province."[58]

Additions to the governor's house (also known as Government House) at the west end of the Plaza included glazed windows and a fireplace and chimney. Inside the high walls that enclosed the courtyard, Governor Grant added a stable and coach house and a laundry with a residential room above. He also expanded the kitchen garden and a grove of fruit trees. Further south on St. George Street, St. Peter's Church had been beautified by the addition of a new tower and steeple that stood more than 70 feet tall.

The most startling changes had been made at the south end of the town where the Franciscan monastery and church was converted into the St. Francis Barracks for British military officers and soldiers. The largest building in British East Florida, known as the "pile of barracks" stood adjoining to the south. Completed in 1772, the huge structure with a brick first floor and two upper stories of wood measured nearly 200 feet long and 40 feet wide. The "verandas [that] wrapped around the upper floors … and tall chimneys, cupola, and weathervane" affixed to the roof, convinced architectural historian Elsbeth Gordon that the huge barrack "dominated the southern waterfront."

The two-decade British governance of East Florida resulted in architectural transformations that changed the appearance of St. Augustine. However, these changes disappeared or were forgotten, and few town residents today realize that St. Augustine was once the capital of a British colony. A striking example of how quickly the British footprints vanished from popular memory can be gleaned from the reminiscences of James Grant Forbes, born in St. Augustine in 1770. At age thirteen, Forbes departed for England with his father, the Reverend John Forbes. He returned 38 years later, after Florida became a United States Territory in 1821.[59]

On return, Forbes was surprised to discover that the Plaza had again been transformed. A new Catholic church faced south on the Plaza, built on a lot that had previously been his father's orange grove. Forbes and his father had lived in an adjoining two-story home at the northwest corner of the Plaza and St. George Street.

When Forbes looked across the Plaza, he noticed a vacant lot at the site that had been occupied by the elegant British Statehouse during his childhood. That structure had been torn down in 1804. Trinity Episcopal Church, completed in 1832, occupies the site today.

Forbes got another surprise when he walked south on St. George Street looking for the Anglican parish church where his father presided from 1764 to 1773. Forbes discovered that St. Peter's Church had been torn down; the Spaniards used it to construct their parish church. A parking lot occupies that site today.

The town's largest structure, the three-story "pile of barracks" had been reduced to a single-story. A fire in 1792 destroyed the wooden upper floors, leaving only the brick first floor that was converted to a prison. No trace of the barrack remains; the St. Augustine National Cemetery occupies the site today.

James Grant Forbes' autobiographical reminiscences bear witness to how transitory architectural features can be in a city that experienced repeated changes of national sovereignty. As a boy, Forbes watched as British craftsmen erected grand public buildings that were dismantled a decade or two later. Walking the streets of St. Augustine as a child, he observed carpenters transforming old Spanish dwellings and creating new structures, yet in only one generation the physical imprint of British occupation was disappearing, as wooden dwellings burned and crumbled. Soon after, even the historical memory of St. Augustine's British era had been incorporated within the absorptive story of Spanish St. Augustine.

NOTES

[1] Robert L. Gold, *Borderland Empires in Transition: The Triple-Nation Transfer of Florida* (Carbondale: Southern Illinois University Press, 1969), Charles Loch Mowat, *East Florida as a British Province, 1763-1784* (Berkeley and Los Angeles: University of California Press, 1943; facsimile edition, Gainesville: University of Florida Press, 1964), and John Jay TePaske, *The Governorship of Spanish Florida, 1700-1763* (Durham, N.C.: Duke University Press, 1964). See also Fred Anderson, *The Crucible of War: The Seven Years War and the Fate of Empire in North America, 1754-1766* (New York: Alfred A. Knopf, 2000), and Colin G. Calloway, *The Scratch of a Pen and the Transformation of North*

America (Oxford, UK: Oxford University Press, 2006).

2 Mowat, *East Florida*, Chapter 1, and J. Leitch Wright, Jr., *British St. Augustine* (St. Augustine, Florida: Historic St. Augustine Preservation Board, 1975), 1-6. See also Robertson to General Thomas Gage, 8 March 1764, New York, enclosing "Report of the State of East and West Florida," Colonial Office Papers Microfilm Roll 5, Volume 83, page 137 (hereafter CO 5,83/137), The National Archive, Kew, UK, and on microfilm at St. Augustine Historical Society Research Library (hereafter SAHSRL).

3 Feliú to Count de Ricla, 25 August 1763, and 5 February 1764, St. Augustine, Archivo General de Indias, Santa Domingo, 86-7-11, No. 11, from file of translations at SAHSRL. Ogilvie's correspondence with the Secretary of State and the Board of Trade in 1763-64 is in CO 5/540, 5/548, 5/549. Robertson to Amherst, 26 September 1763, Jeffry Amherst Papers, 1758-1764, Schedule 3, Vol. 1, Manuscripts Division, William L. Clements Library, University of Michigan.

4 Grant learned of his appointment in June 1763. See Paul David Nelson, *General James Grant: Scottish Soldier and Royal Governor of East Florida* (Gainesville: University Press of Florida, 1993).

5 Grant to Richard Oswald, 20 September 1764, Box 1, File 84-85, James Grant of Ballindalloch Papers, Governorship Series, Scottish Record Office, Edinburgh (hereafter JGP 1/84-85); Grant to James Moultrie, 31 August 1764, JGP 1/75-76.

6 Grant to John Moultrie, 15 May 1767, JGP 2/43.

7 Mowat, *East Florida*, has the most accurate and detailed account of the colonial government. See also Daniel L. Schafer, *St. Augustine's British Years, 1763-1784* (St. Augustine, Florida: St. Augustine Historical Society, 2001), and Wright, *British St. Augustine*. Unless otherwise noted, these are the sources of general information used throughout the chapter.

8 Schafer, *British Years*, 5-15. For Fish's East Florida Claim for property lost after the cession of East Florida to Spain in 1783 see Treasury 77, Papers of the East Florida Claims Commission, NA, Kew, (hereafter T77). See also Jesse Fish, Sr. to William Pitt, Chancellor of the Exchequer, 15 April 1767 (copy in the author's possession, courtesy of Robert H. Pratt, Milwaukee, Wisconsin). See also biographical files, SAHSRL.

9 Schafer, *British Years*, 13-15.

10 Ibid.,76-99. For John and William Bartram at the Picolata Conference see 65-67.

[11] Ibid.

[12] Grant to Egmont, 16 June 1768, JGP 1/350-52.

[13] Grant to Oswald, 31 August 1766, JGP 1/247-51.

[14] For Grant's experimental farm and his indigo and rice plantations see Schafer, *Governor James Grant's Villa: A British East Florida Indigo Plantation* (St. Augustine: The St. Augustine Historical Society, 2000).

[15] Schafer, *British Years*, 28-40. See also Schafer, *William Bartram and the Ghost Plantations of British East Florida* (Gainesville: University Press of Florida, 2010), Chapters 4-6.

[16] Two studies of Turnbull's East Florida plantation and the Mediterranean laborers stand out: E.P. Panagopoulos, *New Smyrna: An Eighteenth Century Greek Odyssey* (Gainesville: University of Florida Press, 1966), and Patricia C. Griffin, *Mullet on the Beach: The Minorcans of Florida, 1768-1788* (Gainesville: University Presses of Florida, 1991). Several dozen letters written by Turnbull, and rare maps of the Smyrnea Plantation can be seen at "Florida History Online," a digital history archive, http://www.unf.edu/floridahistory/. See also Patricia Griffin, "Blue Gold: Andrew Turnbull's New Smyrna Plantation," in Jane G. Landers, ed., *Colonial Plantations and Economy in Florida* (Gainesville: University Press of Florida, 2000), 39-68; and Schafer, *British Years*, 118-151.

[17] The governor's social life is in Schafer, *British Years*, 41-47. Military officers had their own Masonic Lodge.

[18] See 28 February, 25 September, and 13 November 1765, JGP 9/241, 261, 317.

[19] Grant to Moultrie, 1 April 1772, London, JGP 3&4/61-63.

[20] Moultrie to Grant, 3 November 1772, JGP 23/210-18, Grant to Moultrie, 1 April 1772, JGP 3&4/61-3, and Moultrie to Grant, 22 August 1772, JPG 23/181-85.

[21] Moultrie to Grant, 3 June 1773, JGP 24/45-7; Forbes to Grant, 23 February 1773, JPG 24/16-19. See also James H. Schaub, "The King's Road: A National Historic Civil Engineering Landmark," in *Engineering Issues: Journal of Professional Activities, Proceedings of the American Society of Civil Engineers* 103, (13) (July 1977); William R. Adams, Daniel L. Schafer, Robert Steinbach, and Paul Weaver, *The King's Road, Florida's First Highway: A Narrative History of the Road's Construction; with a Description of its Route from St. Augustine*

to New Smyrna; Transcriptions and Explanations of Survey Notes from the Territorial Period; Maps; and Illustrations (New Smyrna Beach: Volusia County Council), and James R. Ward, "Florida's Neglected Treasure," *Florida Times-Union* (Jacksonville) October 17-December 19, 1973.

22 Forbes to Grant, 23 August 1773, JGP 24/16-19. See also Mowat, *East Florida*, 83-104, and "Men at Odds," in Schafer, *British Years*, 169-188.

23 Mulcaster to Grant, 28 August 1774, JGP 24/205-212. Mulcaster was married to the daughter of John William Gerard de Brahm, East Florida's first surveyor general.

24 Moultrie to Grant, 23 December 23 1774, JGP 24/231-38. Drayton to Grant, 29 June 1774, JGP 24/191-93.

25 Mulcaster to Grant, 9 August 1774, JGP 24/197-204.

26 See Mulcaster to Grant, 12 March 12 1774, JGP 24/156-64, 14 May 1774, JGP 24/179-84, and 9 August 1774, JGP 197-204.

27 Forbes to Grant, 1 November 1774, JGP 24/213-18, 20 December 1774, JGP 24/242-44, 29 October 1775, JGP, 24/327-29, and 1 November 1775, JGP 24/318-22.

28 Yeats to Grant, 23 October 1775, JGP 24/299-301.

29 Forbes to Grant, 29 October 1775, and 1 November 1775, JGP 24/318-22 & 327-29.

30 Grant to Yeats, 26 April 1776, Ballindalloch Castle Muniments, Bundle 772 (nomenclature when stored at Ballindalloch, Banffshire, Scotland).

31 Unless otherwise noted, the following were used for East Florida during the American Revolution: J. Leitch Wright, Jr., *Florida in the American Revolution* (Gainesville: University Presses of Florida, 1975), Martha Condray Searcy, *The Georgia Florida Contest in the American Revolution, 1776-1778* (Tuscaloosa: University of Alabama Press, 1985), and Schafer, *British Years*, chapters 12 and 13. For a recent study that focuses on Tonyn, see Roger C. Smith, "The Fourteenth Colony: Florida and the American Revolution in the South" (unpublished PhD diss., University of Florida, 2011).

32 Edward J. Cashin, *The King's Ranger: Thomas Brown and the American Revolution on the Southern Frontier* (Athens; University of Georgia Press, 1989).

33 J. Russell Snapp, *John Stuart and the Struggle for Empire on the Southern*

Frontier (New York: Cambridge University Press, 1995), and John Richard Alden, *John Stuart and the Southern Colonial Frontier: A Study of Indian Relations, War, Trade, and Land Problems in the Southern Wilderness, 1754-1775* (New York: Gordian Press, 1966).

[34] Yeats to Grant, 27 February 1776, JGP 24/349-51.

[35] Forbes to Grant, 1 November 1775, 5 August 1776, JGP 24/318-22 & 423-27.

[36] Moultrie to Grant, 1 August 1776, JGP 24/416-18.

[37] Forbes to Grant, 5 August 1776; Yeats to Grant, 7 August 1776, JGP 24/423-27 & 420-22.

[38] Forbes to Grant, 5 August 1776, JGP 24/423-27.

[39] Katherine S. Lawson, "Luciano de Herrera, Spanish Spy in British St. Augustine," *Florida Historical Quarterly* 23 (1945): 170-176.

[40] Moultrie to Grant, 3 March 1778, 25/13-15, 12 March 1780, JGP 26/8-10.

[41] Ibid., 3 March 1778, JGP 13-15.

[42] Ibid., 12 March 1780, JGP 26/8-12.

[43] Yeats to Grant, 6 May, 5 June 1780, JGP 26/ 14-16 & 17-19. Yeats inoculated two hundred persons with no casualties.

[44] Griffin, *Mullet on the Beach*, 94-101.

[45] Mabel L. Webber, "Josiah Smith's Diary, 1780-1781," *The South Carolina Historical and Genealogical Magazine* (January, 1932).

[46] Carole Watterson Troxler, "Loyalist Refugees and the British Evacuation of East Florida, 1783-1785," *Florida Historical Quarterly* 60 (July 1981): 1-28, and "Refuge, Resistance, and Reward: The Southern Loyalists' Claim on East Florida," *Journal of Southern History* 55 (1989): 563-596. See also Linda K. Williams, "East Florida as a Loyalist Haven," *Florida Historical Quarterly* 54 (April 1976): 465-478 and Schafer, *British Years*, 207-29.

[47] Mowat, *East Florida*, 125-134, Schafer, *British Years*, 230-251.

[48] Yeats to Grant, 18 June 1782, JGP 26/98-99.

[49] Ibid,, 15 September 1782, JGP 106-107.

[50] Mowat, *East Florida*, 139

[51] Moultrie to Grant, 17 June 1783, JGP 26,128-133.

[52] Mowat, *East Florida*, 110, 146.

[53] Yeats to Grant, 14 February 1784, JGP 26/144-146.

[54] Ibid., 19 July 19 1784, JGP 26/158-160.

[55] Ibid.

[56] Tonyn to Lord Sydney [Thomas Townshend], 4 April, 10, 29 August and 10 November 1785, and 11 January 1786, C.O. 5/561.

[57] Griffin, *Mullet on the Beach*, 117, and Schafer, *British Years*, 252-72.

[58] Elsbeth Gordon, *Florida's Colonial Architectural Heritage* (Gainesville: University Press of Florida, 2002), Chapter 4. Also see Elsbeth "Buff" Gordon's brilliantly illustrated book, *Walking St. Augustine, An Illustrated Guide and Pocket History to America's Oldest City* (Gainesville: University Press of Florida, 2015). for comments on the town's architectural history.

[59] James Grant Forbes, *Sketches, Historical and Topographical of the Floridas; More Particularly of East Florida. Facsimile Reproduction of the 1821 Edition.* (Gainesville: University of Florida Press, 1964). Forbes, a colonel in the United States army, became the town's first American mayor.

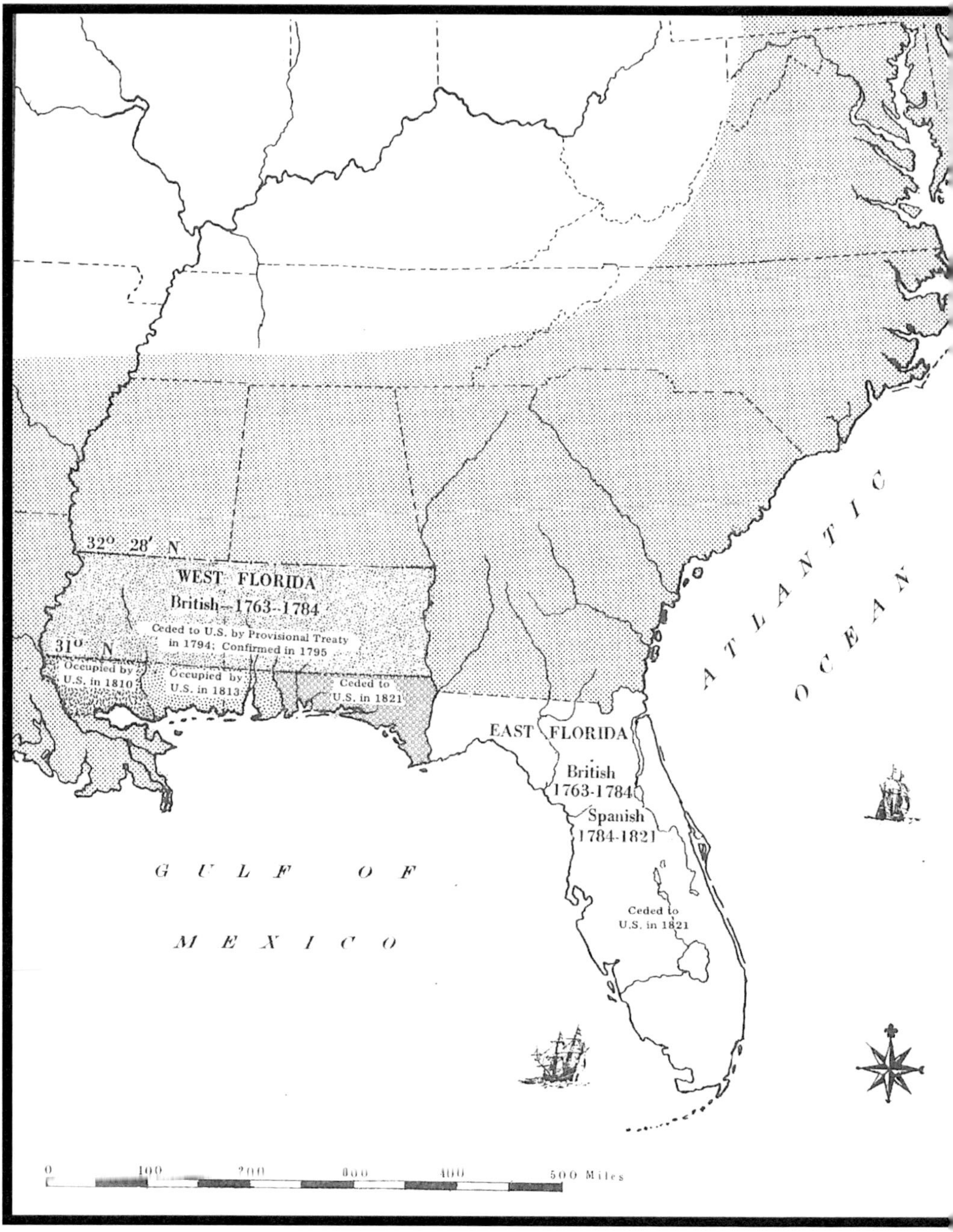

From the 16th century the land called Florida has had a variety of shapes and boundaries. *La Florida* of the Spanish explorers included not only the territory indicated on this map, but also all of present-day Louisiana, Arkansas and much of Oklahoma and Texas. Treaties, annexations, purchases and accessions over the years have reduced Florida to its present size.

6

The Spanish Return

1784 - 1821

James G. Cusick and Patricia C. Griffin

The end of the American Revolution coincided with a remarkable situation in St. Augustine. For nearly a year and a half, two governments existed side by side as the British engaged in a reluctant withdrawal, and the Spanish regime reinstated itself. Spanish Governor Vicente Manuel de Zéspedes, newly arrived, wrote terse communiqués, translated into English by his able assistant, Captain Carlos Howard. They were taken a few doors away to British Governor Patrick Tonyn, whose responses bristled with chilly British formality.

The return of Spanish rule to the Floridas did not mean a return to the world that had existed in the first half of the eighteenth century. Time, warfare, and changes in population reshaped everything. Missions no longer dotted the landscape of the Timucua, Guale, and Apalachee homelands. The Florida colony of 1763, when the Spanish departed, was now two colonies, East and West Florida, set up by the British. Instead of competing with France and Britain for control of North America, Spain faced competition from the United States.

The French Revolution, the War of 1812, and the collapse of the Spanish empire would all affect Florida. Closer to home, conflicts were springing up between the Creek and Seminole and the settlers of Georgia. For the next 37 years, during the era known as the Second Spanish Period, the inhabitants of St. Augustine repeatedly wrestled with one over-arching question: would they make their future with Spain or with another country?[1]

In the immediate aftermath of the American Revolution, however, a host of problems distracted Governor Zéspedes.[2] He faced difficulties with slaves, Indians, and the local populace, as well as a menacing wave of land-hungry settlers just across the border in the United States. Governing Florida meant juggling many concerns: the East Florida-Georgia border, Indian territory, economic development, and loyalty to the Spanish Crown

The exploits of Daniel McGirtt typified the kinds of trouble that would plague Florida's border with the United States. McGirtt, characterized by Governor Tonyn as "the Head and support of a desperate Gang of high Way Robbers," set the border area ablaze in 1784. He quickly became notorious for stealing slaves, rustling cattle, and committing robberies. He was eventually arrested and his goods and property confiscated. Imprisoned in Havana, McGirtt gained release in 1785 and returned to the Georgia coast with plenty of grudges against Spanish officials. There were frequent confrontations between Spanish authorities and freebooters along the Georgia-Florida border over the next three decades.[3]

Gaining the friendship of Native American leaders proved just as challenging. The Creek and Seminole were firmly established in Florida. They favored the British as allies and regarded the Spaniards as potential enemies. The first three governors, Zéspedes, Juan Nepomuceno de Quesada, and Enrique (Henry) White, all worked to negotiate treaties and foster goodwill with native headmen.

The closest group to St. Augustine, the Seminole of the Alachua Savannah, held territory across the St. Johns River and about 80 miles away in modern day Alachua County. Cowkeeper, their *micco* (chief) distrusted the new Spanish regime. However, his successor, King Payne, became a staunch ally. A lively trade sprang up between St. Augustine and the Alachua towns. Besides seeking a market for deerskins and pelts, Payne's people maintained free-range herds with thousands of cattle and horses, which they sold as breeding stock to ranchers.

The territory of the Lower Creek was in West Florida, along the Flint, Apalachicola, and Chattahoochee rivers of western Georgia and modern-day Alabama. The single largest Seminole settlement in Florida was also in this area, on the shores of Lake Miccosukee (near Tallahassee). In times of war, the Creek and Seminole in these towns could mass thousands of warriors, making them a formidable military power, capable of staging raids as far as the Atlantic coast. Nevertheless, they welcomed partners for the deerskin trade, which brought them guns, cloths, tools, and other commodities.[4]

Governor Zéspedes adopted the British practice of establishing trading posts within easy travel distance of Indian settlements. After initial efforts to create a Spanish trading firm failed, Zéspedes turned to an experienced British firm, Panton, Leslie & Company, already operating in the Floridas, and agreed to give them exclusive rights to trade with the Seminole and Creek on behalf of the Spanish government. The firm did most of its business through its western trading posts at Pensacola and St. Marks, although there was an office in St. Augustine.

Friendship with the Indians was so crucial to Spanish rule in East Florida that Zéspedes even appealed to former British Governor Patrick Tonyn to put in a good word with Creek leaders. Tonyn, in a letter to his superior in England, Lord Sydney, said that he found this to be "a very unpleasant task," after years of convincing the Indians of the perfidy of all those of Spanish descent.[5]

The Spanish regime also sought to attract more settlers to Florida. Initially the entire colonial population, clustered near St. Augustine, numbered perhaps 2,000 people, including 216 incoming settlers from Spain and Spanish colonies, 400 to 600 Minorcan, Greek, and Italian settlers, 217 settlers from Europe and the United States, 100 free people of color, and 550 slaves. The soldiers in the garrison, with their dependents, totaled several hundred more. By contrast, the population of the nearby state of Georgia was more than 80,000.

During the 1800s, the population of St. Augustine itself was 2,000 people, while the overall population of the colony doubled to 4,000. There was an influx of new settlers from Ireland, France, and the United States while the free black population grew to about 300 people. The single biggest increase, however, was in the slave

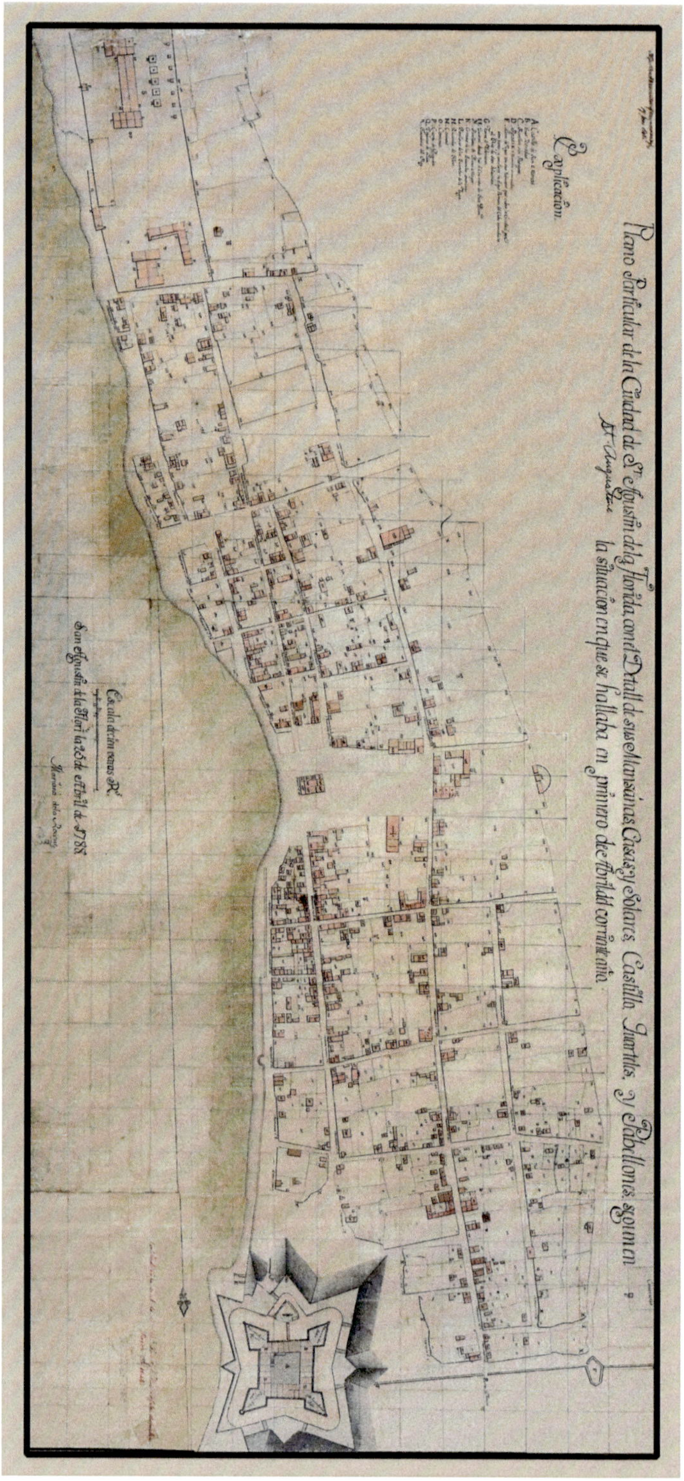

Map of St. Augustine dated April 25, 1788, drawn by Spanish Engineer Mariano de la Rocque, depicts property lines, buildings, and defense works.

population. By 1811, half of East Florida's 4,000 people were slaves.[6]

Although East Florida's population remained small during the Second Spanish Period, it was highly diverse, especially in St. Augustine. Court records indicate that many languages were spoken. Visitors strolling through town could hear conversations in Spanish, English, Catalán, French, and Muscogee. Interpreters were in constant demand, and it was common for the well-educated to know two or three languages, with a reading knowledge of more. People might speak in one language and receive an answer in another. Personal libraries contained books ranging from old classics to works of the Enlightenment.[7]

Colonists from Spain and her colonies filled most government positions. Fifty-four bureaucrats, functionaries, clerks, and servants, along with their families, accompanied Governor Zéspedes. Those of high status included treasury officials Gonzalo Zamorano and Dimas Cortés, notary Carlos Ximénez, hospital physician Bernardo La Madrid, and surgeon Juan José Bousquet.

Others were newcomers of more humble rank. Twenty-five-year-old Gerónimo Álvarez, on the royal payroll as a baker for 20 *pesos* per month, lived with a local Minorcan, Joseph Pons and his family, and later married Pons' step-daughter. Álvarez bought what is now popularly known as the González-Álvarez House, or the Oldest House, for his residence and eventually served as St. Augustine's mayor.[8] Andrés Ximénez, from Ronda, Spain, arrived later. He too married into a Minorcan family, opening a store in a two-story building that still stands, the Ximénez-Fatio House, on Aviles Street.[9]

Other settlers, known as *floridanos,* whose families left the colony in 1763 at the end of the previous period of Spanish rule, returned after twenty years of exile. They arrived from Havana and a rural area near Matanzas, Cuba. They included Antonio Fernández, an intern with the military hospital, his wife Victoriana Guillén, and government employees Joaquín Escalona and Diego de Miranda.[10]

Some settlers, already established in Florida from the days of British rule, stayed, like the Minorcan families, originally from the Balearic Islands, Italy, and Greece. They were encouraged by the return of Spanish rule after their decade-long period of indentured servitude at Andrew Turnbull's New Smyrna settlement. "We rejoice to pass under Spanish dominion," a delegation stated in a petition to Zéspedes, "and we humbly beg Your Excellency to represent us to His Majesty as desirous of being recognized as natural-born subjects."[11]

The Minorcans became the single largest component of St. Augustine's white population. The city became as much Minorcan as Spanish, its culture shaped by the Minorcans' lively festivals and Old World traditions. For livelihood, they raised food crops on small garden plots outside of the city boundary and fished. They had few slaves and lived predominantly in the northwest section of town, sometimes referred to as the quarter. A few became merchants, pooling their resources to buy schooners and brigs. Carpentry and masonry were common trades. Many worked at two or even three occupations.[12]

Some families faced a hard-scrabble life. In a poor section of the quarter, 68 people in nineteen households lived in one-story houses with palm-thatch roofs, arranged in a simple two-room "common plan" typical of St. Augustine. Others, like the family of Bernardo and Agueda Seguí, with their bakery and shipping business, could afford a substantial two-story house of coquina stone, located south of the plaza where the wealthy lived.[13]

Just a handful of settlers from Europe remained in East Florida. The exodus of British residents had severely depopulated East Florida's countryside, where the rural economy faced collapse. The number of families who made their living from small-scale farming, ranching, timber-cutting, citrus, or cultivation of rice and cotton dwindled to just 44 households in the late 1780s. About half worked their land with slave labor and only a quarter planted more than twenty acres of land.[14]

Among them was John Leslie, a native of Scotland and a bachelor, who remained in town to manage the interests of his firm, Panton, Leslie & Company, which controlled trade with the Creek and Seminole. Bilingual and of an adaptable disposition, he was much in demand as an interpreter and arbitrator, and his relationship

Panton, Leslie & Company, an Indian trading company in Spanish East Florida, had their headquarters in this waterfront building on today's Avenida Menendez. In the early 1900s the Institute of Science and History, forerunner of the St. Augustine Historical Society offered its collection of exotica here. The house burned in 1914. A remnant wall still abuts the sidewalk.

with Zéspedes and later Spanish governors was amiable, although detractors thought this a possible result of his ability to secure furniture in the latest mode for Government House.[15]

Francis Philip Fatio, of Swiss origin, remained to oversee his extensive plantation holdings on the St. Johns River, which at their height incorporated 10,000 acres. He had an Italian wife, and, as a gentleman and scholar, spoke six languages. He spent much of his time in town, and, like Leslie, was often called into service as a lay judge. He had interests in citrus, timber, manufacture of tar, pitch, and turpentine, cattle ranching, and he transshipped wines, brandies, and other products. With thriving business interests, Fatio impressed upon Spanish officials the need to strengthen Florida's commerce: "By encouraging settlement and granting privileges to the inhabitants" he wrote in 1785, "East Florida will be able to provide wood for all kinds of construction, planks of superior quality for decks of ships, tar, pitch, rosin, and turpentine, which Spain is obliged to buy on credit in the Baltic."[16]

New York-born Jesse Fish traced his Florida roots to the 1760s. When Florida was ceded to Great Britain, the bilingual Fish stayed and sold property and slaves to the incoming British. When the Spanish returned he reversed that procedure. In his late maturity he married a young wife. Because of her "madcap" qualities he eventually separated from her and their two children to live as a recluse on his Anastasia Island plantation, making the additional mistake of trusting his business dealings to an inept relative. Although he continued to raise and ship oranges whose quality was highly regarded as far away as London, his estate was in financial ruin by the time of his death in 1790.[17]

Francisco Xávier Sánchez was about seventeen when the British took over Florida in 1763. He became a successful planter in the British Period. By the time of the Spanish return he had a mulatto mistress, whose progeny he recognized as his legal heirs. Later, like Fish, he took a young wife, although a more respected one, and when he died in 1807 he was one of the most venerated citizens in town.[18]

Manuel Solana, a rancher and a planter, also prospered through the British years and beyond. In 1783 he was living on the San Sebastian River, where later the Solana ferry crossed over from what is now Bridge Street. By his death in November 1821, he had acquired several houses, including the large two-story building on the corner of present Charlotte and Cadiz streets.[19]

Luciano de Herrera, another holdover from the British Period, had ample reason to welcome the return of Spanish rule. He was never popular with British officials, who correctly suspected him of being a spy. Zéspedes rewarded him for the years he reported to Cuba on events in British St. Augustine, making him overseer of public works and the governor's intermediary in his relations with the Indians.[20]

Zéspedes also tried to attract colonists from other places. In a letter to superiors, he suggested that recent European émigrés to the United States might look favorably on taking up farming and planting in Florida, especially if they received generous allotments of land. "Such Europeans are the most suitable immigrants for this country, for, since they are poor and destitute in America and separated from their respective fatherlands by the Atlantic Ocean, it is presumed they will settle in good faith and with grateful loyalty upon the lands that may be assigned to them for their own by the king's generosity."[21]

In his quest for colonists, Zéspedes even re-evaluated age-old decrees about religious faith. A regulation that new settlers had to practice Catholicism discouraged many Protestant families from seeking entry to Florida. In 1786, this provision was dropped in favor of a loyalty oath to the Spanish crown. The change did not introduce religious freedom, and Protestant churches and public Sunday services were still prohibited, but even so Protestant families began to apply for land. Other religious bans remained in effect, however, preventing Jewish or Islamic people from taking up residence in Spanish territory.[22]

East Florida soon saw a steady flow of settlers from Georgia and South Carolina. In 1791, Thomas Jefferson wrote gleefully to George Washington, praising Spanish policies to open Florida to settlers from the United States. "I wish a hundred thousand of our inhabitants would accept the invitation. It will be the means of delivering to us peaceably, what may otherwise cost us a war."[23]

The biggest demographic shift in the colony was in the slave population. Slave labor became the basis of almost all agricultural operations in East Florida, and of many other tasks. Settlers held slaves as servants, grooms, and valets, and placed them in trades like carpentry and tailoring. Slaves served in ranching, timber-cutting, even the Indian trade. Moreover, a direct slave trade with Africa flourished at the town of Fernandina.[24] Sitiki, a slave in the household of Buckingham Smith, grew up in St. Augustine, and later in life, wrote a memoir that Smith edited. Sitiki's early experience of being kidnapped from West Africa would have been familiar to other enslaved people in East Florida.[25]

Even as slavery came to prominence in East Florida, runaways from across the border in the United States continued to flee into the colony seeking freedom. In December 1786, for example, the slaves Prince and Judy, with their children Polly and Glasgow, fled from the plantation of Jacob Weed in Georgia, and crossed the St. Marys River into Florida. Weed placed a newspaper advertisement to have them seized and returned, describing the family in these terms: "Prince: "6 feet high, strong built and brawny, a carpenter by trade, 30 years of age . . . talkative." Judy: "a smart, active wench . . . also about 30 or upward and country-born, 5' 7 or 8" high." Glasgow: "about 8 years of age, a well looking boy of open countenance and obliging disposition. Polly: "6 years old, lively eyes and gently pitted with the pox." Despite Weed's efforts, Prince and Judy remained in East Florida and in 1788, responding to a proclamation from the governor, Princc presented himself in St. Augustine and formally petitioned for sanctuary. Prince, who took the Spanish name Juan Bautista "Prince" Witten, went on to become a militia captain and landowner.[26]

Spanish laws promising freedom to runaways, established by royal decree almost a century before, stayed in effect until 1790, when protests from the United States convinced Spanish officials to repeal them. After this, runaways sought a different route of escape. Unknown numbers of Africans, *pardos,* mulattoes, and *morenos* disappeared into Indian territory, living as free maroons when possible, or becoming slaves among the Creek and Seminole as an alternative to life as slaves on a plantation.[27]

Slaves owned by settlers within Florida also had some legal avenues to achieve freedom, although only a fraction of the slave population ever succeeded in using them. Under Spanish law, a slave could petition for freedom through *coartación* and manumission, a procedure by which a slave bought himself or herself out of servitude. In 1793, Andaina, a slave woman, sued to be freed from her owner Catalina Acosta. Don Domingo Reyes, who was probably also the father of one of her children, supported her plea. It took four years for Andaina to pay off the sum for her freedom. She eventually managed to have a price set for the release of her children. Despite Andaina's success, most slaves either did not know about *coartación* or were unable to take advantage of it.[28]

Issues related to slavery, runaway slaves, and free blacks grew more heated over time. Slave-holders in nearby Georgia, angry at the constant stream of runaway slaves headed into East Florida, agitated for the United States to seize the territory. Inside East Florida, families of free blacks, or couples with mixed-race children, worried about what would happen to their legal rights if Florida changed hands to another government. Blacks, both free and slave, living among the Seminole and Creek, warned their Indian associates against trusting any group that wanted their lands.

On a day-to-day basis, however, the residents of St. Augustine showed little concern about the future or the outside world. Visitors often remarked on the atmosphere of festivity, much of it tied to Catholic religious celebrations that seemed to permeate the town.

The Catholic Church dominated the Second Spanish Period in Florida, much as it had the First, but in a world that was far more secular. There were about the same number of priests but no friars. Irishman Father Thomas Hassett, parish priest, and Father Pedro Camps, who came to Florida with his Minorcan flock in 1768, served the St. Augustine parish. Between 1783 and 1821, St. Augustine rarely had more than three clergymen for the entire province of East Florida. Catholicism's influence was strongest within the city boundaries.[29]

A long series of festival activities in December 1789 exemplified the pomp and gaiety of public life in St. Augustine. That year, Governor Zéspedes planned a grand commemoration of the ascension of Charles IV to the throne of Spain, an event being celebrated all over the empire. The three-day festivities included public processions through decorated streets, the unveiling of the royal portraits, the blast of cannon salutes, rifle volleys and church bells, parties all over town and theatrical entertainments lit by bonfires in the evening. The merriment ended with the parade of a triumphal float drawn by six magnificent horses. Members of the Minorcan carpenter guild who constructed the elaborate contraption rode in it, red cockades stuck jauntily in their broad hats, flaming torches in their hands. At every corner they stopped to lead the bystanders in huzzahs for Spain's new rulers.[30]

Two days later the annual two-day celebration of the Immaculate Conception took place with the traditional festive illumination of the windows of the town. This barely ended when word was received of the birth of a girl child to the king and queen, so two more days were set aside during that unusually balmy December, to rejoice in the happy birth of the royal *infanta.*

Carnival, just before the austere Lenten period, was a rollicking, sometimes riotous time. A traveler of the day described that "Masks, dominoes, Harlequins, Punchinellos, and a great variety of grotesque disguises, on horseback, in cars, gigs, and on foot, paraded the streets with guitars, violins, and other instruments."[31]

When Lent began, the excitement died down, only to commence again as Easter weekend approached. On Good Friday a man dressed in rags and representing St. Peter delighted groups of boys lying in wait around town by throwing his net to capture them. Holy Saturday found the girls strolling about town during the day, presenting bouquets to young men of their choice. Of all of the activities, the *formatjada* serenade on Easter Eve was the most unusual. In this early "trick or treat" event, gangs of young men went around singing the *formatjada* song at different homes about town. The music ended with a request for the little pastries containing nuggets of cheese. Revelers threatened to put a hex on the house if the cakes were not forthcoming. Even in hard times, the women spent days baking for the Easter feast, and the minstrels were rewarded with goodies dropped from the balconies into their waiting bags; if they were lucky, the man of the house poured them noggins of wine as well. Easter itself was given over to religious celebration and feasting.

St. John's Eve, June 23, was a time of general merrymaking based on the ancient summer solstice celebration. Maskers delighted in dressing up as highborn persons of the opposite sex—the women representing the ancient chivalry on gaily caparisoned steeds, and the men wearing the trappings of the ancient dames. Events sometimes lasted three days, and featured Posey dances, parades, and heavily decorated altars set up all over town where young dark-eyed girls offered bouquets to male passersby who took their fancy.[32]

Dancing and serenades spiced up life between regular holidays. Celebrations of royal births were sporadic additions to the customary yearly holiday round. What most impressed a man who had come to Spanish St. Augustine as a young slave was the festive atmosphere: "The people were the gayest I can imagine. Serenades, processions, balls, picnics, masquerades came the year round in constant succession."[33]

The revelries of the era concealed some of the hard realities and unsightly features of everyday life. In 1790, Governor Juan Nepomuceno de Quesada, together with his young family, left his previous appointment on the swampy mosquito-infested coast of Honduras. When their ship, *La Terrible,* reached the port of St. Augustine, the new governor was appalled at the squalor and chaos. He found scant comfort in the fact that his children had a school to attend in St. Augustine, when over half of the government buildings were collapsing, and he and his family could not occupy Government House because one side had caved in.[34]

He discovered that St. Augustine was used as a dumping ground for undesirables. Criminals in Havana were given the choice of jail in Cuba or army service in St. Augustine. Most who chose the latter deserted promptly on arrival; casements of the Castillo were constantly full of such prison rabble. One night engineer Mariano de la Rocque heard a terrific, clanging, crunching sound as he passed the Castillo. It turned out to be some condemned men trying to dig their way out, using their chains as clumsy shovels.[35]

Aside from minor debilities, the population stayed healthy and epidemic free. A temporary hospital was first located in the barracks, but with the increase in soldiers, it had to be moved. In 1793, a new structure was built just south of the plaza near the bay. Funds were also expended to repair and improve the Castillo de San Marcos, the fortification that was the linchpin to defend the city and harbor.

Sloops and schooners from St. Augustine regularly visited Savannah and Charleston, or went south to Havana, or further afield to Baltimore and New York. The operation of the schooner *Venus,* owned by the Greek settler Pedro Cosifacio, was typical. It made the St. Augustine-to-Charleston run, a popular one since Charleston was an emporium for all sorts of basic goods. The *Venus* came in from Charleston on January 2, 1794, with "sundries" and foodstuffs, and sailed back on January 10 with a shipment of oranges, returning to St. Augustine by February 5 to unload rice, lard, flour, soap, candles, and other cargo.[36]

But many merchants had ambitions beyond coastal trade, and fretted that trade grew very slowly. They blamed the sluggish expansion of commerce on the Spanish Crown's restrictive trading practices. Assessment of customs duties also aggravated them. Import and export duties were fairly high, and customs officers in St. Augustine never took shipping manifests at face value. They opened all casks, barrels, and containers to inventory the contents, carefully recording shipments of textiles by type and yardage with an equally exacting inspection of crockery, spices, wines, and other products.[37]

Governor Quesada was sympathetic to merchant complaints about Spanish limits on trade. He sent futile pleas to Havana and eventually went over the heads of his superiors in Cuba and wrote directly to the king. In 1792, a group of prominent citizens also petitioned the king to open trade between Florida ports and ports of neutral countries, especially those of the United States.

The Crown responded with a new royal *cédula* (decree), promulgated in 1793, loosening some trade restrictions, but stopping well short of what the merchants sought. Fifteen irate settlers sent a petition back to the Crown insisting that the rules about trade were still too restrictive. They also turned on Quesada, charging him with mismanagement and with favoring the business of Panton, Leslie & Co.[38]

Meanwhile, international affairs intruded on St. Augustine. The French Revolution in 1789 started a series of wars that embroiled all of Europe. The new French republic had agents in the United States, and one of these, Edmund Genet, operating from Charleston, South Carolina, encouraged Americans to attack Spanish East Florida. Genet's agitations became the catalyst for a rebellion and border war that broke out in 1794 and 1795.[39]

What became known later as "the 1795 rebellion" demonstrated how quickly life in East Florida could degenerate into chaos. Responding to French promises of aid, armed bands of men began to gather along the Florida-Georgia border, recruited in part by native Georgian Elijah Clarke, a hero of the American Revolution. Other leaders in the group were citizens of the United States who had recently immigrated into East Florida, including John McIntosh. Like Clarke, he was a scion from a noted Georgia family with credentials as a patriot of the American Revolution. In smoky taverns and private homes, these men plotted and gathered recruits. The plan was to overthrow the Spanish colonial government in St. Augustine.

When word of their intrigue reached Governor Quesada, he ordered the arrest of McIntosh and others, and shipped them off to prison in Havana. Upon his release in 1795, McIntosh returned to the Florida-Georgia border bent on revenge. Along with another landholder in East Florida, Richard Lang, he organized an invasion force made up of disaffected Florida colonists and settlers in Georgia. In late June 1795 his force attacked Spanish garrisons at Fort Juana and Fort San Nicolas, both near present-day downtown Jacksonville, and then occupied part of Amelia Island. But the taste of victory was short lived for the rebels. Spanish troops, supported by British and Spanish brigantines, retook the captured positions, and the insurgents fled.[40]

Even though the revolt failed, it caused havoc. Some rebels were apprehended and clapped in irons in the Castillo. Others, having lost all rights to their homes and lands in East Florida, fled to Georgia and vented their anger from across the border. Quesada "might kiss his ass," said one angry exile, "for he did not value him and...could whip him at a fair fite."[41]

The 1795 revolt also raised a critical question for everyone living in East Florida: could the colony maintain itself as part of Spain, or was it destined to become attached to some other nation – Great Britain, France, or the United States?

People in Florida were divided in their sympathies. The Spanish-speaking population, centered at St. Augustine, espoused loyalty to Spain. Free blacks also regarded Spain as the better alternative as did the Seminole of Alachua. English, Scottish, and Irish residents had similar views. They were mostly former British Loyalists. Having been on the losing side of the American Revolution, and lost their homes inside the United States because of it, they had a deep suspicion of the new republic and no desire to see Florida annexed to it. If Spain lost Florida, they hoped it would go to Great Britain. But a sizeable faction of settlers, including those with close ties to Georgia and South Carolina, welcomed the idea of turning Florida over to the United States.

Meanwhile, Governor Quesada was anxious to leave East Florida and its troubles. An old illness had flared up under the stress of his duties and he implored his superiors to transfer him to a place where he could serve the Crown with "zeal and credit," but "with less anguish" than the hardships of Florida afforded.[42]

In his place, the Crown appointed an Irishmen, Enrique (Henry) White. A crusty old bachelor, White arrived in 1796 with a record of previous success in Pensacola as governor of West Florida. Knowledgeable in colonial warfare and in the politics of the borderland, he was competent, well liked and completely dedicated to Spain's interests. He spoke and read English, Spanish, and French, and he proved a wise choice. The province needed someone who could restore order, reassure settlers, and discourage further challenges to authority.[43]

Against the odds, White did just that. The new parish church on the town plaza was completed and White pushed through repairs to the Castillo and other parts of town. In his thirteen years as governor he weathered several crises, thwarted the agitations of William Augustus Bowles among the Creek Indians, and piloted East Florida through a time of increased tensions between Spain and the United States after the Louisiana Purchase. His greatest concern was for the Florida-Georgia border, where violence continually erupted. Dissension along the border, he predicted, "cannot but produce discords, and, in time, a bloody war that might destroy great numbers of innocent people, due to the zealous indiscretion, or evil intention, of some few."[44]

On the whole, however, White's tenure was peaceful. An improvement in the economy worked in his favor. St. Augustine's commerce was finally beginning to pick up, bolstered by trade with the United States. Of 53 ships in the harbor in 1803, 35 hailed from U.S. ports.[45] More money in colonists' pockets, and better credit abroad, brought about a surge of urban renovation as merchants and planters put up more substantial houses. A distinctive style of domestic architecture developed, one that still gives the historic district of St. Augustine a certain Spanish colonial charm. In fact, many of the colonial-era homes that still exist in St. Augustine were either built or remodeled during the Second Spanish Period.

Minorcan craftsmen did most of the building. The foundations and lower floors of houses were fashioned of coquina rock from the quarries of Anastasia Island, with second stories of stone or wood. Street-front balconies were common. Some balconies were right across the street from each other, close enough that people could reach across and touch another person. The myth is that many a romance began this way.

Houses also typically had a *loggia,* a type of porch with walls on three sides, open to the yard at the back of the house on the south or west side. Although glazed or paned windows were now common, walls on the north side of houses usually had no or few windows, to prevent the cold winter winds from penetrating inside. Bedrooms were on the second story. The ground floor might have a *sala* (parlor), the *comedor* (dining room), and a room for a small shop or business.[46]

Wood shingled roofs contrasted with the rustling palm frond thatch that covered some poorer houses and outbuildings. Kitchens were usually separate, removing the heat and danger of fire from the main house. Wells lined with cut coquina penetrated to the level of underlying fresh water, and, as in the past, the yards themselves supported orange, fig, and even peach trees, small kitchen gardens, and chicken coops. The Spanish pink was a particularly favored flower, grown always in pots and used on balconies.[47]

St. Augustine also completed two major projects. The center of community life was the new parish church, finished in 1797, at the northwest corner of the plaza. Originally designed by the military engineer Mariano de la Rocque and constructed by engineer Pedro Díaz Berrio, the church's façade featured Doric columns and a broken pediment, above which rose the graceful *empadaña*-style belfry. The building has since evolved into the Cathedral-Basilica of St. Augustine, although retaining its eighteenth-century facade.[48]

A crucifix recovered from the ruins of Nombre de Dios after the Palmer raid of 1728, was displayed inside the church, near the door, reminding the parishioners of an earlier period of Catholicism in the city. The black congregation occupied the first balcony and *Te Deums* rang out from the choir in the second balcony. Some of St. Augustine's boys had the privilege of standing outside on the wooden platform behind the belfry to ring the bells that hung in the four niches. Holidays or a bishop's visit called forth a joyous peal, while at other times their sad measured beat could be heard tolling the number of years of life of the recently deceased. Every night at nine o'clock they also rang out, halting the faithful wherever they were for a silent prayer.[49]

Another project was the creation of a school to educate the town's boys. Parish priests were alarmed that boys from Minorcan families were speaking the Minorcan dialect of Catalán, their native tongue, or the English they had picked up during the British Period, instead of Spanish. They also wanted boys to receive better instruction in the Catholic catechism. Squeezing money from the budget, officials approved salaries for two teachers, one in mathematics, and one in letters, reading and writing. They allocated a large two-story stone house at the south end of town for a school building. Father Thomas Hassett, who had previously worked with schools in Philadelphia, drafted the regulations and made recommendations about texts. Financed from the Treasury, the school offered a free education, and all boys were expected to attend. Despite this, no Protestant families complied, since instruction in the Catholic faith was required.[50]

Once it opened in 1786, the boys' school was in continuous operation for the rest of the colonial period. The school faced the same issues as modern schools—overcrowding, low teacher salaries, and shortages of supplies. Officials tapped the Treasury and the hospital for teachers and at one point Governor White remitted the sentence of a convict laborer, Joseph Monasterios, and sentenced him to teach instead. As a teacher of reading and writing in 1796, he earned less than the pay of the servant who swept the church.

There were about 200 boys eligible to attend school in 1796, and the roll for Monasterios' class for that year, the only one to survive, has 80 names on it, the youngest being four and the oldest fourteen. Monasterios described daily life in the ground-floor classroom. The schoolroom was supplied with benches and large work tables and measured about 22 feet square. Without enough desks, Monasterios reported, "the students taking writing must wait for the others to finish their assignments before beginning their own; and those learning reading are packed together shoulder to shoulder, and nearly suffocated by reason of the heat."[51]

All lessons were conducted in Spanish. Rules had a surprisingly modern ring. A ruler, kept on the teacher's desk, served as a "latrine pass" to be carried by boys if they needed to be excused. Near the door hung a pendulum, and upon leaving with the pass, a pupil had to set the pendulum in motion, and be back before it stopped swinging.

School hours were long, from roughly sun up to sunset with two hours off in the middle of the day for the boys to return home for dinner and siesta. Teachers were urged to adopt a caring attitude to correct students, and to use corporal punishment sparingly. Facing the sad realities of those days, pupils were expected to attend the funerals of classmates who did not live to maturity. At dismissal, boys were supposed to "go directly home without loitering, or shouting, or committing mischievous pranks in the streets."[52]

The school was the principal educational facility for East Florida, and families who could not or would not take advantage of it had to find other ways to educate their children. Children of the affluent, especially those who were Protestants, received schooling at home from tutors or parents or their older siblings. Some were sent away to boarding schools, others were apprenticed into trades.

Susan Fatio L'Engle, granddaughter of the wealthy Swiss settler Francis Philip Fatio, who owned New Switzerland Plantation, recalled in a memoir the great importance her family placed on education. "It would be hard to decide which language was most used in the family, but I think French was, though my grandmother and [grandfather] usually conversed in Italian. My brother was sent to New York State to school. My sister Mary....was sent to St. Augustine."[53]

The center of town life was the market, which consisted of stalls set up in the town plaza, along with open-air meat and vegetable stands. Sitiki, recalling part of his youth in St. Augustine, vividly described a scene from around 1817: "The market place for meat was at the Plaza in the side of the present market house on the eastern end of a low, one story latticed building....Beef and pork were the meats for the market." He also remembered the King's apothecary and two buildings adjoining this building were two intermediate rooms with supplies for the King's launch. South of this was a building called *La Botica*, the shop of the King's apothecary. To the south and east was the vegetable and fruit market, although fruit was generally sold in the streets from baskets carried on the head. Seafood for sale included fish and stone crabs "taken among the coquina rocks on the south beach or brought from Matanzas." Six cents bought a plate of shrimp or a quart of oysters.[54]

People came to market dressed in a variety of ways. The average man wore a hunting shirt of checked cotton, with "common breeches" and an intricately braided palmetto hat. He might be barefooted, or wearing moccasins if the weather was cooler. Soldiers dressed in the uniforms of their units. Women wore petticoats of cotton, linen, or silk, depending on their social station, and home-fashioned fabric shoes, some even made of satin. Kerchiefs or lace veils controlled their hair, tucked into the open fronts of their bodices, assuring modesty in public.

When the community's elite appeared in public, they wore the latest and highest fashions that they could afford and secure through the uncertainties of import. Slaves were dressed fitting the rank of their owners, and the free blacks according to their own affluence.

Indian men who came to market wore jackets or blankets above their loincloths. Their ears were resplendent with rings of silver and brass and the odor of bear grease rose from their pomaded hair. Slung across their shoulders were haunches of deer and other products of the hunt. They also brought ponies, hogs, wild honey, beeswax, snakeroot, bears' oil, raw and dressed deerskins and sometimes even a slave for exchange. They left town with purchases of powder, lead, cotton clothes and shrouds, beads, combs, looking glasses and carmine to paint their faces.[55]

Throughout the Second Spanish Period, St. Augustine remained a military town. Garrison troops were housed at the south end of town in the pile of barracks, a large wooden structure built during the British Period, and in quarters created from the old Franciscan friary. The latter contained the mess hall and a wing that housed the *presidarios* (convicts) sentenced to work for the army in St. Augustine. A tavern immediately next door did a brisk business, and further west, along today's St. Francis Street, were garden lots that soldiers tended during their off-duty hours. The principal unit garrisoning St. Augustine for most of late colonial times was the Third Battalion of the Cuban Infantry Regiment, whose soldiers wore white linen uniforms with red facings. Other forces, including militia from Havana, supplemented them in times of war.[56]

St. Augustine also relied on local urban militia units for its defense, with units for the Spanish, the Minorcans, the Irish, and the free blacks. The militia for free men of color in St. Augustine had an especially distinguished record, and its members were noted for their skill at frontier fighting. They gained their skills under a black military officer, George Biassou, veteran of the wars of the Haitian Revolution, who came to St. Augustine with his family and retinue in 1796.

Biassou was a leader of the slave revolt in Haiti (Sainte-Domingue), then became an officer in the Spanish army's Black Auxiliaries of Carlos IV. Proud and disdainful, he caused a sensation when he arrived in St. Augustine, drawing an annual salary from the Crown of 3,840 *pesos* and cutting a dashing figure in his uniform. More importantly, he inspired the local black militia, and was a symbol of status and freedom to other free blacks.[57]

During the 1790s and afterwards, the free black militia garnered a reputation for prowess rarely matched by other militia units, friendly or foreign. Black troops helped to patrol the frontier and restore order after the 1795 revolt. Their presence near the border was a constant source of friction with the frontier families of

Camden County, Georgia, who repeatedly accused Spanish officials of raising a "Negro Army" to terrorize them.[58]

As the first decade of the 1800s came to a close, St. Augustine and East Florida needed its military. The colony's fate was again balanced on a knife's edge. The Louisiana Purchase, vehemently protested by the Spanish Crown, had embittered relations between the United States and Spain. Then, in 1808, Napoleon Bonaparte cast Spain into chaos when he deposed Charles IV from the throne, placed the heir Ferdinand under house arrest, and put Spain under a French military occupation.

Spain splintered into factions, some favoring Napoleon, others backing a new regency government that ruled in Ferdinand's name from the heavily fortified seaport of Cádiz. The disarray in Spain encouraged liberation movements in the Spanish colonies, including the 1810 Hidalgo Revolt in Mexico and, that same year, a successful move in part of West Florida to break away from Spain and declare independence. Within months, the United States stepped in to incorporate the "Republic of West Florida" as a U.S. territory.[59]

Although this turmoil did not immediately engulf East Florida, the overthrow of the Spanish Crown did cause panic. The entire financial apparatus of the colonial government and the military depended on funding from the Crown. Prominent planters and merchants in Florida, afraid of social collapse, toyed with the idea of declaring independence, like their counterparts in West Florida, or seeking U.S. intervention. Would the future mean rule by Spain, France, or Britain? Suddenly an American affiliation seemed a wise choice.[60]

There were also agents in the United States who wanted to annex East Florida. The former governor of Georgia, George Mathews, appeared at the Florida-Georgia border in 1810 to hold secret talks with prominent Spanish subjects of East Florida. He sent optimistic reports to the administration of U.S. President James Madison, saying key planters in East Florida would support a move of the colony to the United States. Prompted in part by these reports, Congress authorized Mathews to keep an eye on the situation. If East Floridians declared independence from Spain, or if Great Britain or any other power tried to move troops into the area, Mathews could request assistance from the U.S. military and take possession of the colony.[61]

All of this came to a head in 1812, as the United States prepared to declare war on its old adversary, Great Britain. Instead of merely watching the situation in East Florida, Mathews fomented a rebellion, using his own forces, dubbed Patriots, to encourage the residents of East Florida to throw off Spanish rule. The plan was a disaster, and a major embarrassment to the Madison administration. Before word of it reached Washington, Mathews' forces, joined by U.S. infantry and Marines, crossed the border, captured the town of Fernandina, and advanced to St. Augustine. There they were stopped, in part by the strength of the city's defenses and in part by orders from the Madison administration to cease hostilities.[62]

This began the so-called "Patriot War," a border conflict that eventually merged into the War of 1812. Mathews's attack on Spanish territory was wildly popular in Georgia. "We rejoice to learn that active operations have commenced against the Floridas," wrote the editor of the *Savannah Republican*. "Better late than never." Georgia militiamen rushed south to the aid of American forces and the Patriots, hopeful of capturing St. Augustine.[63]

The acting military governor of St. Augustine, Cuban-born Juan José de Estrada, was determined to hold the city for Spain. "Rest assured," Estrada wrote to the captain general in Cuba, "that this place is in a state to make a vigorous resistance, and that in the event of the enemy possessing himself of it, that it will be only of its ruins, under which I shall be found buried." Soon thereafter a new governor, Sebastián Kindelán y O'Regan, arrived from Havana with military reinforcements and supplies. The Spanish garrison, the militia of St. Augustine, and the Seminole war parties of Alachua joined together to defend the province.[64]

In contrast to the short-lived revolt that shook East Florida in 1795, the Patriot War turned into a military occupation that dragged on through 1812 and 1813. St. Augustine was well protected, but destruction in the countryside was extraordinary. Virtually every homestead between the Georgia border and Cape Canaveral was looted or burned. Roving bands of men knocked down fencing for firewood, confiscated livestock, and slaughtered cattle to deny them to Spanish forces. As many as 10,000 head of cattle were rustled or killed. The fields all around St. Augustine resembled a butcher yard, bloodily spattered with the rotting corpses of steers, cows, and calves. Elsewhere raiding parties emptied corn houses and cotton houses, carted off household furniture, and invaded slave quarters, seeking people to kidnap and sell. Off the coast, a pair of privateers preyed on St. Augustine's shipping.[65]

At St. Augustine, everything was a stalemate. U.S. forces could not take the Castillo, the key strategic point, and Spanish forces would not come forth to open battle. The hot oppressive summer of 1812 saw breakdowns in morale and discipline on both sides, as well as rising sickness among the occupying troops. They were encamped at the old site of Fort Mose north of town, short on food, tents, and potable water. Their commander, Lieutenant Colonel Thomas Adam Smith, had no control over Patriot groups, who foraged and raided at their own discretion. At times he despaired of maintaining order and health among his hungry and depleted forces. "In truth I am truly tired of this Damned Province," he said about six months into the American occupation of Florida, "and would not remain (if it rested with me) one month longer in my present situation for a fee simple to the whole of it." A medical orderly from Virginia expressed the situation more succinctly. He characterized the U.S. encampment as "pregnant with sickness and death."[66]

Inside St. Augustine, things were not much better. Governor Kindelán was running out of food, and even had to confront a mutiny from part of the garrison. In early September, he composed a desperate letter to his superiors in Cuba. "All or the greater part of the Province is in rebellion. Amelia Island, the St. Marys River, the St. Johns River, are in the possession of the troops of the United States. The Treasury has not a *real* or any credit. The port is blockaded."[67]

The urban black militia saved the day for Kindelán. Even as he wrote his foreboding message, they were out trying to sever enemy lines of communication and force a retreat from St. Augustine. Their unit was led by Lieutenant Juan Bautista "Prince"

Witten—the same who had escaped from slavery across the St. Marys River with his wife and children back in 1786.

On the evening of September 11, 1812, he and his men, assisted by maroons and warriors from the Seminole, ambushed a contingent of twenty-two U.S. soldiers with a supply train for the troops encamped at Fort Mose. The militia pinned down the troops, mortally wounded Captain John Williams, the Marine in command, and took away the wagons. It was a turning point in the conflict. "About 50 coloured militia inhabitants....saved by their Bravery and fidelity the City of St. Augustine from being taken & Plundered," one resident later recalled. Within days, Lieutenant Colonel Smith abandoned his advance position and pulled his weakened force of sick troops back to the safety of their base on the St. Johns River.[68]

Fighting shifted away from St. Augustine as the Georgia militia mounted an offensive against the Seminole. Daniel Newnan, with 117 Georgia volunteers, headed to Alachua seeking out Seminole war parties, and fought a pitched battle with them.[69] Finally in the spring of 1813, U.S. forces received orders to withdraw from East Florida. The War of 1812 against Britain was going badly, and the United States could no longer afford to tie down troops in Spanish territory.[70]

St. Augustine parish church and the monument to the Spanish Constitution of 1812. Engraving in *American Magazine of Useful and Entertaining Knowledge*, June 1835.

Settlers in Florida emerged from the Patriot War exhausted, bitter, and broke. The one piece of good news they received was that the Spanish government at Cádiz had promulgated a constitution. Under the Constitution of 1812, the eligible males of St. Augustine engaged in its first popular election. Gerónimo Álvarez took office as *alcalde* (mayor), heading an *ayuntamiento* (town council), that included Minorcan Francisco Pons, Fernando de la Maza Arredondo, the younger, Eusebio María Gómez, Francisco Rovira, and Vicente Llarena. Bernardo Seguí was selected to serve as secretary.[71]

The creation of the city's first elected municipal government did not go entirely smoothly. Mayor Álvarez wrangled constantly with Governor Kindelán over the extent of mayoral powers. At one point Kindelán, in frustration at having to share political power, complained harshly of Álvarez's "natural stupidity, which led him to commit [the] worst outrages." Álvarez, for his part, was intent on making the position of mayor one of true authority, and not simply a nominal office. He implemented a night patrol of the city and oversaw an 1813 census. In 1814, the City Council completed a monument to the new constitution, an obelisk bearing a commemorative tablet, which still stands in the town plaza.[72]

Ultimately, the damages left in the wake of the Patriot War and the War of 1812 ended hopes for stability or prosperity in the Spanish province. People tried to rebuild and to regroup. But in 1816, American troops crossed the border again to destroy a town of runaway slaves and black maroons along the Apalachicola River, a place known as the Negro Fort. The following year, Scottish adventurer Sir Gregor McGregor took the town of Fernandina, holding it in the name of the republics of Venezuela, New Granada, Mexico, and Río de la Plata. The intruders rebuffed two military expeditions dispatched against them from St. Augustine.

It was not Spain but the United States that eventually restored order at Fernandina. In December 1817, the administration of President James Monroe sent in troops and placed the town under military control, staunchly refusing to relinquish it. Only a year later, General Andrew Jackson brought U.S. soldiers across the border to fight the Seminole. The First Seminole War (1817-1818) came nowhere near St. Augustine, but by the time Jackson withdrew he had shown once more that American troops could operate inside Spanish territory with impunity. There seemed to be no peace, no respite, anywhere.[73]

Ceding Florida to the United States was now openly discussed. The Treaty of Ghent, which ended the War of 1812, had already established that portions of West Florida, seized by the United States in 1813, would remain in U.S. hands. This, and the general tribulations shaking Spain's overseas empire, made it evident that the United States would eventually annex Florida. Negotiations between U.S. Secretary of State John Quincy Adams and Spanish ambassador, Luis de Onís led to the Adams-Onís Treaty, drafted in 1819 and finally accepted in both Madrid and Washington in 1821. St. Augustine was about to enter its next era, as a city in a U.S. territory. Many of the colonial residents who had grown up in St. Augustine decided to stay and become American citizens. From them came families that still call the "Oldest City" their home today.

NOTES

1 Paul E. Hoffman, *Florida's Frontiers* (Bloomington: University of Indiana Press, 2002): 225-242; William S. Coker and Susan R. Parker, "The Second Spanish Period in the Two Floridas," in *The New History of Florida,* ed, Michael Gannon (Gainesville: University Press of Florida, 1996): 150-166.

2 Helen Hornbeck Tanner, *Zéspedes in East Florida 1784-1790* (Jacksonville: University of North Florida Press, 1989), 38-52; Susan R. Parker, "'I am neither your subject nor your subordinate,'" in *Clash Between Cultures, Spanish East Florida, 1784-1821, El Escribano* 25 (1988): 52-53.

3 Joseph Byrne Lockey, *East Florida, 1783-1785: A File of Documents Assembled and Many of Them Translated* (Berkeley: University of California Press, 1949), 214, 358-367, 598; Tanner, *Zéspedes*, 44-47.

4 Susan R. Parker, "So in Fear of Both the Indians and the Americans," in *America's Hundred Years' War: U.S. Expansion to the Gulf Coast and the Fate of the Seminole, 1763-1858,* ed., William S. Belko (Gainesville: University Press of Florida, 2011), 36-40; James G. Cusick, "King Payne and his Policies, A Framework for Understanding the Diplomacy of the Seminoles of La Chua,

1784-1812," in ed., Belko, *America's Hundred Years' War,* 41-53.

5 Tanner, *Zéspedes,* 80-94; Lockey, *East Florida,* 29, 320-326.

6 Population figures were compiled from Sherry Johnson, "The Spanish St. Augustine Community, 1784-1821: A Re-Evaluation," *Florida Historical Quarterly* 68 (July 1989): 42; Patricia C. Griffin, *Mullet on the Beach, The Minorcans of Florida, 1768-1788* (Jacksonville: University Press of North Florida, 1991), 117-118, 121; James G. Cusick, *The Other War of 1812: The Patriot War and the American Invasion of Spanish East Florida* (Athens: University of Georgia Press, 2007), 41; Susan R. Parker, "Men without God or King: Rural Settlers of East Florida, 1784-1790," *Florida Historical Quarterly* 69 (October 1990): 135-155; Donna Rachal Mills, *Florida's First Families, Translated Abstracts of Pre-1821 Spanish Censuses* (Tuscaloosa: Mills Historical Press, 1992); Tanner, *Zéspedes,* 126.

7 James G. Cusick, "Ethnic Groups and Class in an Emerging Market Economy: Spaniards and Minorcans in Late Colonial St. Augustine" (Ph.D. dissertation, University of Florida, 1993), 236-241.

8 "Employees for the Hospital at St. Augustine" and "Government Employees Destined for St. Augustine," Lockey, *East Florida,* 198-199, 202-204; Jean Parker Waterbury, *The Oldest House, Its Site and Its Occupants 1650 (?) to the Present* (St. Augustine Historical Society, 1984), 11-16.

9 Jean Parker Waterbury, *The Ximénez-Fatio House, Long Neglected, Now Restored* (St. Augustine Historical Society, 1985).

10 Johnson, "The Spanish St. Augustine Community," 38.

11 "Memorials of the Italians, Greeks and Minorcans, St. Augustine, July 12, 1784," in Lockey, *East Florida*, 232-233.

12 Griffin, *Mullet on the Beach,* 114-124, 150-151.

13 Griffin, *Mullet,* 154-168; Jean Parker Waterbury, *Where Artillery Lane Crosses Aviles Street: The Seguí-Kirby Smith House* (St. Augustine Historical Society, 1987).

14 Parker, "Men without God or King," 142-143, 147-150; James G. Cusick, "Across the Border: Commodity Flow and Merchants in Spanish St. Augustine," *Florida Historical Quarterly* 69 (January 1991): 277-299; Hoffman, *Florida's Frontiers*, 244-260.

15 Tanner, *Zéspedes*, 35-36. Lockey, *East Florida*, 255-256. Janice Borton

Miller, "The Struggle for Free Trade in East Florida and the Cédula of 1793," *Florida Historical Quarterly* 55 (July 1976): 49-51.

[16] Susan R. Parker, "Success Through Diversification: Francis Philip Fatio's New Switzerland Plantation," in *Colonial Plantations and Economy,* ed., Jane G. Landers (Gainesville: University Press of Florida, 2000), 69-82; Report by Francis Philip Fatio, March 16, 1785, Section 7, East Florida Papers, Reel 16.

[17] Robert L. Gold "That Infamous Floridian, Jesse Fish," *Florida Historical Quarterly* 52 (July 1973): 1-17.

[18] Jane G. Landers, "Francisco Xávier Sánchez, *Floridano* Planter and Merchant," in ed.Landers, *Colonial Plantations and Economy*, 83-97.

[19] Tanner, *Zéspedes,* 93, 123.

[20] Lockey, *East Florida*, 203.

[21] Arthur Preston Whitaker, *Documents Relating to the Commercial Policy of Spain in the Floridas, with Incidental Reference to Louisiana* (DeLand: The Florida State Historical Society, 1931), 53.

[22] Jane Landers, *Black Society in Spanish Florida* (Urbana: University of Illinois Press, 1999): 74-76.

[23] Thomas Jefferson to George Washington, 2 April 1791, in *The Papers of George Washington,* see Founders Online, https://founders.archives.gov/; Janice Borton Miller, *Juan Nepomuceno de Quesada, Governor of Spanish East Florida, 1790-1795* (Washington: University Press of America, 1981), 77-94.

[24] Landers. *Black Society,* 177. A *peso* was worth approximately one U.S. dollar in the early 1800s.

[25] Patricia C. Griffin, *Sitiki, The Odyssey of an African Slave* (Gainesville: University Press of Florida, 2009).

[26] Jane G. Landers, *Atlantic Creoles in the Age of Revolutions* (Cambridge: Harvard University Press, 2010), 34-35, Landers, *Black Society,* 79-81; Frank Marotti, *Heaven's Soldiers, Free People of Color and the Spanish Legacy in Antebellum Florida* (Tuscaloosa: University of Alabama Press, 2013), 15-17, 116.

[27] Landers, *Black Society*, 82

[28] Ibid., 141-143.

29 Tanner, *Zéspedes*, 54-57; Griffin, *Mullet,* 22; Michael V. Gannon, *The Cross in the Sand* (Gainesville: University Press of Florida, 1965), 86-95.

30 Tanner, *Zéspedes*, 196-203.

31 *Narrative of a Voyage to the Spanish Main in the Ship Two Friends: The Occupation of Amelia Island, a Facsimile Reproduction of the 1819 Edition* (Gainesville: University Presses of Florida, 1978): 163; Griffin, *Mullet*, 172-175.

32 Griffin, *Mullet,* 73-77.

33 Griffin, *Sitiki,* 33-34

34 Miller, *Quesada,* 6-11.

35 Ibid., 28-30.

36 "Description of the commerce of East Florida, written by Luis Fatio, November 17, 1790, in Whitaker, *Documents,* 125-139; James G. Cusick, "Hello Sailor! St. Augustine as a Seaport, 1784-1800," *El Escribano* 47 (2010): 34.

37 Cusick, "Across the Border," 284.

38 Miller, "Royal Cédula," 55-58; Whitaker, *Documents,* 176-199.

39 Charles E. Bennett, *Florida's 'French Revolution,' 1793-1795* (Gainesville: University Press of Florida, 1981).

40 Bennett, *Florida's 'French Revolution,"* 117-118; Hoffman, *Florida's Frontiers,* 248-252; Richard K. Murdoch, *The Georgia-Florida Frontier, 1793-1796: Spanish Reaction to French Intrigue and American Designs* (Berkeley: University of California Press 1951), 42-43, 84-92, 124-133; Miller, *Quesada,* 125-166.

41 Cusick, *Other War,* 51.

42 Miller, *Quesada,* 168-169.

43 Roger C. Harlan, "A Military History of East Florida during the Governorship of Enrique White, 1796-1811." Master's thesis. Florida State University, 1971).

44 Harlan, "A Military History," 180.

45 Cusick, "Across the Border," 287.

46 Albert Manucy, *The Houses of St. Augustine, 1565-1821* (St. Augustine Historical Society, 1962), 41-61; Elsbeth K. Gordon, *Florida's Colonial Architectural Heritage* (Gainesville: University Press of Florida, 2002): 139-163.

47 Albert Manucy, *Sixteenth Century St. Augustine, The People and Their Homes* (Gainesville: University Press of Florida, 1997), 83-108; Griffin, *Sitiki,* 31.

48 Mariano de la Rocque to Governor Quesada, June 27, 1793, East Florida Papers, Library of Congress Manuscript Collection Reel 73; Gordon, *Architectural Heritage*, 123-127.

49 Gannon, *Cross in the Sand*, 108-110; Griffin, *Sitiki,* 33.

50 James G. Cusick, "The Boys' School in Colonial St. Augustine, 1786-1820" *El Escribano* 42 (2005): 23-46.

51 Ibid., 37-39.

52 Ibid ., 31-35; Father Thomas Hassett's *Reglas y Instrucciones*, Rule 24, East Florida Papers, December 25, 1786, Reel 16.

53 Susan Fatio L'Engle, *Notes on My Family and Recollections of My Early Life* (New York: The Knickerbocker Press, 1888), 16, 50-51.

54 Griffin, *Sitiki,* 30-31.

55 Ibid. 28, 32-33.

56 Prosecution of *presidario* Jose Betancurt for murder of silversmith Manuel Tobar, May 9, 1807, Section 64, East Florida Papers, Reel 120.

57 Landers, *Atlantic Creoles*, 55-94.

58 Cusick, *Other War*, 6-7, 184-185

59 Hoffman, *Florida's Frontiers*, 353-361.

60 Cusick, *Other War*, 1-3. Rembert W. Patrick, *Florida Fiasco, Rampant Rebels on the Georgia-Florida Border, 1810 1815* (Athens: University of Georgia Press, 1954), 16-54

61 Cusick, *Other War,* 30-32; Hoffman, *Florida's Frontiers,* 260-268.

62 Patrick, *Florida Fiasco,* 40-47, 83-98.

63 *Savannah Republican,* April 11, 1812.

64 Cusick, *Other War,* 145-148, 165-166. Quotation is from a report contained in Estrada to Thompson, April 15, 1812, Admiralty 1/502, Public Records Office (London).

65 Cusick, *Other War,* 193-208; Frank Marotti, *The Cana Sanctuary, History Diplomacy, and Black Catholic Marriage in Antebellum St. Augustine, Florida* (Tuscaloosa: University of Alabama Press, 2012), 29-49.

66 Cusick, *Other War*, 211; Lieutenant Colonel Thomas A. Smith to Captain William R. Boots, September 4, 1812, copy in the Smith Letterbook, T. Frederick Davis Papers, P.K. Yonge Library of Florida History, George A. Smathers Library, University of Florida

67 Kindelán to Apodaca, September 12, 1812, Section 2, East Florida Papers, Reel 12.

68 Marotti, *Cana Sanctuary,* 73-93, quote on 77.

69 Patrick, *Fiasco,* 195-210. James W. Covington, *The Seminoles of Florida* (Gainesville: University of Florida Press, 1993), 28-33.

70 Cusick, *Other War,* 236-278.

71 Alejandro Quiroga Fernández de Soto, "Military Liberalism on the East Florida 'Frontier': Implementation of the 1812 Constitution," *Florida Historical Quarterly* 79 (Spring 2001): 452-453. Susan Richbourg Parker, "Response to the Spanish Constitution of 1812," *El Escribano* 48 (2011):73.

72 Quiroga Fernández de Soto, "Military Liberalism," 455-456, 461, 464.

73 Hoffman, *Florida's Frontiers*, 264-281.

OSCEOLA
WAR LEADER – SEMINOLE INDIANS
CAPTURED 1838

7

"Dull Old Place' or a 'Garden of Eden"

1821 - 1877

T. W. Upchurch

In 1862, Calvin Shedd was a 36-year-old lieutenant with the Seventh New Hampshire Regiment, assigned to garrison duty in St. Augustine. Soon after arriving in the town, Shedd wrote his family and noted: "Saint Augustine is a dull Old Place now, & I should think there was not much life here at any time." Yet despite the dullness of the place, he saw potential. In the same letter he continued: "This must be a nice place for Northerners to live in Winter & it is strange to me that more do not Especially the rich anyone could make a Garden of Eden here at a quarter of the expense that some spend north on an ordinary affair."[1] While ancient by American standards, St. Augustine for much of the early nineteenth century was small, remote, and struggled to grow and prosper. Yet even in the midst of war, Shedd saw the same charm and potential that Henry Flagler and others would see in just a few years.

St. Augustine had persevered for some 250 years as both a Spanish and British town, yet it had never grown or prospered in the way so many other European cities and colonies in North America had flourished. When the two Spanish colonies of East Florida and West Florida were transferred to the United States in 1821, they became a single American territory, divided administratively at the Suwannee River. During the British and second Spanish periods, the Apalachicola River had been the boundary between the two

LEFT. Portrait in ceramic tile of Osceola. Tile portrait is located on east wall of Webb Building, 18 St. Francis Street (Oldest House complex). Created by Manuel Real Alarcón in Valencia, Spain, in 1958 for the St. Augustine Historical Society, the tile arrived at SAHS in August of 1959. Photograph by James Quine, 2014.

Florida colonies. Pensacola was the capital in the west, and St. Augustine in the east until 1824, when Tallahassee was established as the capital of the territory. In 1825, the population of the territory was less than 13,400, with about thirteen percent of the people living in St. Augustine.[2]

The town's growth and economic prosperity were hampered by a number of factors, most prominently the inlet. It was historically capricious; sandbars constantly shifted, both preventing larger ships from entering and endangering those that did attempt to cross over the bars into the harbor. James Grant Forbes, a native of the city, wrote in 1821 that ships drawing more than six feet of water could not enter the harbor safely because of the sandbars. He stated that the harbor was dramatically impacted by the winds, but downplayed the breakers that surrounded the inlet, claiming they were "not as dangerous as they appear."[3]

William Hayne Simmons described an ambitious plan to improve St. Augustine's harbor in his 1822 book, *Notices of East Florida*. The first half of the nineteenth century was an era of great canal building in America; the most successful example, the Erie Canal, was completed in 1825. Visionaries and schemers discussed construction of a canal to connect the St. Johns River with the harbor in St. Augustine by way of Six Mile Creek. Simmons wrote that "it is thought by many, that bringing the waters of the St. John's into the harbour of St. Augustine, would have the effect of deepening the bar, by the increased momentum that would thus be given to the tide, at its ebbing."[4] This idea was never acted upon.

Mary Anderson, the matriarch of the Anderson family that would impact the city for the next hundred years or more, described her family's attempt to enter the harbor in 1829: "In our first attempt to cross we were almost lost-the wind having died away when we were only half over leaving us at the mercy of the Breakers-here was a scene of terror which I never saw before equaled. I never experienced such a relief in my life was when I set foot once more on the shore."[5]

As the Americans raised their flag over the Castillo de San Marcos in July 1821, it eloquently symbolized the transfer to the United States. Charles Vignoles described the appearance of the town as "ruinous, dirty, and forbidding."[6] There were perhaps as many as a thousand houses in St. Augustine, occupying a space approximately "three quarters of a mile in length and a one quarter in breadth."[7]

Historically, the town's population was diverse, including at one time a "small settlement of Germans, with a church of their own" in addition to an Indian settlement.[8] The Spanish-speaking population of the town was large enough that as late as 1840, political advertisements were still printed in both Spanish and English.[9] The presence of the significant Minorcan group created a large Catholic population. "Minorcans," the collective term for descendants of Minorcan, Greek, and Italian colonists originally recruited to operate Andrew Turnbull's failed plantation in New Smyrna, occupied as much as a quarter of the town. Europeans, Anglo-Americans, free blacks, and slaves filled the remainder."[10]

Nationally, it was a period of rising tensions between Catholics, who were often European immigrants, and Protestants, known as "nativists." This nativist, anti-Catholic sentiment, grew out of longstanding tensions between the two groups of Christians. Ethnic stereotyping of Catholics contributed to these tensions, as did nativist concerns about economic competition from newly arrived (often Catholic) immigrants.[11] With near equal numbers of both Catholics and Protestants, these tensions flared in St. Augustine in 1848, with the publication of a guidebook, *Sketches of St. Augustine,* by Rufus King Sewall, a minister of the fledgling Presbyterian Church. He wrote the book together with B. E. Carr, a local merchant and operator of the Magnolia Hotel on St. George Street, with the aim of encourage people to visit St. Augustine by extolling its virtues as a "resort for invalids."[12]

In his book, Sewall wrote that the Minorcans were of "servile extraction" and that the men "lack enterprise." He denounced the local Lenten celebration of Carnival and a post-nuptial custom called Sherivaree (chivarée). Sewall described Sherivaree as a gathering of rowdies and noisemakers at the home of the newlyweds and who finally dispersed when "bought off" with whiskey or money.[13] When the published book arrived in town, Sewall immediately faced angry protests from the Minorcan population, which was particularly offended by the "servile extraction" comment. As Thomas Graham explains: "In local society, the Minorcans had come to be regarded by some as an inferior social caste, and the reference to slave origins in a society practicing Negro slavery was a direct affront to the dignity of Minorcans."[14] The protests forced Sewall to leave town and the first edition of *Sketches* was sold locally only after the offending pages had been cut out.[15]

Charles Vignoles had earlier described the Minorcans in some detail in his 1823 book, *Observations upon the Floridas*. He wrote that they formed a "numerous, industrious and virtuous body of people," a group separate and distinct from the "the indolent character of the Spaniard and the rapacious habits of some of the strangers who have visited that city since the exchange of flags." He found Minorcans often busy in "laborious but useful occupations," as farmers, hunters, and fishermen. He continued: "crime is almost unknown among them; speaking their native tongue, they move about distinguished by a primitive simplicity and honesty. . . ."[16]

John Lee Williams also offered his observations about the town and its residents in the mid-1830s, which paint St. Augustine as remarkably diverse. He contended that "the languages usually spoken are English, Spanish, French, and Lingua Franca" and that half of the population "are natives of the United States" while the others were Minorcans. Further, there were 151 "colored persons free" (8.7 percent) and 571 slaves (32.8 percent). Williams also provided a list of occupations represented among St. Augustine's residents, occupations that included ten lawyers and five "segar makers."[17]

He noted the "splendid catholic church" and "the new trinity church, a very neat edifice of the gothic order." He continued: "The Presbyterian church in the south part of the town, has lately been enclosed, and finished in a plain but neat style. A small Methodist church was built in 1833 on Charlotte-street." [18] He claims half the city's population of 1,739 inhabitants was Catholic and the balance divided between the three Protestant denominations.[19]

Until freed as a result of the Civil War, black slaves were a part of the day-to-day life of St. Augustine. At the time of the 1830 census, approximately half of the city's population was black or mulatto; this percentage decreased to 32% by 1860. Five individuals owned more than twenty slaves, while two-thirds of the population owned none. While the majority of the black population was enslaved, approximately one in ten were free blacks. Daniel Schafer argues these free blacks were contributing members of the community: "St. Augustine had long been home to educated free blacks who owned property, held responsible jobs, and led productive lives....In fact, many had been slave owners."[20]

In addition to the natural, shallow, condition of its inlet, another reason St. Augustine did not prosper as many other communities did is that a plantation economy never developed, although it was not for lack of trying. For example, the first Andrew Anderson purchased 31 slaves in 1839 to work a mulberry plantation that was never economically viable.[21] When Josiah and Hannah Smith arrived in St. Augustine in 1817 during the Second Spanish period, they brought with them thirteen slaves, overwhelmingly male, between sixteen and twenty-eight-years-old. They were the type of slave that would have been used for heavy agricultural work. Like the Andersons, the Smiths were not successful, whatever ambitions they might have had to be plantation owners. When Hannah Smith died a widow in 1855, she still owned thirteen slaves, although the composition had radically changed. Her slaves were all female except for one, four were deemed to be "aged Negroes," and one was described as "insane." Whatever her economic and personal motivations in the 1850s for owning these slaves, it does not appear it was for intensive agricultural work. [22]

For a period of time, oranges did flourish in St. Augustine. During the early 1830s, the city exported approximately 2.5 million oranges a season, with a value of about $72,000. The Anderson family had a 20-acre grove surrounding their home, Markland, now owned by Flagler College.[23] William Simmons purchased some 1,800 acres near the St. Johns River, which he devoted to oranges. However, the citrus industry was devastated by the freeze of 1835 when the temperature hovered around 7 degrees Fahrenheit for several days.[24] Pastor Sewall, in his guidebook, describes the impact on the city, albeit somewhat melodramatically:"At one fell stroke, the labor and profit of years of toil-the inheritance of many

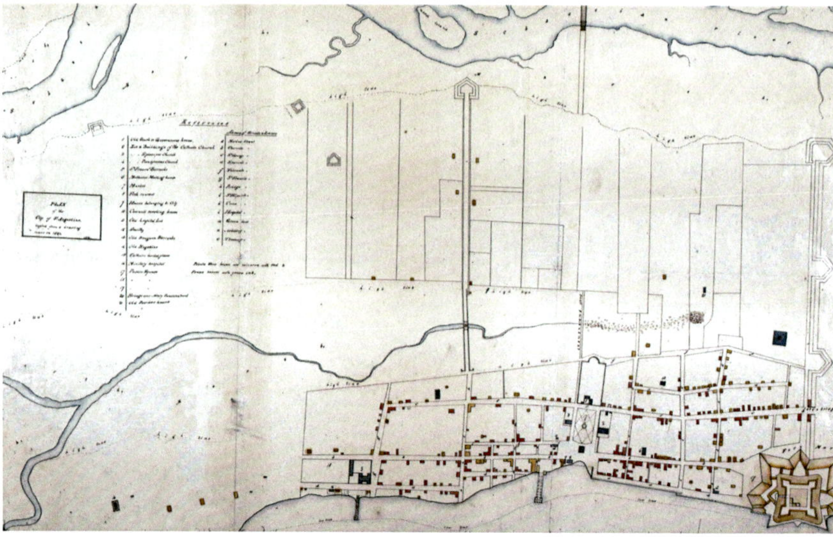

Anonymous. Plan of the City of St. Augustine copied from a drawing made in 1831. Original in National Archives, Record Group 77, Map #L-46.

generations-the little all of many families, were swept away! The resources of the city were dried up! Many were hurled in a night from the seat of affluence, into the lap of poverty and distress!"[25]

After describing the bucolic atmosphere of the "rustic village" of St. Augustine where prior to the freeze, houses peeped from among the "clustered boughs and the golden fruit of their favorite tree" and the "foreign invalid cooled his fevered limbs and imbibed health from the fragrant air," John Lee Williams discussed the destruction wrought by the freeze: "Dry unsightly poles with ragged bark, stick up around her dwellings and where the mocking-bird once delighted to build her nest, and tune her lovely sound, owls now hoot at night, and sterile winds whistle through the leafless branches. Never was a place more desolate."[26]

While Williams predicted the orange industry would recover within the next ten years, he did not foresee that the damaged trees were susceptible to infestation of orange coccus or "scale," which effectively destroyed the industry.[27]

Although nineteenth-century America was primarily an agricultural society, the economy of St. Augustine did not become dependent on a cash crop because the land would not support it. James Forbes wrote in 1821, the year Florida came under American control, that the sandy soil in the neighborhood of the city "may give it the appearance of being the worst in the province." However, he argued it produced two crops of Indian corn "some years, and garden vegetables always in great perfection," all in addition to the oranges and lemons, exceeding those of Spain and Portugal.[28] What Forbes describes is subsistence farming–bounty to sustain a family, but not sufficient to sell and grow wealthier.

Yet, soon after St. Augustine became a part of the United States, people suffering from respiratory illnesses such as tuberculosis began to discover the city for health reasons. Ralph Waldo Emerson typified these medical tourists. Historian Thomas Graham described Emerson's visit: "Ralph Waldo Emerson, who tarried in St. Augustine in the year 1827 with a pain in his chest, was one of those who endured loneliness and homesickness. He spent his time sitting in the sun, strolling along the beach, visiting the town's antiquities and sailing on the bay. The gentlemen among his fellow boarders whiled away the time whittling walking sticks from orange branches. Meetings of the Bible society, temperance society, court sessions, election days, and slave auctions provided some relief from the dull affairs of society."[29]

John Lee Williams described St. Augustine as "a place of great resort for invalids, affected by pulmonary and bronchial complaints." He noted that accommodations were rapidly improving and that soon, "persons of the first rank will be under no necessity for visiting Italy or the south of France, for the improvement of their health." However, Williams may have been overly optimistic about St. Augustine's ability to "soon" compete with the south of France. Accommodations did improve at existing establishments like the Union Hotel on the bayfront, arguably the oldest hotel in town and the City Hotel, also an early business. The Florida House opened in 1835 and B. E. Carr opened the Magnolia Hotel in the 1840s.[30] By the 1850s the town could accommodate approximately 300 visitors. But it wasn't until some fifty years after Williams's remarks, with the opening of Henry Flagler's Hotel Ponce de Leon, that the city could compete with European destinations.[31]

Political and military events impacted the city. The origins of the Second Seminole War can be traced to the Treaty of Moultrie

Creek, signed near St. Augustine in 1823, in which some thirty-two Seminole leaders agreed to move from North and Central Florida to a four-million-acre tract between the Peace and Withlacoochee rivers, a land Florida Governor William P. Duval described as "the most miserable region I ever beheld." The Seminoles soon realized the Governor was right about the poor quality of their new lands and slowly began to return to their former lands, now being settled by Americans.[32]

The returning Seminoles clashed with the constantly arriving new white settlers; this growing conflict created the impetus to find a "solution" to the "Indian problem." The administration of President Andrew Jackson strongly advocated removal of Native American tribes to lands west of the Mississippi River. In order to implement that policy, Federal agents induced fifteen Seminole leaders to sign the Treaty of Payne's Landing in May 1832. The Federal government argued the Indians had agreed to move west in three years, while the Indians contended they had only agreed to first inspect the western lands before putting the decision whether to move to a tribal vote. At an impasse, warfare erupted in 1835. At the time it was known at the time as the Florida War, but is now called the Second Seminole War.[33]

While most of the fighting occurred in Central Florida, St. Augustine and the surrounding environs did experience Seminole raids and other events. In January 1836, Florida militia skirmished with a band of Seminoles at John Hanson's sugar plantation just west of the San Sebastian River on Tocoi Road.[34] Further, General Thomas S. Jesup ordered the seizure of the prominent Seminole leader Osceola and some of his followers under a white flag in October 1837 at a site west of St. Augustine near the current location of Treaty Park. Imprisoned in Castillo de San Marcos, some twenty Seminoles escaped from the fortress in November, but not Osceola. He died the following year in January at Fort Moultrie, South Carolina.[35]

In 1840, a small raiding party attacked a theatrical troupe that was traveling from the ship's landing point on the St. Johns River into St. Augustine. Three of the actors were killed; three others and their driver managed to escape to the city. The next year, the leader of the raid, Coacoochee, appeared at Fort Cummings in Central Florida to negotiate with government envoys. The Indians came in costumes taken from the hapless actors; Coacoochee was dressed as Hamlet, "his aides appeared as Horatio and Richard III."[36]

During the war, the population of St. Augustine swelled to perhaps 3,000 people as refugees from the interior of Florida sought protection in the town for themselves and their slaves. Further, the city saw a large number of U.S. Army troops and volunteers from several states come through the town, whether stationed in the city, on leave, or to recover, often from malaria or other fevers.[37]

William J. Hardee, a recent West Point graduate and a lieutenant in the Second U.S. Dragoons, was deployed to Florida to fight the Seminoles. In May 1840, he became ill and was sent to St. Augustine to recover. It was there that he met and married Elizabeth Dummett. Elizabeth's father owned two tracts of land, one near the Tomoka River and the other near the Indian River, where he grew sugar cane. Due to the outbreak of the war and resulting Indian raids, the Dummetts had abandoned their property and sought protection in St. Augustine in 1835.[38]

After the Seminole War, Hardee continued his military career. He served as commandant of West Point, wrote a manual, *Rifle and Light Infantry Tactics,* which was the most widely used military manual during the Civil War, and lent his name to the "Hardee Hat," the regulation dress hat for enlisted men in the Union Army during the American Civil War.[39]

Elizabeth Dummett Hardee died in 1853, leaving her husband and four children, including a son known as Willie. Hardee entrusted the care of his children to his unmarried sister-in law, Anna Dummett, who was also caring for six other nieces and nephews at her home on the corner of St. George and St. Francis streets. At the outbreak of the Civil War, Hardee resigned his commission in the U.S. Army and joined the Confederate Army, ultimately rising to the rank of lieutenant general.[40] Although a senior Confederate commander, in the waning days of the Civil War, Hardee personally lead a cavalry charge of Terry's Texas Rangers, a unit that included his only son Willie, at the Battle of Bentonville (N.C.). While the charge was successful, seventeen-year-old Willie was killed. [41] His name is inscribed on the monument to St. Augustine's Confederate War Dead in the plaza.

Another sojourner in the city during the Seminole War was John T. Sprague. Arriving in St. Augustine in 1839 as a first lieutenant in the Eighth United States Infantry, he met and married Mary Worth, the oldest daughter of Colonel William Jenkins Worth.[42] He remained in Florida through 1848, missing the Mexican-American War, while serving as Officer in Charge of Indian Affairs and Disbursing Agent for the Army. However, he used his time in Florida to write and publish *The Origins, Progress and Conclusion of the Florida War,* which remains authoritative on the military history of the Second Seminole War. During the Civil War, he served as adjutant general of the state of New York, where he was responsible for recruiting troops for the Union Army. He returned to Florida during Reconstruction and was placed in charge of the Freedman's Bureau in Florida and later became the military commander of the District of Florida. Historian John K. Mahon wrote of Sprague's service during Reconstruction "Wearing his two hats, Colonel Sprague was the keystone of reconstruction in Florida during the touchy period of military domination dictated by the radical Republicans. This was delicate duty, and it is to the colonel's credit that he seems to have done it well." He retired from the Army, only to be appointed major general of the Florida Militia, which he commanded until at least 1876. However, he maintained his connections with St. Augustine, serving on the Board of Trustees of the Buckingham Smith Benevolent Association.[43]

Important improvements to the city's infrastructure were made during this period. The Spanish had constructed a seawall extending from the Castillo to the public market (plaza), that was described as seven feet high, with a base of eight feet, and tapering to five feet at the top. This section needed to be rebuilt because it "had been mostly torn up and the stone removed by the United States authorities" and to have the seawall extended to the St. Francis Barracks because great injury has already been sustained, by one or two eastern gales, for want of this barrier." The wall was constructed of coquina although the capstones came from Port Deposit, Maryland, and was completed in 1841-42.[44]

At the same time, the causeway and bridge across the San Sebastian was built.[45] "Across the creek, an excellent stone causeway is erected. The St. Sebastian's is crossed by a bridge 500 feet long, and a causeway is extended over the marshes, about seven hundred yards."[46]

As the chaos, the excitement, and the opportunities of the Seminole War subsided, St. Augustine found itself drifting back towards its former self as a quiet, even dull little town. Fernandina and Jacksonville in East Florida eclipsed St. Augustine in population and prosperity, while, generally, East Florida was surpassed by Middle Florida as its plantation-based economy boomed in the 1840s and 1850s.[47]

In the 1840s, East Florida opposed statehood, as the region continued to lose economic and political power to Middle Florida. Thomas Graham argued that East Floridians, led by Robert R. Reid, David Levy, and James D. Wescott, all with strong St. Augustine roots, feared the new state would be dominated by Middle Florida and that the state could not afford the expense of statehood.[48] If population growth was an indication of political power, then their fears were well founded. By the 1840 census, 62 percent of Florida's population of some 54,500 residents lived in Middle Florida, 28 percent lived in East Florida, and the remaining 10 percent lived in West Florida, which was closely identified with Alabama.[49] As the momentum for statehood grew, East Florida's leaders argued for splitting Florida once again between East and West Florida with the Suwannee River serving as the boundary.[50] They saw this proposal as a means to insure political power for St. Augustine and East Florida.

Daniel Schafer argued that antebellum politics were dominated by the "Nucleus." Individuals like Richard K. Call, were early appointees of presidents, like Monroe and Jackson, and merged with wealthy migrants from Virginia to become part of a "conservative ruling class" that strongly identified with the Whigs. Reid, Levy, Westcott and others organized as Jacksonian Democrats in opposition to these Whigs.[51] The parties were in heated disagreement over banking laws; the Whigs supported abundant and inexpensive credit to fund economic growth, for credit backed the territorial government. In fact, government bonds were issued. With the disruption caused by the Seminole War and the national economic panic of 1837, the territorial government was forced to make good on its guarantee, which resulted in higher taxes for all Floridians.[52]

However, the distinctions between Whigs and Democrats were not easy for St. Augustine politicians. While Robert Reid opposed Whig banking policies, he and other prominent St. Augustinians had investments in the Southern Life Insurance and Trust Company of St. Augustine, a banking company that ultimately failed.[53] Further, although David Levy Yulee had deep St. Augustine ties and was a Democrat, he was instrumental in the crusade for Florida's admission to the Union in 1845. He and David Westcott were elected Florida's first two United States senators. [54]

The sectional conflict that tore at the nation in the 1850s, reverberated in St. Augustine. One tangible manifestation of this "impending crisis" between the North and South was the formation of the Florida Independent Blues, more commonly known as the St. Augustine Blues, a local militia. Historians Thomas Graham and David J. Coles have placed the formation of the unit in 1860, after John Brown's abortive slave rebellion and the collapse of the Democratic Party Convention. However, the company may have been formed as early as July 15, 1854.[55]

The American Civil War Museum & White House of the Confederacy in Richmond, Virginia, holds the company flag. The flag has a deep blue field with a star across the top for each of the seven Deep South states that had left the Union between December 1860 and February 1861. In the center is a cotton boll surrounded by hibiscus blossoms and below these, the motto: "Any Fate But Submission."[56] Attached to the flag is a short streamer or tie: embroidered on one end is "Florida Independent Blues" and on the other "Organized July 15, 1854."

The significance of the date the unit was organized is not clear, although the U.S. Congress had passed the Kansas-Nebraska Act on May 30, 1854, potentially opening new territories to

Flag of the Third Florida Infantry, Company B . From the collections of The American Civil War Museum & White House of the Confederacy, Richmond, Virginia.

slavery.[57] While arguably the South received greater concessions in the compromise than did the North, perhaps the acrimony created by the political debate made southerners, or at least St. Augustinians, doubtful the compromise would hold and preserve the Union. Therefore, the young men of the town organized to protect their political interests, as did other young men in both the North and the South in the years leading up to the Civil War.

After Abraham Lincoln's election in November 1860, citizens in St. Augustine were increasingly pressured to take sides and declare whether they would remain loyal to the Union or support the Confederacy. While there is no question that a majority supported secession, there were citizens that remained loyal to the Union. Buckingham Smith sat out the war in New York City.[58] Andrew Anderson, despite having joined the St. Augustine Blues, thought better of his decision and like his neighbor Buck Smith went to New York, where he trained as a physician.[59] While a slave owner, his mother Sarah Anderson, certainly harbored Unionists sentiments, but stayed in St. Augustine throughout the war. As a woman, she was never at risk of being forced into the army, a threat that stared her 22-year old son squarely in the face. As a woman, her Unionist sentiments might well have been more tolerated than if held by a man. She was not alone; her associate, Sarah Mather, also endured the war in St. Augustine, despite having Unionist sentiments.[60]

At least one notable St. Augustinian served in the Union Army during the Civil War. Stephen Vincent Benet was born in St. Augustine in 1827 of Minorcan ancestry. His father, Pedro, known locally as the "King of the Minorcans," was wealthy enough to send Stephen to preparatory school in Virginia. Stephen subsequently graduated from West Point and taught there as an "instructor of Ordnance and the Science of Gunnery" throughout the war. After the war, he rose to the rank of brigadier general and served as chief of ordnance for the army for sixteen years.[61]

Those that stayed loyal to the Union, regardless of the depth of their loyalty, were a distinct minority; most St. Augustinians supported secession and the subsequent war effort. Two of the town's sons served as Confederate generals. William Wing Loring, born in North Carolina, moved with his family to St. Augustine early in the Territorial Period. He volunteered for military service in the Second Seminole War at the age of fourteen and lost an arm in the Mexican War. He served as a general throughout the Civil War, primarily in the Western Theater of operations. Afterwards, he was employed as an officer in the army of the Khedive of Egypt. He died in New York City in 1886.

Loring was as restless in death as he was in life. He was cremated and his ashes originally interred in New York City, only to be removed to Evergreen Cemetery in St. Augustine the following year. In 1920, with great pomp and circumstance, his remains were moved to their current resting place under the obelisk erected in his honor at the corner of King and Cordova streets.[62]

Edmund Kirby Smith was born in 1824 on Aviles Street in what today is known as the Seguí-Kirby Smith House; the structure is home to the St. Augustine Historical Society's Research Library. His father served as a federal judge. Like Benet, he attended preparatory school in Virginia and graduated from West Point. As a young officer, he too served in the Mexican War and fought Indians in Texas. Like so many of his peers at the start of the Civil War,

Union Soldiers in Front of Monument and Church. Engraving in *Leslie's Illustrated Newspaper,* December 13, 1862.

he surrendered his commission in the U.S. Army and accepted a position in the Confederate Army.

Kirby Smith played a significant role in Braxton Bragg's ill-fated invasion of Kentucky in 1862. The St. Augustine Blues, having been mustered into the Confederate Army as Company B, Third Florida Infantry, also participated in this operation.[63] Kirby Smith subsequently commanded the Trans-Mississippi Department of the Confederacy, an assignment that covered countless hundreds of square miles and involved precious few men. Further, once the Mississippi River came under the control of Union forces after the fall of Vicksburg in July 1863, the department was of negligible importance to the overall war effort. Some remember Kirby Smith with pride as the last Confederate general to surrender at the end of the war. This distinction however has much more to do with geography than principle; physical distance and slow communication made the process of surrender difficult. After the war, he served with distinction on the faculty of the University of the South in Sewanee, Tennessee, for almost twenty years. Kirby Smith also has the honor of being one of the Floridians to be commemorated in Statutory Hall in the U. S. Capitol.[64]

St. Augustine played an insignificant military role in the Civil War. Early in the conflict, the Confederate government made the decision not to defend the east coast of Florida. Any potential benefit of defending the coast simply did not warrant the cost of deploying men and materials to protect the area from Federal intrusion. Therefore, when Federal forces captured Fernandina, Jacksonville, and St. Augustine in March 1862, Confederate forces had already abandoned the town.[65]

Throughout the remainder of the war, St. Augustine served as a Union garrison. The military value of the town to the Federal forces was perhaps as minimal as it was for the Confederates; the difference was that the Federal Army did not suffer from the same shortages of men and equipment that the Confederates faced and thus could afford to maintain the garrison. While the Federal occupation prevented the harbor from being used by blockade runners and the garrison served to pacify the interior of the country, the town also served as a place for Federal troops to rest and recuperate far from the front lines in Virginia and Tennessee.[66]

Leander Harris, a member of the Fourth New Hampshire Regiment, was stationed in St. Augustine shortly after its occupation by Federal troops in 1862. In a series of letters to his wife, Emily, he described his experiences in St. Augustine, an "out-of-the-way hole." He despaired that St. Augustine was so quiet and so far from the excitement of the war, that he felt he was "playing soldier" as opposed to being a real soldier on the frontlines.

St. Augustine looked quite foreign to a New Englander like Harris. "There is nothing American in the looks of the town, everything appears just as it left the hands of the old Spanish settlers." Like countless visitors, before and after, Harris described the narrow streets, the bayfront, and the Castillo. But the war had brought new sites to see, including the wreck of the *Jefferson Davis*, a Confederate privateer that had run aground in the town's inlet on August 17, 1861. Harris told his wife that he had a piece of wood from the wreck and intended to use it to make a cane for his father.

Despite the suffering caused by mosquitoes, he marveled at the profusion of flowers in the town and he professed that he and his fellow soldiers were "living high" on melons, figs and grapes. He regularly commented on the fine musical abilities of the regimental band and noted that three soldiers had drowned when their sailboat capsized in the bay.[67]

He wrote that he had seen his first "real live" nun. After describing her dress and veil, he concluded: "I think she looked as good and pure as it is possible for a poor mortal to be." Harris was also struck by his encounters with "Florida Crackers." Suggesting they were far beneath the character of good New Englanders, he continued: "They manage to live, and raise a flock of children without doing any work. They live on clams, fruit, and fish and anything else they can pick up. That they live for I do not see."

Like sacrificing a pawn in a chess match, the Confederates felt they could give up the coastal region of Florida. However, they could ill afford to allow Federal military excursions into the interior of Florida. If the Federal Army invaded the state west of the St. Johns River, it could potentially disrupt the movement of cattle and other foodstuffs to feed the Confederate Army or worse, knock Florida out of the war and restore the state to the Union. Therefore, the Confederacy assigned Colonel J. J. Dickison and the Second Florida Cavalry to East Florida. They "harassed the enemy when its harassment was needed, fought pitched battles when the moment demanded, and guarded large and important areas of the state so that vitally needed food and supply lines from Florida to the rest of the South could be kept open."[68]

The experience of Emily Southwick and her young family illustrates the cat and mouse game between Dickison and the Federal forces, but also provides insight into the lives of ordinary people during an extraordinary time. Emily, English by birth, married an older man, Lyman Southwick, whom she described as a "seafaring man." Lyman was from Rhode Island and for a period operated a coastal schooner between St. Augustine and Charleston. He appears to have been in St. Augustine by 1829, but died prior to the Civil War, leaving Emily and four children.[69]

The family lived on 30 acres of land, known as Arenta, on the west bank of the San Sebastian River. The farm spread out from the southwest corner of the stone causeway that forded the river down to Oyster Creek.[70] They grew peaches and oranges and the land supported a great deal of oak wood. They also had milk cows. The house was two stories, with a coquina fireplace and cypress clapboards. The kitchen was built out from the house and the storehouse was three times as large as the home. There were "a good many" other buildings on the property.[71]

Emily's oldest son, Stephen, perhaps just sixteen, had joined the St. Augustine Blues prior to the war. Stephen did not join the Confederate Army when the Blues were mustered in, perhaps because he was not yet eighteen. But his mother describes pressures on her oldest child to enlist. In her claim filed with the Southern Claims Commission after the war, she states he was "pressed" into Confederate service.[72] In January 1862 he mustered into Company D, Eighth Florida Infantry and became a part of Robert E. Lee's Army of Nothern Virginia. In September he was captured at the Battle of Antietam. Although he was subsequently paroled, he died of disease at Chimborazo Hospital Number 4 in Richmond in October.[73]

After Stephen's death, Emily Southwick remained on her farm with her daughter and two younger sons until 1863, when Colonel Dickison, the Confederate cavalry officer, presented her with a choice. She must either move into St. Augustine, then under Federal control, or across the St. Johns River into Confederate controlled territory. The implication was that her family, her sons in particular, were providing information to the Union troops on the operations of Dickison and his men in the interior of St. Johns County. Other families in the area were faced with the same ultimatum; some families went west to the Confederates, but others, including the Southwicks, went into St. Augustine.[74]

Abandoning her property, she lost all but the five milk cows, which she took with her when she moved into St. Augustine. Her home and other buildings were literally dismantled and the lumber used for military purposes. As a refugee in town, she was forced to support herself: "I took five cows + with their milk + sewing I got along poorly with only now and then a little help from the Commissary." After the war, the family remained impoverished; one witness stated they were forced to build a "palmetto shed" for shelter.[75]

The war made refugees of countless residents of the town. Some, like Andrew Anderson and Buckingham Smith, were forced by circumstances to leave because of their Unionist sentiments.

Emily Southwick, although she later professed to be a Unionist despite her son Stephen's service in the Confederate Army, was forced to move because she was in the wrong place. The war made Confederate sympathizers into St. Augustine refugees as well. Many left town immediately before the arrival of Union forces in 1862. The Union Army also forced Confederate sympathizers from town in September 1862 and in February 1863.[76]

The end of the Civil War saw St. Augustinians searching for ways to remember their dead, celebrate their freedom, and help recently freed blacks. As occurred throughout the South, women organized the Ladies Memorial Association of St. Augustine to memorialize Confederate veterans who died in the war with a monument. Anna Dummett, the sister-in-law of General Hardee, is credited with being the driving force behind the association, founded in September 1866. The association asked Colonel Sprague, as the military leader of Reconstruction in Florida for permission to build the monument, but he would not allow it to be erected on public property. However, Bishop Augustin Verot, dubbed the "Rebel Bishop" by historian Michael Gannon for his Confederate sympathies, allowed the ladies to erect the monument on Catholic Church property in 1872.[77]

With the end of Reconstruction in 1877, the monument was rebuilt in its current location at the east end of the plaza. The names of forty-four St. Augustine men who died for the Confederate cause were inscribed on the monument including that of Anna Dummett's nephew, William J. "Willie" Hardee. However, Stephen Decatur Southwick's name is missing.

We do not know why Stephen Southwick's name is not on the monument. One explanation is that he was simply forgotten. Despite the confusion wrought by war and the destruction of some Confederate military and other government records, this explanation seems unlikely. Given the relatively small size of the community, the four decades the Southwick family had lived there, the marriage of his uncle into the Minorcan community, and the obvious importance the community placed on the sacrifice of its Confederate veterans, it is hard to imagine that Southwick's sacrifice was simply forgotten or unknown. Another explanation may be that Southwick was left out because of his mother's self-professed

Unionist sentiments. Just as his mother had to explain her son's Confederate military service as she claimed to be a Unionist; his sacrifice for the Confederate cause may well have been questioned given his mother's professed loyalty to the Union. Or perhaps Southwick's situation was considered and simply found wanting by the members of the Ladies Memorial Association of St. Augustine.

The conflicts and the acrimony of the war years continued to embroil the residents of the St. Augustine long after the peace. When Sarah Mather died, an anonymous letter written to the *St. Augustine Evening News* questioned her allegiance to the Union during the Civil War, alleging "Her Loyalty came with the landing of the Federal troops." A few days later, Andrew Anderson came to her defense in his own letter to the paper, arguing she was in fact a strong Unionist. As evidence, he claimed that Mather had been threatened with expulsion by Confederate authorities in the months prior to the Federal occupation.[78]

While the postwar years were a time of remembrance for the white community, it was a time of celebration among newly freed blacks. In a letter to Buckingham Smith dated July 23, 1870, George W. Atwood described the black community's reaction to the passage of the Fifteenth Amendment. He relates that there was a procession with a "Car of Liberty" that included 36 black children representing each of the states and a "Black goddess of Liberty." The car was pulled by six horses and followed by an ensemble of blacks with banners and music. The group made its way to the plaza to hear speeches and then a "Grand Dinner" was held under the trees at Markland. Following dinner, the group made its way by boat to the lighthouse for more speeches, including one by Jonathan C. Gibbs, Florida's Secretary of State and an African-American. Atwood concluded, "The day was fine, and the people (colored) seemed to be *perfectly* happy."[79]

Despite the obvious joy over emancipation and the newfound power to vote among black men, newly freed slaves were desperate for social services. In 1865, just months after the end of the war, Roman Catholic Bishop Augustine Verot recruited eight sisters of the Order of St. Joseph in Le Puy, France, to come to St. Augustine and teach black children. Despite having to learn

English themselves, within two years they had about sixty pupils. Adult black citizens also attended the sisters' classes. The bishop was motivated by both a sincere desire to address the social needs of the recently freed slaves, but also to respond to the active effort of northern Protestants who had begun working among freed persons before the war was over. [80]

Buckingham Smith was responsible for another effort to address the needs of blacks in St. Augustine. Smith, a widower and childless at the time of his death in 1871, left a large portion of his estate for "the use of the black people of St. Augustine." Dr. Oliver Bronson, as the executor of Smith's will, was responsible for implementing this bequest. He created the Buckingham Smith Benevolent Association, using the funds available through Smith's estate to carry out this work. The Association was governed by a five-person board whose membership included Bronson and his son, Oliver Bronson, Jr., Dr. Andrew Anderson, James W. Allen, and Colonel John T. Sprague. However, the day-to-day work of the Association was carried out through the efforts of the Board of Lady Managers consisting of thirty women: ten Catholics, ten Episcopalians, and ten "other non- Episcopalian Protestants." For the first twenty years of its existence, the Association operated a home for infirmed blacks, although it also housed young black children as well. The home was located on present day Granada Street on the site of the Flagler College gymnasium.[81]

Utilizing the same space and staff, the Association also opened a school for black children; at one time there were as many as 21 students enrolled in the school. Both the school and home were closed in 1894, as the Association looked for more efficient ways to serve the black community in St. Augustine. The Association continues it work today, although its methods have changed, its mission remains.[82]

Calvin Shedd had seen the potential for St. Augustine during his brief posting in the city during the Civil War, the opportunity to be a "Garden of Eden." However, it would take a man of Henry Flagler's vision, wealth, abilities, and connections to transform the town from a "dull, old place" into a Gilded Age resort.

NOTES

1 Letter from Calvin Shedd to his family dated October 12, 1862. Calvin Shedd Digital Collection, Special Collections, University of Miami Libraries. http://scholar.library.miami.edu/shedd/letters/62oct12.html (accessed June 13, 2014). All punctuation and spelling in transcribed copy.

2 East Florida included the Florida peninsula from the Atlantic Coast to the Suwanee River. The population estimate for East Florida is found in Daniel L. Schafer, "U.S. Territory and State," in *The New History of Florida,* ed., Michael V. Gannon (Gainesville: University Press of Florida, 1996 and 2013), 215 [1996]. The population figure for the town is as of 1830. George E. Buker, "The Americanization of St. Augustine, 1821-1865," in *The Oldest City: St. Augustine Saga of Survival,* ed., Jean Parker Waterbury (St. Augustine: The St. Augustine Historical Society, 1983), 154-155.

3 James Grant Forbes, *Sketches Historical and Topographical of the Florida; more Particularly of East Florida* (New York: C.S. Van Winkle, 1821), Quadricentennial Edition of the Floridiana Facsimile Reprint Series, (Gainesville, Florida: University of Florida Press, 1964), 88-89. Charles Vignoles, writing in 1823 argues that although the channel into St. Augustine was deeper, 12 to 13 feet, it was "very detrimental to its increase as a commercial town." By way of comparison, he writes that the entrance to the St. Marys River was from 20 to 28 feet and the mouth of the St. Johns River as only twelve feet. *Observations upon the Floridas*, (New York: E. Bliss & E. White, 1823) Bicentennial Floridiana Facsimile Series (Gainesville, Florida: University Presses of Florida, 1977), 35-36, 67. He was of the opinion that the mouth of the St. Marys was the only good harbor on the east coast of Florida. "Florida," *Encylopaedia Metropolitana* 29 vols. (London, 1817-1845). Included as a supplement to facsimile edition described above, 16.

4 William Hayne Simmons, *Notices of East Florida, with an Account of the Seminole Nation of Indians* (Charleston, 1822), Bicentennial Floridiana Facsimile Series (Gainesville: University of Florida Press, 1973), 10.

5 Thomas Graham, *The Awakening of St. Augustine: The Anderson Family and the Oldest City, 1821-1924* (St. Augustine: St. Augustine Historical Society, 1978), 1.

6 Vignoles, *Encyclopaedia*, 17.

7 Forbes, *Sketches of the Floridas*, 88.

8 Ibid.

[9] Buckingham Smith Papers, Manuscript Division, New York Historical Society.

[10] Schafer, "U.S. Territory and State, 214-215 [1996].

[11] Daniel Walker Howe, *What Hath God Wrought: The Transformation of America, 1815-1848* (New York: Oxford University Press, 2007), 826-827.

[12] R. K. Sewall, *Sketches of St. Augustine with a view of the History and Advantages as a Resort for Invalids* (New York: George P. Putnam, 1848). Facsimile Reproduction (Gainesville: University Presses of Florida, 1976); Introduction by Thomas Graham. viii-x.

[13] Ibid., 40, 66-67. As to Sherivaree, Sewall writes: "It is an excessively annoying exhibition, to say nothing of its ill-manners, and gross violation of the peace and good order of society." John Lee Williams, writing approximately eleven years before Sewall, shared the pastor's disdain for Sherivaree. However, Williams is more nuanced in his criticism of Carnival. He blames the Americans for turning Carnival, which was celebrated by the Spanish and Minorcans "with much taste and gaiety," into a drunken affair. John Lee Williams, *The Territory of Florida* (New York: A. T. Goodrich, 1827) Floridiana Facsimile & Reprint Series (Gainesville, Florida: University of Florida Press, 1962), 117.

[14] Ibid., xxvii.

[15] Ibid., xxvi, xlix.

[16] Vignoles, *Observations*, 72.

[17] Ibid., 118-121.

[18] Ibid., 118, 120

[19] Ibid.

[20] Graham, *Awakening*, 19. The population figure for free blacks was for 1840. Daniel Schafer suggests that the largest slave owners were holdovers from the Spanish Colonial Period. Schafer, "U.S. Territory and State," 225 [2013].

[21] Graham, *Awakening*, 19, 41.

[22] T. W. Upchurch, "Special Gifts and Acts of Charity: The Buckingham Smith Benevolent Association, 1871-1894," *El Escribano* 47 (2010): 71-92; 75.

[23] Graham, *Awakening*, 38-39. Sewall, *Sketches*, 44. To place the revenue of

$72,000 from oranges into context, John Lee Williams states that during this period city taxes, in the form of business licenses "on stores, taverns, groceries, carts, and slaves" generated approximately $1500 annually. Williams, *Territory of Florida*, 121.

[24] Buker, "Americanization," 161, 163.

[25] Sewall, *Sketches*, 45. Describing St. Augustine in 1837, John Lee Williams wrote: "The town is, in fact, embosomed in a grove of orange trees." He then inserts an asterisk directing his writer to the bottom of the page and states "1834, before the great frost." *Territory of Florida*, 117.

[26] Williams, *Territory of Florida*, 19.

[27] Ibid.; Graham, *Awakening*, 38-39

[28] Forbes, *Sketches*, 88.

[29] Graham, *Awakening*, 61

[30] Graham, Awakening, 59. Buker, "Americanization," 170

[31] Graham, *Awakening*, 61

[32] Schafer, "U.S. Territory and State," 216 [1996].

[33] Ibid.

[34] Buker, 161, 165

[35] Brent R. Weisman, "Florida's Seminole and Miccosukee Peoples," in *The History of Florida*, ed. Michael Gannon, (Gainesville: University Press of Florida, 2013), 209.

[36] Buker, "Americanization," 169-171

[37] Ibid.,164

[38] Robert Redd, *St. Augustine and the Civil War* (Charleston: The History Press, 2014), 98.

[39] "William J. Hardee (1815-1873)," Government and Politics: Military; *New Georgia Enclycolpedia*. http://www.georgiaencyclopedia.org/articles/government-politics/william-j-hardee-1815-1873 (accessed May 24, 2014). "The Famous Hardee Hat," *Civil War Talk*. http://civilwartalk.com/threads/the-famous-hardee-hat.73380/ (accessed May 24, 2014).

40 Redd, *St. Augustine and the Civil War*, 98. "William J. Hardee (1815-1873)," Government and Politics.

41 Nathaniel Chearis Hughes, Jr., *Bentonville: The Final Battle of Sherman and Johnson* (Chapel Hill: University of North Carolina Press, 1996), 204, 205. Two other generals with St. Augustine connections were present at Bentonville: William Wing Loring, a Confederate general, discussed below, and John M. Schofield, a Union general. After the war, Schofield would serve as Secretary of War under Andrew Johnson, commandant of West Point, and commanding general of the United States. From the 1890s and until his death in 1906, he and his family were residents of St. Augustine. Ibid., Redd, *St. Augustine and the Civil War*, 112-13. Schofield served as a pallbearer at Loring's funeral in New York City; the connection between the two generals is not clear. *New York Times*, January 3, 1887.

42 Worth, a veteran of the War of 1812, the Second Seminole War, and the Mexican American War was commemorated in the naming of Fort Worth, Texas and Lake Worth, Florida; and is buried at Worth Square at the intersection of Broadway and Fifth Avenue in New York City. Arvin W. Turner," Worth, William Jenkins,"*Handbook of Texas Online,* published by the Texas State Historical Association http://www.tshaonline.org/handbook/online/articles/fwo28, (accessed May 25, 2014.) Mary Worth Sprague predeceased her husband and is buried in the National Cemetery in St. Augustine.

43 Ben E. Pingenot, "Sprague, John Titcomb," *Handbook of Texas Online* (http://www.tshaonline.org/handbook/online/articles/fsp30), accessed May 25, 2014. Uploaded on June 15, 2010. Published by the Texas State Historical Association. John K. Mahon, "Introduction," *The Origins, Progress, and Conclusion of the Florida War* by John T. Sprague, (New York: D. Appleton & Company, 1838), Quadricentennial Edition of the Floridiana Facsimile & Reprint Series (Gainesville, University of Florida Press, 1964), xix. Upchurch, *Special Gifts and Acts of Charity*, 78-80.

44 Williams, *Territory of Florida*, 119. Letter from F. S. Dancy to Buckingham Smith, August 28, 1870. Buckingham Smith Papers, New-York Historical Society.

45 Ibid.

46 Williams, *Territory of Florida*, 120.

47 Schafer, "U.S. Territory and State," 214-215 [1996].

48 Graham, *Awakening,* 56.

49 Schafer, *U.S. Territory and State*, 225 [2013].

50 Graham, *Awakening*, 56.

51 Schafer, "U.S. Territory and State," 234-35 [2013].

52 Ibid.

53 Graham, *Awakening*, 35-36.

54 Schafer, "U.S. Territory and State," 236 (2013).

55 Graham, *Awakening*, 86-87; David J. Coles, "Ancient City Defenders: The St. Augustine Blues," *Civil War Times in St. Augustine*, ed. Jacqueline K. Fretwell, (Originally appeared as Volume 23 of *El Escribano, the Journal of the St. Augustine Historical Society*), 65-90, 65.

56 G. Edward White argues: "No word better captured white southerners' sense than preserving slavery meant preserving their own freedom than 'subjugation.' Slaveholders and non-slaveholders both described the prospect of northern political control of the South as 'galling in its tyranny,' conceding that 'it is better to spend our all in defending our country than to be subjugated and have it taken away from us." *Law in American History* (New York: Oxford University Press, 2012), 1:387.

57 Stephen Douglas, an Illinois Democrat, was the author of the Kansas-Nebraska Act that repealed the Missouri Compromise of 1820. That earlier legislation had prohibited slavery in the northern portion of the Louisiana Purchase; the Kansas-Nebraska Act lifted that prohibition and in its placed allowed the voters in a territory to determine if the territory would enter the Union as a free or slave state. The effect was to potentially open new territory to slavery. The aftershock of its passage destroyed the national character of the Democrats and Whigs and effectively reduced them to sectional parties. Indignation over the bill was felt most intensely in the North: for example, Abraham Lincoln was "aroused…as he had never been before." James M. McPherson, *Battle Cry of Freedom: The Civil War Era* (New York: Oxford University Press, 1988), 127.

58 Sitike, *The Odyssey of an African Slave*, ed., Patricia C. Griffin (Gainesville: University Press of Florida, 2009), 110.

59 Graham, *Awakening*, 119.

60 Ibid.,112.

61 Redd, *St. Augustine in the Civil War*, 93-95. “Stephen Vincent Benet, Brigadier General, United States Army,” *Arlington National Cemetery Website*, http://www.arlingtoncemetery.net/svbenet.htm (accessed June 6, 2014). He is the grandfather of the American poet of the same name.

62 Redd, *The Civil War in St. Augustine*, 107-111.

63 For a general discussion of the Kentucky invasion and the role of Florida troops, see Jonathan C. Sheppard, “Another Luminous Page to the History of Florida: September-October 8, 1862.” *By the Noble Daring of Her Sons: The Florida Brigade of the Army of Tennessee* (Tuscaloosa: The University of Alabama Press, 2012).

64 Redd, *The Civil War in St. Augustine*, 114-116.

65 Thomas Graham, ““The Home Front: Civil War Times in St. Augustine.” *Civil War Times in St. Augustine*, 25. Graham, *Awakening,* 100.

66 George E. Buker, “St. Augustine and the Union Blockade,” *Civil War Times in St. Augustine*, 6.

67 Letters from Leander Harris to Emily S. Harris, April 7, 13; May 9; June 1, 8, 9; July 13, 1862. Milne Special Collections and Archives, University of New Hampshire Library, MC 193.

68 Samuel Proctor, “Introduction,” Mary Elizabeth Dickison, *Dickinson and His Men: Reminiscences of the War in Florida*, (Louisville, KY: Courier-Journal Job Printing Company, 1890), Floridiana Facsimile & Reprint Series (Gainesville, University of Florida Press, 1962), xii.

69 1850 and 1860 Federal Censuses enumerated on October 27, 1850 and July 9, 1860 respectively. Claim #16178 of Emily Southwick, Commission on Claims (Southern Claims Commission: 1871-1880) National Archives and Records Administration, Record Group 217; Claim date December 13, 1878. Shipping Notices published in the *East Florida Herald* and the *Florida Herald Southern Democrat,* Southwick biographical files, St. Augustine Historical Society Research Library. Lyman’s younger Bradford married Catherine Ann de Medici in St. Augustine in 1836, of a Minorcan family. He also appears to have been involved in shipping and in St. Augustine at the same time as his brother. See also “Genealogy of the Descendants of Lawrence and Cassandra Southwick of Salem, Massachusetts: the original emigrants and the descendants who have since borne his name by James M. Caller and Maria A. Ober (Salem, MA: C.H. Choate and Co, 1881).

70 Deed Book P, pages 252-53, November 17, 1851, St. Johns County, Florida, Public Records.

71 Southwick Claim. The reference to the fireplace is found in R. A. Speissegger, "Early history of New Augustine." (self-published, 1946), copy at St. Augustine Historical Society Research Library. While the author provides a number of interesting tidbits about the Southwicks, some of which can be collaborated, there are a number of glaring mistakes in his account that unfortunately calls into question the reliability of this source.

72 Southwick Claim. Elsewhere in her claim she states her son was "decoyed away," implying he was tricked into Confederate service. John Canova, who filed an affidavit in support of Southwick's claim stated: "I think they crowded Mrs. Southwick's son Decatur to go. He told me they were going to compel him to go."

73 David W. Hartman and David Coles, comp., *Biographical Roster of Florida's Confederate and Union Soldiers, 1861-65* (Wilmington, N.C.: Broadfort Publishing Company, 1995), 814. The 8th Florida fought at the Sunken Road in the central part of the Antietam battlefield, together with the 2nd and 5th Florida Regiments. All the units suffered from a lack of leadership due to the death, wounding, or incapacity of their field officers. Colonel Richard Floyd of the 8th Florida, having been confined to a Virginia hospital, arrived on the battlefield during the fight. He searched desperately for his unit. Ultimately he found men from his regiment who advised him that everyone in the unit had been "killed, wounded or dispersed." It appears Stephen Southwick was one of the ones "dispersed." Zack C. Waters and James C. Edmonds, *A Small but Spartan Band: The Florida Brigade in Lee's Army of Northern Virginia* (Tuscaloosa: University of Alabama Press, 2010), 37-38.

74 Southwick claim.

75 Ibid.

76 Graham, "The Home Front," 19-45, 30, 34.

77 Greenleaf, "History of the Confederate Monument."

78 *St. Augustine Evening News*, January 9, 1895.

79 The 15th Amendment was ratified on February 3, 1870. Emphasis in the original. Buckingham Smith Papers. The lighthouse mentioned here is the predecessor of the current tower (built 1874) and was located east of the current tower.

80 Michael V. Gannon, *Rebel Bishop: The Life and Times of Augustin Verot* (Milwaukee: The Bruce Publishing Co., 1964), 130-133, 139-40, 144.

[81] T. W. Upchurch, "Special Gifts and Acts of Charity: The Buckingham Smith Benevolent Association, 1871-1894," El Escribano 47 (2010): 71-92, esp. 74, 77, 84, 85. Dr. Bronson donated the land for the building and built and furnished the home; the bequest from the Smith Estate was then invested to generate income to support the home.

[82] Ibid., 89-90.

8

St. Augustine Enters the Modern Era

1877 - 1941

Thomas Graham

The dominant shaping force in St. Augustine society since the 1870s has been an almost relentless tide of new residents from the North. This surge of population growth became most extreme in the last decades of the twentieth century, but it began back in the final decades of the previous century. The crucial question during all this time has been: how to accommodate this flood of people and still maintain the unique character of America's Oldest City?

The first indications of what was to come appeared in the 1870s when a few wealthy Northerners built large winter homes in St. Augustine. George L. Lorillard of the Lorillard tobacco empire exemplified the newcomers. He erected a fine house on North St. George Street and surrounded it with a tropical garden. Other prominent newcomers were Henry and Frances Ball, wealthy New Yorkers, who purchased a large orange grove just on the western outskirts of town and raised an impressive mansion in the middle of their trees. These fine wooden "cottages" and the elegant carriages in which their owners traveled stood in stark contrast to the old stone houses left over from Spanish time and the humble horse carts of the natives.

William Astor, son of the patriarch John Jacob Astor, in about 1870 purchased the rickety Tocoi Railway that connected St. Augustine with the St. Johns River. It was the town's primary connection to the outside world. Following his death Astor's son,

LEFT: Post card of Ponce de Leon Hotel.

William, Jr., rebuilt the roadbed, added new iron rails, and put two locomotives and new passenger cars to work on the line. When the first of the new locomotives chugged into town, a crowd of people turned out to see this wonder of modern technology since some St. Augustine denizens had never seen a locomotive before.

The most unusual visitors to St. Augustine came unwillingly as prisoners of the United States government. These were parties of Western Indians taken from their families in the West. In May of 1875 a contingent of Kiowas, Comanches, Cheyennes, and Arapahoes arrived at Fort Marion (Castillo de San Marcos) to be incarcerated. Captain Richard Henry Pratt assumed responsibility for their custody. Pratt treated the Indians in an enlightened manner, allowing them to police themselves and attend classes taught by local schoolmistresses. They also fashioned trinkets to sell to curious winter season tourists and were sometimes allowed out to work in town or take pleasure trips to the beach. Captain Pratt would go to Carlisle, Pennsylvania and establish a school for young Indians, including some from the St. Augustine group. A decade later, in April of 1886, groups of Apaches began arriving at Fort Marion until as many as 447 people were being held in confinement in and around the fort. These would remain for one year. Captain Pratt returned to St. Augustine to recruit some youngsters to become students at his school.[1]

In January of 1880 ex-President U. S. Grant, his wife Julia, and son Fred came to Florida on their way to visit Cuba and Mexico. They took the little Tocoi railroad to St. Augustine. A boisterous crowd met them at the bridge over the San Sebastian River and escorted them past decorated buildings on King Street to the St. Augustine Hotel on the Plaza. A band played "Hail to the Chief." Grant had a particular reason for coming to St. Augustine: his wife Julia was the sister of Brigadier General Frederick Dent, commander of the troops stationed at St. Francis Barracks. The former president and his party spent several days in town touring the sights and being feted in the evenings before continuing on their way.[2]

Three years later in the spring of 1883 President Chester A. Arthur paid a somewhat less celebratory visit to St. Augustine for a brief period of rest. He shook hands at a reception in the Magnolia Hotel, but otherwise spent his time quietly walking the streets to see the historic sites and taking a steam launch ride down the Matanzas River.

St. Augustine began to take on a few of the aspects of a modern town. In 1882 a paid police force was established consisting of a captain and four patrolmen. A fire engine was purchased, but it was served by volunteer firemen, and its hose was designed to suck water from the nearest body of open water, not a fire hydrant, since a city water system would not be built until the 1890s. Yet most houses in town had back yard privies, and only a few hotels had laid sewer pipes into the bay. Cows and horses remained free to roam the streets.

In 1885 the State of Florida contributed to the enrichment of the town's environment by establishing the Florida School for the Deaf and the Blind on a five-acre tract of land donated by local hotel owner Captain E. E. Vaill. Although begun on a very modest scale, the school would grow over the years, with its students and teachers enriching the community.[3]

The man who would transform St. Augustine, Henry M. Flagler, first came to St. Augustine in the winter of 1878 with his wife Mary, who suffered from a pulmonary disease. Flagler ranked as one of the wealthiest men in America, having been an early partner with John D. Rockefeller in the establishment of Standard Oil Company. Flagler would later say of St. Augustine, "I did not form a very favorable first impression. I must admit." The old, dirty, run down town with its boarding houses full of sick people depressed him, and he left after spending just one night. Mary would pass away a few years later, and following her death Flagler remarried. In December of 1883 he brought his new wife Ida Alice to St. Augustine, and they remained until March. The following winter, when Flagler himself was suffering from poor health, he, his wife and his daughter Jennie Louise returned to St. Augustine. A new hotel, the five-story San Marco, had just opened on a large lot north of the City Gate and west of Fort Marion. Flagler marveled at the "wonderful change" in the old city. The San Marco was as good as any resort hotel in the country, and it was filled—not with sick people—but with affluent Northerners who had come South simply to get out of the cold winter weather and enjoy themselves.

Flagler planned on returning to St. Augustine to spend winters in the future, and it occurred to him that other wealthy men from the North would also like to enjoy spending time in town during the cold season. Why not build a hotel to meet their desires? Flagler had already made the acquaintance of one of the town's leading old-time citizens, Dr. Andrew Anderson, and they agreed that Flagler would purchase the eastern portion of Anderson's Markland orange grove property as the site for the hotel. Saltwater marsh covered most of the area, so Flagler would have to engage in a major filling project to create usable dry land. To further develop his plans, Flagler and Anderson proceeded to quietly buy both large and small tracts of land around the hotel site to create a broad expanse of property where Flagler could fulfill his dream of remaking the old city.

Flagler also brought Franklin W. Smith into his plan. Smith, a Boston businessman, had built his Villa Zorayda as a winter home in 1883. Designed in an exotic Moorish style, the house was one of the first in America to be constructed entirely of poured concrete. An amateur architect, Smith had revived a building technique once known to the Romans. Newly invented Portland Cement allowed for a stronger mix of concrete than that available to the ancients. Flagler realized that this fireproof, hurricane-proof building material would be suitable for a much larger hotel.

At the same time Flagler recruited the manager of the San Marco, Osborn D. Seavey to be his principal advisor in the hotel business. He also hired the builders of the San Marco, James McGuire and Joseph McDonald, to be his builders. Returning to New York, Flagler engaged young Thomas Hastings, the son of his former Presbyterian minister, to draw a picture of a hotel that McGuire and McDonald would turn into a reality. However, Hastings and his partner John M. Carrère soon showed Flagler that he needed the skills of professional architects if he wished to create a truly monumental hotel. By this time Flagler's dream had evolved into the goal of building the finest resort hotel in the country and remaking St. Augustine into the Newport of the South. At the time Newport, Rhode Island, was the summer playground of the wealthiest families.

On December 1, 1885, workers began digging the foundations of the Hotel Ponce de Leon. Flagler mixed local sand and coquina shell with Portland Cement to make the concrete for the foundations and walls. Wooden forms were built and the liquid concrete poured into the forms, twelve to eighteen inches in depth After the concrete had hardened for a couple of days, the wooden forms would be removed and reassembled at a higher level. To make the spaces over arches and windows stronger, railroad-track iron would be dropped into the concrete for reinforcement. No large building had ever been constructed this way, but the work went forward without major incidence. Orange terra cotta decorations were added to the walls to create a pleasing contract between the bright ornamentation and the gray walls. Although the walls rose quickly, it soon became clear that the building would not be ready to open in time for the 1887 season.

Flagler hired well regarded firms to furnish the interior of his hotel. The New York company of Pottier & Stymus supplied the oak floors and carved woodwork. Louis C. Tiffany's glass company provided the stained glass windows and helped with some of the interior decorations. George W. Maynard and Herman Schladermundt painted the ceiling murals. Thomas Edison's company provided the dynamos and electrical system that gave the hotel its incandescent lights. The Otis Brothers company supplied three elevators: two for guests and one for luggage. Flagler drilled several deep artesian wells seeking fresh water for the hotel's plumbing, but found only sulfur water. A few years later he would build a fresh water reservoir four miles outside town and pipe water in. Following the custom of the day, only a few of the hotel's suites had private bathrooms. Most of the guests shared common bathrooms at the ends of the hallways.

In April of 1887 a fire broke out one night in the St. Augustine Hotel on the Plaza. There was no hope of saving the hotel, so those who turned out to fight the fire—soldiers from St. Francis Barracks, workers from Flagler's hotel, local men—concentrated their efforts on preventing the flames from spreading to the rest of the city.

Musicale and Cotillion, at Cordova To-night.

DINNER.

BLUE POINT OYSTERS — **LITTLE NECK CLAMS**

Chicken Giblet. — Consommé, Macaroni.

Canape Madison.

Sliced Tomatoes. — *Olives.* — *Salted Almonds.* — *Sliced Cucumbers.*

Boiled Sheepshead, Egg Sauce.

Parisienne Potatoes.

Boiled Ham, Champagne Sauce.

Roast Loin of Pork, Shaker Apple Sauce. — Roast Ribs of Beef, Dish Gravy.

Roast Capon, Chestnut Stuffing.

Green Peas. — *Sweet Corn.*

Boiled Potatoes. — *Sweet Potatoes.* — *Mashed Potatoes.*

Sirloin of Beef, à la Flamande.

Granadine of Lamb, à la Soubise.

Chicken Sauté—Provencale.

Rice Croquettes, Brandy Sauce.

String Beans. — *Hominy.* — *Stewed Tomatoes.*

PERSICO PUNCH.

Broiled English Snipe, on Toast.

Lettuce Salad. — *Currant Jelly.*

Queen Pudding, Cream Sauce.

Peach Pie. — Washington Pie.

Fancy Kisses. — Assorted Fancy Cake. — Maizena Cake.

Baba au Rhum. — Macaroons.

Vanilla Ice Cream.

Bananas. — San Mateo Oranges. — Malaga Grapes.

Mandarin, and Tangerine Oranges. — Apples.

Assorted Nuts. — Figs. — Layer Raisins.

Stilton, Roquefort, and American Cheese. — Bent's Water Crackers.

Coffee.

TUESDAY, January 31, 1893.

☞ The water used in Hotel Ponce de Leon for drinking and culinary purposes, is distilled, and absolutely pure.

The Plaza limited the fire's path to the south (although the roof of the Public Market burned), but the Catholic cathedral to the west caught fire and burned to the ground, leaving only its coquina walls standing. To the north the firefighters valiantly prevented the flames from jumping to the Florida Hotel and thereby saved the northern part of the city.

A new concrete row of business buildings replaced the St. Augustine Hotel and the Catholic church was rebuilt. Henry Flagler secretly provided some of the funds for restoring and improving the church. A new bell tower rose beside the historic façade of the church. One of St. Augustine's regular winter guests, the New York architect James Renwick, who had designed St. Patrick's Cathedral, drew up plans for the new tower.

Across King Street from his Hotel Ponce de Leon, Flagler erected the Hotel Alcazar, with its Baths and Casino. This complex had been conceived as an auxiliary hotel to handle the overflow from the Ponce de Leon and as a place of amusement for winter guests. The ground floor of the Alcazar held shops where ladies could shop for clothing or fine curios. Behind the main building were the therapeutic baths intended to restore the health of those suffering from a variety of diseases. Finally, to the rear of the complex stood the large Casino with a huge indoor swimming pool surrounded by a promenade and on the upper level a dance floor.[4]

In order to ensure that guests from the North would be able to reach St. Augustine in convenience and comfort, Flagler purchased the newly completed railroad connecting St. Augustine with Jacksonville. He converted the track from narrow gauge to standard gauge, and in 1890 Flagler threw the first bridge across the St. Johns River at Jacksonville so that trains could run all the way through from New York. In future years Flagler's Florida East Coast Railway would be extended all the way to Palm Beach, Miami, and, finally, Key West.

Flagler opened his Hotel Ponce de Leon for a celebration by a few invited guests on January 10, 1888. Two days later the iron gate of the entrance was raised and thousands of townspeople poured in to wonder at the interiors of the building that they had watched rise from the former marshland during the past two years. (Each January

LEFT: Menu, Hotel Ponce de Leon, January 31, 1893.

St. Francis Street Scene, Soldiers Drilling in Front of Barracks.
Signed by Felix de Crano. Oil on canvas, 18¼ x 28¼ inches, circa 1900. St. Augustine Historical Society art collection.

thereafter the ceremonial opening of the hotel to all the public for a few hours became a major ritual in town.) That winter the hotel paid host to the social elite of the nation. In February, President Grover Cleveland and his wife Frances paid a brief visit and shook hands with thousands of citizens as they filed through the Rotunda of the hotel. Although the Hotel Alcazar remained unfinished, the front hotel section had been sufficiently completed so that guests could take rooms there beginning in March, when the Hotel Ponce de Leon filled beyond its capacity.

At the end of the season, Flagler acquired another hotel in the heart of St. Augustine. While Flagler had been building his hotels, Franklin W. Smith erected the Casa Monica Hotel diagonally across King Street from the Ponce de Leon, and it opened for guests just five days after Flagler's hotel. Smith had served as his own architect for the Casa Monica, and he designed it in the same Moorish style as his own Villa Zorayda. Unfortunately, Smith ran out of money before he had completed the building, and Flagler provided the funds to finish the building. When the Casa Monica failed to attract enough patrons to make a profit, Flagler purchased the hotel and renamed it the Cordova.

At the rear of the Hotel Ponce de Leon Flagler provided seven studio lofts for artists to occupy and show their paintings to potential customers among the winter visitors. Martin Johnson Heade, a Northerner who had settled in St. Augustine before Flagler, became the most famous of the artists to occupy one of the studios. Today his landscapes and still life flower studies are in high demand by museums and collectors.

Flagler's building projects extended beyond his hotel and railroad ventures. He erected Grace Methodist Church and Memorial Presbyterian Church and donated the site of Ancient City Baptist Church. He purchased the land and erected the buildings of Alicia Hospital, which would later be renamed Flagler Hospital. He built the City Building, which housed government offices, a marketplace, and fire station—as well as rental space for businesses. To relieve overcrowding in the county's old wooden jail, he donated a new jail on the outskirts of town (today's "Old Jail" tourist attraction). He laid large new sewer pipes from his hotels to carry waste far out into Matanzas Bay and allowed others to connect to his sewers. His Model Land Company sold real estate to newcomers wishing to find a place to build their homes.

Flagler's advent brought enough people to town to double its population from the 2,293 residents recorded in the 1880 census to 4,742 counted in 1890. However, when Flagler's building projects were completed, the town's population stabilized and actually shrank a little during the decade of the 1890s.

Yellow fever had long been a scourge in the Caribbean area and southern United States. Its cause remained unknown, nor was there a known cure. Many of those stricken by the disease would die a horrid death since the microbes attacked the victims' internal organs. Thus any outbreak of yellow fever would cause an immediate, panicked exodus from the infected area, followed by a strict quarantine to prevent anyone from entering or leaving the affected town. During 1888 yellow fever appeared in Tampa and then in nearby Jacksonville. In response the city government of St. Augustine, where the fever had not emerged, imposed a quarantine to keep anyone from entering the city. Guards armed with shotguns were placed at all approaches to the town. St. Augustine's reputation as a health resort was at stake. Fortunately the city escaped without a single reported case of fever, but the following winter tourist season would see a dramatic decline in Northerners venturing into the Ancient City and all of Florida.

St. Augustine had long been known for its sandy streets, but Henry Flagler's advent began a period of street paving to modernize the town. In 1888-1889 Flagler, at his own expense, laid asphalt paving on the streets surrounding his hotels and down Valencia Street to the new railroad terminal, Union Station. The city government used the less expensive expedient of wooden cypress blocks to pave St George Street, the streets surrounding the Plaza, and several other well-traveled streets in town. (Flood waters during an 1893 hurricane dislodged many of these wooden blocks.) Most of St. Augustine's streets, however, would be paved with oyster shell or simply remain sand. In 1897 a new era dawned when St. George Street was paved with brick. Thereafter additional streets around town received pavements of either brick or asphalt.

St. Augustine provided a variety of entertainments to keep its winter guests amused. Tennis became one of the most popular sports of the late 1880s and early 1890s. Guests at Flagler's hotels could play on the four courts behind the Alcazar, and here the annual Tropical Tennis Tournament would be played each year, attracting some of the best tennis players in the country.

In 1890 Ponce de Leon Park opened just to the east of Union Station. Baseball impresario Albert Spalding had advised Flagler on construction of the field. Flagler intended to lure professional teams from the North to play winter baseball. Spalding's Chicago Colts (later renamed the Cubs) leased the field that year and played games with the Philadelphia Phillies, who were training in Jacksonville. The Brooklyn Bridegrooms (later called the Dodgers) also came to town for games. The next year the Cleveland Spiders (later Indians) visited town to play a three game series against the Pittsburghs (later the Pirates).

Some of the waiters at Flagler's hotels played for the semi-professional all-black team the Cuban Giants. However, games between black and white professional teams had ceased by this time, and professional baseball eliminated the few black players already part of various white teams. A few rare games between black and white teams still were contested in St. Augustine, but soon racial segregation was extended to baseball as it had been to the rest of society. Flagler dismantled his field after just a few seasons because professional teams found that they could not pay their expenses playing games in Florida during the winter.[5]

In 1895 a golf association was formed in town to sponsor play of the ancient game of Scotland that had just made its appearance in America. The golfers managed to obtain an agreement with the U.S. War Department to play matches on the land around Fort Marion. The course consisted of three links that formed a triangle around the fort. Three times around made a complete nine-hole game. Both the teeing areas and the "greens" around the holes were made of sand. Eventually the course would be extended across San Marco Avenue to establish a nine-hole course. The Flagler hotels created their own course at the south end of town on the edge of the salt marshes. Flagler would abandon this primitive course after a few years, but others later revived the course so that the area came to be called "Little Links."

In 1891 Flagler's influence reached out twenty miles into the county southwest of town to establish a farm intended to provide fresh vegetables for his hotels but also to serve as an experimental station to find out what crops would grow in Florida's soil and climate. Flagler called it "Prairie Garden Farm," and brought in a distant cousin Thomas Horace Hastings as manager. When it came time to establish a railroad station there, Flagler suggested the name "Hastings."

Since the area had always been low and wet, farmers first tried rice as their primary crop, although they also produced standard variety kitchen garden crops. However, within a few years farmers in the area discovered that Irish potatoes thrived on the land, and Hastings became one of the largest producers of potatoes in the Eastern United States. Flagler's original farmland soon was divided into town lots, and a thriving community grew up around the railway station, with several churches and its own school.[6]

Development also reached out north of town in 1890 when the St. Augustine and North Beach Railway opened service to

North Beach. This rail line crossed the marshes north of the Fort Mose site and reached the beach over a bridge with an iron swing-span. A dance pavilion and newly created streets and house lots were designed to make the area both a popular place to visit and a settlement of beachside cottages. Unfortunately, the resort did not attract enough patrons to justify its continued existence, and it soon passed away. Not until 1900 would Frank and Kate Usina settle on North Beach and establish a successful beach resort, but their guests arrived by boat, not train. Just to the south of the Usinas, Paul and Ellen Capo established a similar beach resort on what was coming to be called Vilano Beach. In the 1920s new owners would build the elaborate Surfside Casino on the site, but beach erosion would wash away this attraction in the 1930s.[7]

In downtown St. Augustine a private bridge company built a wooden bridge across Matanzas Bay to Anastasia Island. The bridge opened for traffic on January 1, 1896, and a few years later a small steam engine replaced the horses that pulled carloads of tourists over the bay and down the island to South Beach. This bridge ended the days when yacht races could be held up and down the bay, and some critics complained that the scenic vista across the water had been spoiled by a prosaic wooden bridge.

Mundane but important questions of public policy on bridges and streets were subject to lively debates in the City Council. Although the Republican Party had been relegated to minority status on a state wide level with the end of Reconstruction in 1877, Republicans still contended on even terms with Democrats in St. Augustine. The Republican Party drew most of its strength from black voters, and, as the 1890 census reported, the town's population was almost evenly divided between white and black citizens. Most Republican office holders were white, but between 1877 and 1904 about two dozen black Republicans held various offices in St. Augustine and St. Johns County.

In the election of 1888, when many white residents had fled town because of the yellow fever epidemic, the Republicans swept the election. White Democrats responded with a concerted effort to suppress black voting. The state legislature passed a law requiring payment of a poll tax in order to vote, while it also divided St.

Augustine into four wards, with most black voters relegated to just one ward–Lincolnville. John Papino usually held one of the two seats from this ward. During a meeting of the City Council in November of 1902, town marshal Charles Benet shot Papino during a heated dispute over purchase of new police uniforms. Papino lived, and Benet was never brought to trial. In the 1903 election the voting for councilmen returned to being held on a city-wide basis since black voting had dropped precipitously. No more black men would serve on the city council until Henry Twine in 1983.[8]

Because of its long connection with Cuba and the presence of many Cuban cigar makers in St. Augustine, the city paid careful attention to the revolution that broke out in Cuba in the 1890s. Jose Martí, the great Cuban patriot, paid a visit to St. Augustine in 1892 to organize a club that would advocate Cuban independence. Although townspeople supported Cuban independence, many were alarmed when the battleship *Maine* blew up in Havana harbor and the United States subsequently declared war on Spain. The county commissioners sent a letter to the Secretary of War declaring, "In the event of hostilities between the United States and Spain, Saint Augustine is in greater peril from attack by hostile force than any city in the country." The letter explained that St. Augustine lay in clear view of ships at sea, it was the largest city south of Charleston located directly on the coast, and, moreover, the Spanish would remember St. Augustine as an important military outpost.[9]

To partly allay such fears the government moved one of the large Civil War vintage cannon from the fort to an emplacement near the lighthouse, although it is doubtful that this gun would have served any useful purpose in case of an attack. St. Augustine's two volunteer militia units, the Rifles and the Light Infantry, took trains for Tampa to join the army gathering for the invasion of Cuba. However, since Florida had exceeded its quota of volunteers, the Light Infantry was turned around and sent home. Moreover, since the U.S. Army preferred to use regular troops in Cuba rather than state militia, the Rifles spent the war in Alabama and then Fernandina before being mustered out without ever seeing combat.

St. Augustine played only a very minor part in the conflict. Some soldiers charged with crimes were imprisoned in Fort

Marion until they could be put on trial. Many soldiers stationed in Jacksonville or just passing through on their way to points south, walked the streets of town or went to the beach as tourists. Undoubtedly they wrote home telling their families about St. Augustine, and following the war the tide of settlers coming to St. Augustine and to all of Florida increased.[10]

Ironically the war ended St. Augustine's long tradition as a military base. During the war the troops stationed at St. Francis Barracks were called into active service, and St. Augustine's post was abandoned. The grounds of the Barracks compound had proven simply too small to sustain a modern military base. St. Augustinians regretted losing the soldiers, who had been an active part of the community and an important financial resource for the local economy. In 1907 the State of Florida leased the Barracks as headquarters for the state militia, although no troops would be stationed there. In 1915 the nearly empty building caught fire and burned down to an empty stone shell. However, the walls proved strong enough to justify rebuilding, and in 1921 the Federal government gave the site to the State of Florida as headquarters for the Florida National Guard–a function that it continues to serve today.[11]

By 1900 modern times had arrived in America's oldest city. During the previous decade bicycling had become more than just a fad and emerged as a common feature of life in town. As more streets were paved, bicycles became a practical way of getting around and a means of leisurely touring sites around town. Just a half-dozen years later, the first automobiles appeared on city streets. Both bicycles and autos raised controversies as collisions with pedestrians became fairly common events. The City Council passed ordinances requiring bells and lights on bicycles, while automobiles were limited to very low speeds. Yet most citizens welcomed the decrease in horse-drawn conveyances on the streets since horses had long been a safety hazard as well as a source of pollution.

Teddy Roosevelt, often called America's first modern president, visited the town in the fall of 1905. Citizens decked-out their homes and places of business with flags and greenery to welcome their head of state. Although Roosevelt often criticized Standard Oil as an evil enterprise, Henry Flagler, a leading partner in Standard Oil, opened his Hotel Ponce de Leon out of season to accommodate the President. Roosevelt gave a speech from the ramparts of Fort Marion to a large crowd of citizens.[12]

St. Augustine took a long stride into the modern age in 1907 when the St. Johns Light & Power Company began providing electricity for both the city and operation of an electric trolley line around town and across Matanzas Bay to South Beach beyond the lighthouse. By 1908 the line extended as far north as the Deaf and the Blind School on San Marco Avenue. A few years later extensions to the line were made into West Augustine and another mile farther down the beach to what was then called Chautauqua Beach. Over the years the trolley system would never make much of a profit, and in 1924 service in town was discontinued, although trolleys would still run over the bridge across Matanzas Bay to the beach until 1930.[13]

Flagler's Florida East Coast Railway operations became one of the town's major employers. The highly skilled, well paid mechanics in the shops were capable of renovating and repairing the locomotives and rolling stock of the railroad. In addition to the station itself, the railway maintained a headquarters building and a hospital on King Street. Just to the east of the station a neighborhood of small cottages sprang up where workers could live and be close to their place of employment. In 1908 Flagler erected a YMCA building on Valencia Street. For a brief time only railway employees could use the facility, but quickly it was opened to all the young men in town. Later on in the 1920s the FEC's operations had grown so much that a new facility called the Miller Shops opened about a mile north of town.

In 1907 civic leaders revived the Ponce de Leon Celebration that had been first held in 1885 and repeated in 1890. During three days schools and businesses were closed as hundreds of townsmen dressed up as Spaniards, Indians, Frenchmen, English Redcoats, and Florida pioneers to reenact scenes from St. Augustine's past and parade along the streets of town. Bands played, fireworks rent the night sky, power boats raced on the bay, and a myriad of other amusements occupied the time of both local residents and winter visitors. Of course, the primary objective of the celebration was to keep the tourists in town for another week. The Ponce de Leon Celebration continued to be an off-and-on event through the 1920s.[14]

On April 2, 1914, just as the winter season was drawing to a close, fire broke out in the venerable Florida House hotel. This old wooden structure had been fortunate to survive the fire of 1887, but this time it and a five block section of town north of the hotel perished in a huge conflagration. The new city hall next door, as well as the colonial era Vedder and Sanchez buildings, which housed the collection of the St. Augustine Historical Society, collapsed into rubble. It would take decades for new buildings to rise on the vacant land created by the fire.[15]

In 1914 St. Johns County issued more than half a million dollars worth of bonds to raise funds to construct a road paved with bricks from the north to the south boundaries of the county. Because the roadbed was only nine feet wide, oncoming cars were obliged to pull part way off the road to pass each other. Opening of the road to Jacksonville was celebrated in October 1915, when a "Dixie Highway Motorcade" arrived from Chicago. Local autos, decorated with flags and bunting, escorted the intrepid motor pioneers into St. Augustine. A tally of automobiles passing across the county line in November of 1915 showed a total of more than 1,000 cars rolling along the improved road. Most, of course, were headed south for the winter season.

This original road headed west to Hastings before turning south, sending tourists traveling to places such as Palm Beach and Miami miles out of their way. So in 1927 the county opened a new road leading directly south from St. Augustine to Daytona Beach. When the United States Bureau of Public Roads imposed a numbering system on the nation's primary highways to replace the existing jumble of road names, St. Augustine's north-south road became Highway US 1.

For a few years St. Augustine became the locale for shooting silent movies. With its historic buildings, seaside locale, and lush tropical vegetation, the Ancient City could stand in for any number of romantic settings from medieval Spain to darkest Africa. The first movie filmed in St. Augustine appears to have been a travelogue "short" entitled *A Trip to St. Augustine*, made in 1906. In 1910 *A Honeymoon Through Snow to Sunshine* included some local scenes. After several Northern film companies established studios in Jacksonville, cameramen and actors became familiar sights on St. Augustine streets. The 1914 film *A Florida Enchantment* told a story set in the Hotel Ponce de Leon. Theda Bara, the first movie "vamp," attracted attention in 1917 when she stayed in town while making a film. The Chamber of Commerce attempted to attract some publicity by having her plant a palm tree on the plaza. When

Local men and boys played "British" soldiers and Zulus in 1914 film, *Rorke's Drift*.

the movie companies began moving out of Jacksonville in 1917 to relocate in Hollywood, St. Augustine's days as a film center gradually drew to a close.[16]

America's involvement in World War I was too brief to have much lasting impact on St. Augustine. Wartime restrictions on travel reduced the number of tourists coming to town in the winter of 1918, but by the next season the Roaring Twenties were in full swing.

Many U.S. presidents have visited St. Augustine, but none spent so much time here as Warren G. Harding. He first came as president in late January of 1921 following his victory in the previous November's election when he stayed in the Hotel Ponce de Leon. He spent three weeks adding the final members of his cabinet and planning his administration. In February of 1922 and 1923 President Harding again returned, but these times for shorter visits. On each of these visits he enjoyed his favorite pastime, playing golf, on the course north of town. The Flagler System had opened the St. Augustine Links and clubhouse in January 1917. The noted golf course designer Donald Ross planned the course.[17]

During the 1920s St. Augustine gained an important new industry: shrimping. Local people had long caught shrimp with hand-thrown cast nets, but the early twentieth century witnessed the advent of motor-powered fishing boats pulling trawl nets that allowed fishermen to catch shrimp in large quantities. In 1922 Sollecito Salvador, Salvatore Versaggi, and Antonio Poli, all Italian immigrants, brought their shrimp boats from Fernandina to St. Augustine. Almost immediately other fishermen followed, and St. Augustine became home port to a fleet of shrimp boats. By 1923 more than a million pounds of shrimp, packed in barrels filled with ice, were being shipped to northern markets by rail each year. In 1930 two hundred boats were operating out of St. Augustine, and processing plants along the San Sebastian River employed 1,000 workers who "headed" and "shelled" each day's harvest. However, during the 1930s many boat owners moved on to the Gulf of Mexico or north to Georgia. Still as late as the 1970s as many as 100 boats operated out of St. Augustine in the winter shrimping season.[18]

Although the Florida Boom of the 1920s centered on Southern regions of the peninsula, St. Augustine caught the contagion for development. The six-story Florida National Bank building rose in the center of town, overshadowing the old Catholic cathedral—as if announcing that a new age had replaced the old. (Belatedly the City Commission voted to restrict all future buildings to a height of 35 feet.) The most important changes in town came as a complementary unit: a new bridge to Anastasia Island and a revolutionary residential development on that island.[19]

In 1925 the citizens of St. Augustine overwhelmingly voted to sell a one million dollar bond issue in order to finance improvements to the City water works and to build a modern replacement for the old wooden bridge that had stood since 1895. The new concrete and steel alloy bridge would rise in a graceful arch over the bay, with four towers at the sides of a center draw span. The whole structure would be done in the popular Mediterranean style. Work began in the summer of 1925.

Shortly after construction began on the bridge, David P. Davis, a noted land developer from Tampa, announced that he had purchased 1,500 acres of marshland on the northern tip of Anastasia Island and that he would build a modern planned neighborhood consisting of a hotel, yacht club, apartment houses, and hundreds of individual homes. In order to turn his mud flats into dry land, Davis built a seawall around the top of the island and had dredges pump in sand from the bay's bottom. "Davis Shores" opened sales offices both in town and in the center of the development.

Unfortunately, just a few months later the Florida Boom started to lose steam due to over speculation. As land prices collapsed, Florida's economy slumped into recession three years before the whole nation slid into economic depression. Building in Davis Shores ceased after only eleven buildings had been completed. Davis himself disappeared while on a sea voyage to Europe. He either fell overboard accidentally or committed suicide. The hotel and the yacht club never materialized, and it would not be until the 1950s that houses began to fill the lots that had stood vacant for a generation.

Before construction of the bridge even began, Dr. Andrew Anderson, Henry Flagler's old friend, donated two Carrera marble lions to guard the entrance to the bridge. He did not live to see the opening of the Bridge of Lions in April of 1927. The completion of the new bridge may be taken as the end of the Roaring Twenties in St. Augustine. The population of the town had been growing steadily since 1900 and then almost doubled during the 1920s—although much of that increase came about simply because the city limits were extended to include areas outside the historic town to the west and north, as well as to the northern portion of Anastasia Island.[20]

During the Depression various New Deal agencies constructed buildings in St. Augustine that have remained landmarks down to the present. The Federal Emergency Relief Administration built the Civic Center on San Marco Avenue that today serves as the Visitor Information Center. It was completed in 1935. In that same year the Works Progress Administration modernized and enlarged the old Spanish Governor's House on the Plaza, which had been serving as the Post Office, by adding a south wing. It continued as the Post Office and federal government building until 1964 when the State of Florida took it over as headquarters of the historic preservation movement. In 1937 the administration building at Fort Matanzas was completed by the W. P. A. It now serves its original purpose and also houses a small orientation room. At St. Augustine Beach the Works Progress Administration built an ocean pier flanked by two coquina stone hotel buildings as a way of promoting development on Anastasia Island. These were occupied by the fall of 1940. Today a new pier has replaced the original and the one surviving hotel building continues in use as a multi-purpose community center.[21]

Civic and business leaders had long appreciated that the town's unique Spanish heritage and "Ancient City" ambiance attracted tourists. When St. Augustine received a new city charter in 1925, the State gave the municipality eminent domain powers to acquire and preserve "ancient landmarks, sites, buildings, and remains." The first building to be accepted in trust by the City was the 1740 vintage Peña-Peck House on St. George Street. With the advent of hard times some city fathers came to believe that enhancing the historic character of the town might attract more visitors. The restoration of Williamsburg, Virginia, which was ongoing at the time, provided an example of how an historic attraction might be created with a nation-wide draw.

Mayor Walter B. Fraser hoped to find a wealthy patron, such as Williamsburg's John D. Rockefeller, Jr., who would be able to finance a "restoration and preservation" effort in St. Augustine. The Carnegie Institution of Washington, D. C., offered to initiate the movement by funding a survey of the city's historic records and archaeological resources. Unfortunately, World War II intervened to halt this endeavor. The Carnegie Institution put up most of the funds to purchase the Fernández-Llambias House on St. Francis Street in 1938. The St. Augustine Historical Society provided the $2,500 needed to complete the purchase. In 1952 work began to restore the Fernández-Llambias House. Funds from a 1937 act of the Florida Legislature to support a restoration and preservation program in St. Augustine underwrote much of the work.[22]

The Great Depression itself may have done the most to preserve the historic fabric of the Ancient City since it halted the population growth that led to the destruction of the local character of so many other Florida towns. St. Augustine's old homes survived because there were no newcomers tearing them down to build something new. St. Augustine ended the decade of the 1930s with a population count of 12,090—a loss of twenty-one souls.

NOTES

1 Edward R. Joyce, "St. Francis Barracks: A Contradiction of Terms," *El Escribano* 26 (1989): 87-88.

2 Jessica A. May, "Ulysses S. Grant's Visit to Saint Augustine," *El Escribano* 46 (2009): 1-30.

3 Thomas Graham, *Mr. Flagler's St. Augustine* (Gainesville: University Press of Florida, 2014), 377-378

4 Thomas Graham, "Flagler's Grand Hotel Alcazar," *El Escribano* 24 (1989):1-32.

5 Graham, *Mr. Flagler's St. Augustine*, 226.

6 Ibid., 262-263.

7 Beth Rogero Bowen, " Usina's Original North Beach," *El Escribano* 47 (2010): 93-120.

8 Canter Brown, Jr., *Florida's Black Public Officials, 1867-1924* (Tuscaloosa: University of Alabama Press, 1998).

9 Graham, *Mr. Flagler's St. Augustine*, 364-365.

10 Ibid., 364-368.

11 Joyce, "St. Francis Barracks," 89-90.

12 Graham, *Mr. Flagler's St. Augustine*, 433-435.

13 Edward A. Randolph, "Street Railways of St. Augustiine," *El Escribano* 24 (1987): 85-101.

14 Graham, *Mr. Flagler's St. Augustine*, 236-236, 463-464.

15 Thomas Graham, "The St. Augustine Historical Society," *El Escribano* 45 (2008): 5-6.

16 Shawn C. Bean, *The First Hollywood: Florida and the Golden Age of Silent Filmmaking* (Gainesville: University Press of Florida, 2008).

17 Susan Richburg Parker, "Golfing, Fishing and Politics: President Harding's Visits to St. Augustine," *El Escribano* 46 (2009): 31-50.

18 "Industries: Mariculture" file, SAHSRL Vertical Files..

19 Beth Rogero Bowen, *St. Augustine in the Roaring Twenties* (Charleston: Arcadia Publishing, 2012).

20 Beth Rogero Bowen, *Bridge to a Dream* (St. Augustine: St. Augustine Historical Society, 2010), 11-19.

21 Susan Richbourg Parker, "The St. Augustine Beach Hotel: A New Deal Project," *El Escribano* 42 (2005): 84-98.

22 Graham, "St. Augustine Historical Society," 20; Jean Parker Waterbury, "The Fernandez-Llambias House," (St. Augustine: St. Augustine Historical

Society, 1997) 2-6,13-16, William R. Adams, "Preserving the Ancient City," *El Escribano* 39 (2002): 151-159.

9

From Winter Newport to Spanish Williamsburg

1941 - 2015

Paul L. Weaver, III

Beginning in the middle of the twentieth century, St. Augustine looked increasingly toward a heritage tourism-based economy. While St. Augustine marketed its ancient streets, buildings and appearance soon after it became part of the United States in 1821, during the post-World War II period, the restoration of the Colonial City became a dominant theme and the backbone of its historical presentation to the public.

At the end of World War II, there were many questions about the future development of St. Augustine. Visioning for the city is not a new idea. There was "visioning" historically as well. From 1885 until 1913, Henry Flagler, his disciples, and many leaders and residents of the city envisioned St. Augustine as the "Winter Newport," a counterpoint to Newport, Rhode Island. Newport developed as a prominent summer seasonal destination for Flagler and other members of a wealthy, primarily northeastern elite.[1] During the 1930s, St. Augustine Mayor Walter B. Fraser and others, with funding and technical support from the Carnegie Institution, created a new vision for the city. Instead of the Winter Newport, which had long since faded, Fraser and other city leaders envisioned St. Augustine as "the Spanish Williamsburg."[2] The model became Williamsburg, Virginia, where John D. Rockefeller was funding

LEFT: Coast Guard Training on Fort Green by Lucy L'Engle,1943. Gouache and watercolor on paper, 13¼ x 20 inches.

reconstruction of the Commonwealth's colonial capital. The plan for a Spanish Williamsburg was interrupted by World War II and not more fully implemented until the late 1950s. While neither the Winter Newport nor the Spanish Williamsburg visions fully achieved their lofty goals, both were major influences on the city's tourism-based economy and both left major impacts on the physical development of the "Ancient City."

By 1945 St. Augustine, with the rest of Florida, emerged from the Great Depression on the back of a growing defense industry, construction of military bases, and tourism. The Ancient City, like much of the state, had suffered longer than most. The state's Great Depression, in reality, began with the collapse of the Florida Land Boom in 1926. Real estate magnate D.P. "Doc" Davis and his Davis Shores development at the northern end of Anastasia Island paralleled this that same year at the local level. His ambitious plan created a brief local real estate boom in the mid-1920s.[3] However, Davis Shores barely got off the ground and left only a few scattered buildings as monuments to its failure.

As one of the few states to show a population increase during World War II, Florida was an important location for military bases. In St. Augustine the Hotel Ponce de Leon was used as a Coast Guard Training Center. St. Augustine was, in fact, a birthplace of the Coast Guard Reserve. One of the first classes to graduate from Reserve officer training did so at St. Augustine in May 1941 at the Ponce de Leon Hotel. From 1942 to 1945, thousands of young recruits received their initial and advanced training there, among them, the artist Jacob Lawrence and actor Buddy Ebsen, an alumnus of the University of Florida.[4]

St. Augustine also received GI wartime tourists from other military bases throughout North Florida. Particularly important was nearby Camp Blanding, located on the shores of Kingsley Lake near Starke, Florida, and one of the largest training bases in the country. At one point during World War II the population of Camp Blanding would have made it the fourth largest city in Florida. Military personnel from naval facilities in Jacksonville, such as Cecil Field, Naval Air Station Jacksonville, and Mayport provided a steady stream of visitors to the Ancient City as well.[5]

One of the most popular local destinations was the St. Augustine Alligator Farm. W. I. Drysdale and F. Charles Usina purchased the attraction in 1936 and, after a disastrous fire, immediately began to rebuild the facilities, expand the collection, and mount a national publicity campaign. To fill the void created by the decline in civilian tourism, they actively promoted the attraction to servicemen stationed at Camp Blanding and other nearby military facilities. Thousands of servicemen who visited St. Augustine and the Alligator Farm during World War II helped promote the city's attractions during subsequent decades. "60 Minutes" commentator Andy Rooney and novelist Sloan Wilson, who wrote *The Man in the Gray Flannel Suit,* numbered among them.[6]

The physical development of Florida cities, which stalled following the collapse of the Florida Land Boom, the onset of the Great Depression, and World War II, resumed with vigor in the late 1940s as the state entered a period of unparalleled growth. Many veterans who had served at numerous military bases in Florida during the war returned at its close to seek permanent residency. Some came to live, but most visited St. Augustine, as it became one of Florida's premier tourist destinations.

In the postwar era, St. Augustine faced developmental pressure similar to virtually every Florida city. Condominiums, high-rise hotels, apartment buildings, and modern tourist-related business blocks replaced many historic hotels and residences in much of the state. Parking lots, shopping malls surrounded by asphalt, suburban sprawl, erosion of the central commercial district, and strip development along major thoroughfares and highways characterized many Florida communities. St. Augustine was not exempt from developmental pressures and would face many challenges in updating its infrastructure and managing economic growth while still preserving its historic sites and buildings in the years following 1945.

In the first years after World War II, preservation of historic buildings in St. Augustine was limited to private initiatives. One of the first successful adaptive uses of a historic building in Florida after the war was the conversion of the Alcazar Hotel to the Lightner Museum. The hotel, built by Henry Flagler, had closed in 1932 and lay dormant during the last years of the Great Depression and World War II. In 1946, Chicago publisher Otto C. Lightner purchased the building to house his extensive collection of Victoriana. Lightner opened the museum two years later, and subsequently donated it to the City of St. Augustine. The Museum is housed in the former health facilities of the hotel, including the spa and Turkish Baths and its three-story ballroom. This was the first of many successful conversions of historic buildings to new uses in post-World War II St. Augustine.[7]

Florida, mainly because of its warm climate and flat topography, became a focal point for military flight training, particularly the aviation branches of the United States Army and Navy. Military aviation industries continued to grow in the Sunshine State after the war. This trend was reflected in St. Augustine with the construction of a Fairchild Engine and Aviation Corporation Plant at St. Augustine Municipal Airport in June 1954.[8] Fairchild was an aircraft and aerospace manufacturing company based at various times in Farmingdale, New York; Hagerstown, Maryland; and San Antonio, Texas. Fairchild was lured to St. Augustine through an incentive package that included a gift of 155 acres of land near the St. Augustine Airport in 1954 and a lease that allowed it to pay a fee of just one dollar each time it used the Airport facility during its early years of operation. In 1964 the St. Augustine Airport Authority was established with a special taxing district. The Airport Authority had the capacity of financing the improvements needed for Fairchild to fulfill its contracts.[9]

The Fairchild Plants primarily re-fitted existing planes such as the B-26 Bomber. Employment reached a peak of 1,400 workers during the height of the Vietnam War when the plant was used for maintenance and modification of existing aircraft. During the Vietnam War years, the Fairchild Plant, then known as Fairchild-Hiller converted C-119Gs into AC-119Ks gunships, primarily for use over the Ho Chi Minh Trail. With the end of the Vietnam War, demand for military aircraft declined. Largely because of this decline, Fairchild-Hiller ended its operation at the Airport in 1976 after a twenty-year tenure. The area lost 200 jobs and a payroll in excess of two million dollars. Grumman St. Augustine Corporation took over the Fairchild-Hiller facility in 1980. Grumman continued the tradition of Fairchild, repairing and refitting aircraft for the United States and some foreign governments. Probably the most prominent was the F-14 Tomcat program. Grumman remained an important component of the local economy and one of the few truly industrial plants in St. Johns County.[10]

On January 13, 1963, 1,300 employees of the Florida East Coast Railway walked off their jobs or refused to cross picket lines in a strike. About 100 workers lived in the St. Augustine area. Bombings and shootings marked the first eight months of the strike. Ed Ball insisted a verbatim report be made of sensitive mediation discussions with mediators sent by the National Mediation Board. Ball's intransigence on this matter stifled attempts to quickly resolve the strike. The strike resulted in the termination of passenger service in 1968 by the FEC although freight service continued. The fourteen-year long strike ended in 1977. The Florida East Coast Railway had been an essential partner in the development of tourism for St. Augustine and the east coast of Florida. The railroad that had brought so many winter visitors to St. Augustine and then to points farther south for eight decades no longer would carry passengers, no matter their reason or destination.[11]

After World War II, the shrimp docks located just across King Street from the headquarters of the Florida East Coast Railway, saw the continuing decline of shrimping. Then, in 1949, when Felix and Johnny Salvador, Porter Cooper, and "Bluff" Petersen discovered pink shrimp off Key West and the Dry Tortugas Islands, shrimpers moved their trawling to the Florida Keys. This was "the final call for St. Augustine shrimp boats" and boat building began to fill the economic void created by the departing fleet. While there were small family boat builders, DESCO Marine dominated the St. Augustine production of shrimp trawlers. In June 1987 DESCO ended its shrimp-boat building business with the launch of the *Penny Ann*.[12] The 75-foot fiberglass trawler was ordered and purchased by Ed Bumgardner of Savannah, Georgia. After almost 50 years of building shrimp boats, the sun had finally set on DESCO.

The expansion of local, state, and federal road systems became one of the major developmental activities during the years

A cannon on the gundeck of Castillo de San Marcos overlooks the creation of land for widening of then-Bay Street, later renamed Avenida Menendez.

Cars drive along the new traffic lanes. Just east of bulkhead, a remnant of dock for sightseeing boat *Victory* II stands.

following World War II. In the immediate aftermath of the war, residents of St. Augustine grappled among themselves and with federal officials over widening the bayfront roadway between the Bridge of Lions and San Marco Avenue, in close proximity to the Castillo de San Marcos.[13] Expansion of the nation's transportation system was a major catalyst for the historic preservation movement at all levels of society and government. President Dwight D. Eisenhower signed into law the National Interstate and Defense Highways Act of 1956, establishing the interstate highway system and providing an easy and efficient way for troops to deploy if under attack. Road construction destroyed many historic properties in subsequent years. Development of the interstate highway system, along with urban renewal were the two major catalysts for the National Historic Preservation Act of 1966. The act was intended to preserve historical and archaeological sites in the United States. It created the National Register of Historic Places, the list of National Historic Landmarks, and the State Historic Preservation Officers.[14]

Residents of St. Augustine faced a conflict between transportation and historic preservation similar to that created by the Interstate Highway program. Despite protests from the St. Augustine Historical Society, in 1947 federal planners approved a plan for a new seawall, expanded parking, and opened two additional lanes of traffic to what was then Bay Street (later Avenida Menendez).[15] The plan greatly extended the area beyond the Spanish-era seawall, and the new traffic lanes closely skirted the Castillo de San Marcos. In September 1953 the final plan was presented to the St. Augustine City Commission. Over the next several years the issue polarized the community. While a majority of voters supported a referendum on the widening and the City Commission voted 3-2 to approve the plan, many in the city, including the St. Augustine Historical Society led by its then-president, X. L. Pellicer, voiced strong opposition. The Florida Supreme Court in its review of a suit by a private citizen and resident of St. Augustine, J.O. Miller, eventually decided the issue. The court ruled unanimously in favor of the Bayfront Plan, while recognizing it was in the public interest to preserve the ancient landmarks of St. Augustine.[16] Unfortunately, historic preservation still lacked the force of law. There was, as

During and after restoration of 42 Spanish Street.

yet, no local ordinance to protect historic sites, no State Historic Preservation Officer and no National Register of Historic Places to protect the city's historic resources from private and public development.

Historic preservation came of age in St. Augustine during the late 1950s. The bayfront expansion undoubtedly created an awareness of a need for protection of the city's historical resources. The eventually constructed four-lane boulevard along the bayfront was just one of a number of new developments in an era of fast growth that threatened the remnants of the city's past. Until 1959, private initiatives were the only examples of historic preservation in St. Augustine other than the National Park Service Program at the Castillo de San Marcos. For example, the St. Augustine Historical Society purchased three colonial buildings in the early 1950s to prevent their destruction.[17] The St. Augustine Historical Society rehabilitated the Triay House (42 Spanish Street) and the Fornells House (62 Spanish Street) and sold them to private persons with restrictive covenants intended to ensure their preservation. The Society also did preservation work on two other colonial structures already under its care: the Paredes-Dodge House in 1948 at 56 St. George Street and extensive renovations to the Fernández-Llambias House in 1954 at 31 St. Francis Street.[18]

With the 400th anniversary of the city's founding approaching in 1965, local officials turned to the state legislature for assistance. On June 19, 1959, Governor LeRoy Collins signed into law a bill creating a St. Augustine Historical Restoration and Preservation Commission. The seven-member commission was authorized "to acquire, restore, preserve, maintain, reconstruct, reproduce, and operate for the use, benefit, education, recreation, enjoyment, and general welfare" St. Augustine's "historical and antiquarian sites."[19]

The historic preservation movement in St. Augustine had its antecedents in the 1930s with the formation of the Carnegie Institution program. Beginning in 1935, St. Augustine Mayor Walter B. Fraser initiated interest in historic preservation based on the Williamsburg model. Funded by John D. Rockefeller, the Williamsburg program sought to return the original capital of

Virginia to its colonial period appearance through restoration and reconstruction of historic buildings. Fraser and other city leaders envisioned St. Augustine as the Spanish Williamsburg.[20]

In 1935 Mayor Fraser approached the Carnegie Institution for funding and technical support of the St. Augustine Restoration Program. As a result, Verne Chatelain, former Chief Historian of the National Park Service, was hired to undertake a historic sites survey of the city. A committee of distinguished scholars was formed to oversee the survey that included Chatelain, Dr. Waldo Leland, Dr. Herbert Bolton, and Dr. Francis Lingelbach, along with John C. Merriam, president of the Carnegie Institution. The Carnegie Institution, the City of St. Augustine, and the Works Progress Administration provided funding for the project. The ambitious program produced little, in part because World War II interrupted it. It did, however, serve as the model for the program started by the State of Florida in 1959. Verne Chatelain's study, *The Defenses of Spanish Florida* was the most substantive accomplishment.[21]

Employing concepts formulated in the 1930s by the Carnegie-sponsored study, the St. Augustine Preservation Commission proposed a program to restore or reconstruct colonial structures throughout the "Walled City," or colonial *presidio*. In late 1960, it undertook its first physical venture, restoration of the Arrivas House at 46 St. George Street, and looked to the Florida Legislature for financial assistance to expand its efforts. It received an appropriation of $150,000, but was required to dip into that small pool of money to fund its staff activities. Little or nothing remained for the acquisition of additional properties or for the actual task of restoration. The recurrent pleas of trustees for capital support to pursue the restoration program fell on deaf ears in Tallahassee. The legislative practice of merely funding staff salaries while ignoring capital expense needs remained in place for the succeeding 36 years.[22]

By the end of 1961, after two years of work, the Commission had but one partially completed project–Arrivas House–to show for its efforts. Looking elsewhere for funds, the Commission created a private foundation to solicit private and other public or foundation assistance. For at least the first two decades of the program, the City of St. Augustine and St. Johns County made annual contributions to the Commission for the acquisition and restoration of specific historic properties.[23]

The Commission selected north St. George Street as the focal point for the program popularly referred to as the "Restoration Area." That part of the city contained a distressed commercial sector, which community leaders wanted revitalized. One block, moreover, harbored a cluster of five surviving colonial buildings, the closest such concentration in the city. They stood directly west of Castillo de San Marcos, offering the possibility of creating an interpretive program linked to the city's most visible and popular historic site. Between 1961 and 1984, the Commission (renamed the Historic St. Augustine Preservation Board in 1968) restored, reconstructed, or preserved some forty buildings within the colonial city, most of them in the blocks bounded by Fort Alley and Hypolita streets on the north and south, and between St. George and Charlotte streets.[24] The City of St. Augustine contributed to the program's interpretive effort by limiting St. George Street to pedestrian traffic from the City Gate to Hypolita Street.

Other legislative developments cast early doubt on the State's commitment to St. Augustine's program. Preservation boards modeled after the St. Augustine example were created in Pensacola, Key West, Tallahassee, and four other locations, providing competition for legislative monies, which, in any case, were always limited. In its 36 years of operation, 1960 to 1996, the state-sponsored commission (or board) received less than $200,000 in capital outlay expenditures for the purposes of acquiring, restoring, or reconstructing historic buildings.[25] Especially after the creation of the rival Pensacola Commission in 1968, it was easily apparent that, barring some legislative miracle, St. Augustine would never receive a State appropriation sufficient to complete even a modest part of its original plan for the colonial city's restoration.

Paralleling and in many ways linked to St. Augustine preservation efforts was the Quadricentennial Celebration of St. Augustine's founding in 1565, observed from 1959 to 1965. The Florida Legislature established a State Quadricentennial

Commission that oversaw a six-year celebration marking the 400th anniversaries of both Pensacola in 1959 and St. Augustine in 1965.[26] In Pensacola, 1959 marked the commemoration of the 400th anniversary of Tristán de Luna's 1559 expedition that established the city as the first European settlement within the current United States. De Luna's settlement was abandoned in 1561, and while another attempt was made to settle the site a few years later, it was not until 1696 that a settlement was permanently established at Pensacola.[27]

The administration of U.S. President John F. Kennedy established a National Quadricentennial Commission in 1963 and the U.S. Post Office marked the occasion of St. Augustine's anniversary with a special postage stamp. The amount of federal money dedicated to the Quadricentennial was relatively small compared to the amount raised locally, said to be over six million dollars. The main federal contribution was the Park Service's reconstruction of the Cubo Defense Line constructed of earthworks and logs extending from the fort to the City Gate. A number of building and restoration projects were undertaken in anticipation of the Quadricentennial. Overall an estimated 70 structures were preserved or reconstructed throughout the city, including some of St. Augustine's most notable landmarks in the historic colonial center of the city.[28] The St. Augustine Amphitheatre was built for the Quadricentennial. Local funds helped pay for construction of the 2,000-seat facility, with its seats that came from the Polo Grounds in New York. A play, *Cross and Sword*, written by renowned playwright Paul Green was commissioned to tell the story of Spanish colonization of the nation's first city. It was performed with many local residents in the cast, and drew visitors for years before finally closing in 1996. In 1973, the Florida Legislature designated it as the official state play.[29]

As part of the Quadricentennial Celebration, the Roman Catholic Diocese of St. Augustine erected a tall cross in the vicinity of the site where Pedro Menéndez de Avilés landed. The cross, 208 feet tall and constructed of stainless steel, marks the spot where Menéndez placed a small wooden cross that symbolized the beginning of the continuous practice of Christianity in the United

States. The cross was dedicated in 1965 but not completed until 1966.[30]

Near the cross is a statue of Father Francisco López de Mendoza Grajales, the priest who accompanied Menéndez and gave the first mass for the Spaniards who landed at St. Augustine.[31] In 1958, Ivan Mestrovic, a world-renowned Croatian sculptor, politician, and architect and friend of Archbishop Joseph Hurley, completed a statue of Father López that portrays him in priestly vestments preaching the Gospel. The statue stands eleven feet tall and is made of bronze with a polished granite base. Mestrovic and his wife attended the April 13, 1958, dedication of the statue, which was moved to its present location, near the Michael Gannon Footbridge, in 2010. In 2014, the Father López Statue was listed on the National Register of Historic Places.[32]

Since the late nineteenth century, St. Augustine had been part of the Jim Crow South. Black residents had been denied the vote, barred from white public accommodations, and their children forced to attend segregated, second-class schools. Civil rights protests broke out in St. Augustine in reaction to these conditions between 1963 and 1964. At the time the city was nearing its 400th anniversary celebration. The local movement was part of a wider, national African-American civil rights movement. It was a major event in St. Augustine's long history and had a significant role in bringing about the passage of the Civil Rights Act of 1964. St. Augustine had a long-standing policy of segregation, and the city became the focus of civil rights protests in large part because of the events celebrating St. Augustine as the nation's oldest continuous settlement. The white community sought to promote St. Augustine's history, while the black community pointed out an inconvenient truth: blacks were treated as second-class citizens, denied opportunities for employment, access to government facilities and public accommodations such as hotels, motels and restaurants, and assigned to separate facilities in hospitals or public transportation.[33]

Robert Hayling, a local dentist and a representative of the National Association for the Advancement of Colored People, initiated protests that eventually ended segregation in St. Augustine. In 1963, Dr. Hayling, a resident of the historic Lincolnville neighborhood, organized campaigns against local segregated public facilities and discriminatory policies. On January 8, 1963, White House Press Secretary Pierre Salinger announced President John F. Kennedy's appointments to the St. Augustine Quadricentennial Commission, formed to promote the celebration of the founding of St. Augustine. Hayling questioned why no African-Americans were included. On February 23, 1963, the NAACP formally requested that Vice President Lyndon B. Johnson, who was scheduled to swear in the members of the all-white National Quadricentennial Commission, not visit St. Augustine. On March 7, Vice President Johnson wrote to local NAACP leaders, promising, "no event in which I will participate in St. Augustine will be segregated." His aide George Reedy consulted with Dr. Hayling to ensure a smooth visit, promising all events would be integrated and that the White House would arrange a meeting between black and white leaders of St. Augustine the day after the vice president's visit. On March 11, Johnson swore in members of the Quadricentennial Commission. Only a dozen African-Americans, including Hayling, were given tickets to the gala for Johnson at the Ponce de Leon Hotel. They were confined to an alcove table in the back, out of sight, and were guarded by Secret Service agents. The next day, Hayling and other members of the NAACP in St. Augustine arrived for their anticipated meeting with city commissioners, but instead were escorted to an empty room with a tape recorder. Vice President Lyndon B. Johnson had by then departed St. Augustine.[34]

While much of the protest in St. Augustine, particularly in 1964, focused on public accommodations such as hotels, motels, and restaurants, early desegregation efforts initially were aimed at government-owned facilities and programs. For example, by the fall of 1963, despite the 1954 Supreme Court ruling in Brown vs. Board of Education, St. Augustine still had only six black children attending white schools.[35] Segregation and discrimination by the City of St. Augustine were also issues with the local African-American community. In June 1963 segregation of the municipally owned miniature golf course and the city-supported public library became an issue.[36]

A scheduled meeting between the NAACP and the St.

Augustine City Commission on June 21, 1963, was to focus on the city's racial policies. The meeting became informal when only two commissioners, Harry Gutterman and H.L. McDaniel, appeared and the commission failed to reach a quorum. Despite assurances the previous night from Gutterman that all facilities under control of the City were integrated, on June 22 a group of blacks were turned away from the municipal putting course leased to Bert Stone.[37]

On June 28, 1963, the St. Augustine City Commission met in regular session. Members of the St. Augustine branch of the NAACP, headed by Hayling and represented by Henry Twine, a future city commissioner, presented a petition concerning discriminatory policies of the City. Attorney Leander J. Shaw, Jr. of Jacksonville spoke on behalf of the NAACP. Shaw was to become one of Florida's most distinguished jurists, eventually becoming Chief Justice of the Florida Supreme Court.[38]

The NAACP petition addressed six areas of concern, including desegregation of all City-owned facilities. City Attorney Robert Andreu, later a county judge, addressed the petition stating the City had no ordinance restricting or prohibiting the use of municipal facilities based on race. Shaw responded by stating a black citizen had been told that he could not use the mini golf course. Andreu concurred that the request had been refused and that access to the public library had also been denied. Andreu then contacted the administrators of both facilities and received letters that he read into the record. The first letter was from E.J. Cosgrove, treasurer of the Free Public Library Association, and included a letter that he wrote to the librarian, Mrs. Flesher. That letter stated that the library's facilities were open to anyone regardless of race or color. Andreu then read into the record a letter from Earl Masters, chairman of the Community Playground Association. Masters stated that there were no restrictions based on race for the facilities operated by the Association on Bay Street (now Avenida Menendez). Shaw asked if Negroes could be denied the use of the golf course. Andreu said they could not be prevented from playing based on race. The only restriction, he said, would be if they were not properly dressed, intoxicated, or for some other legitimate reason not based on race. Andreu clarified that the City of St. Augustine did not own the library but contributed funds to it, but did own the golf course, which was managed by the Playground Association.[39]

Through its actions in June 1963, the City of St. Augustine ended informal policies of segregation of the golf course and public library. This was the first desegregation of public facilities in St. Augustine. Desegregation of public schools would not occur until the fall of 1963. The desegregation of public accommodations in St. Augustine would be harder to achieve, and the slowness in doing so would subject St. Augustine to much negative publicity in the coming year. The Civil Rights activities in St. Augustine would play a major role in the passage of the Civil Rights Act of 1964. The desegregation of the municipal mini golf course was the first chapter in this important historical event. In 2014, partly because of its association with the civil rights movement, the St. Augustine Miniature Golf Course was listed in the National Register of Historic Places.[40]

When Hayling's efforts to integrate public accommodations prior to the 400th anniversary celebration failed, he and other local civil rights leaders appealed to the Southern Christian Leadership Conference (SCLC) for help. That request brought key leaders like Dr. Martin Luther King, Jr., Reverend Ralph Abernathy, Reverend Andrew Young, Hosea Williams, C.T. Vivian, and Fred Shuttlesworth to St. Augustine. The SCLC called on New England universities to send volunteers to the city for the March 1964 demonstrations. By the end of one week of protests, police had arrested hundreds of demonstrators, including a delegation of rabbis and the 72-year-old mother of Massachusetts Governor Endicott Peabody. White vigilantes terrorized local businesses that dared to serve African-Americans.[41]

In early June, Martin Luther King, Jr., came to St. Augustine and took part in a sit-in at Monson Motor Lodge. The iconic image of Monson Lodge owner Jimmy Brock pouring acid in a pool filled with civil rights demonstrators was published throughout the world. That same month, the SCLC arranged for baseball star Jackie Robinson to address a civil rights rally in Lincolnville. The publicity surrounding these two events hastened Congress' passage of the Civil Rights Act on June 20, 1964. President Johnson signed

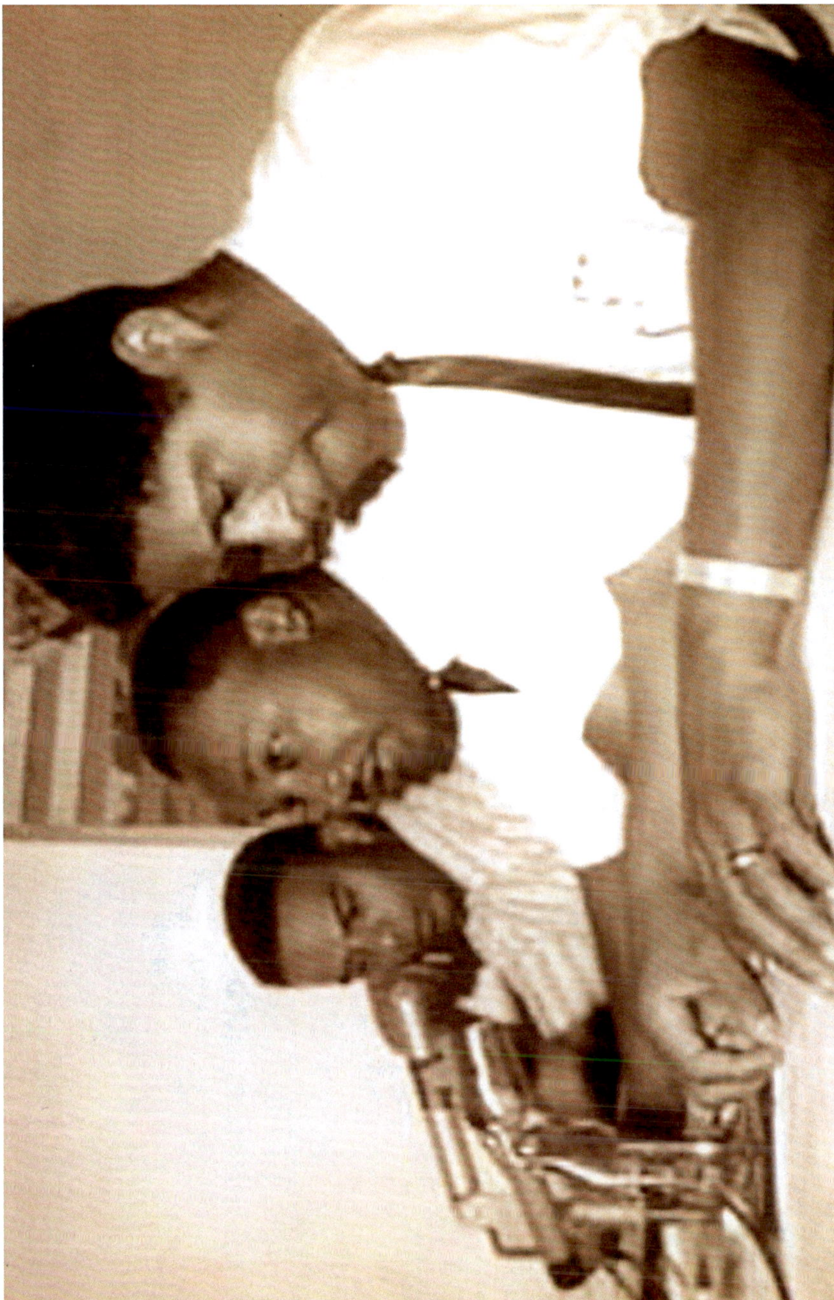

Andrew Young, Dr. Martin Luther King Jr., and Dr. Robert B. Hayling during civil rights demonstrations in St. Augustine.

the Act into law on July 2. Local segregationists initially refused to comply with the new law, but opposition soon ended. The end of segregation in St. Augustine demonstrated that communities could not uphold segregation in the face of determined resistance and federal legislation.[42]

Unfortunately, St. Augustine received much negative publicity and federal support for the restoration program disappeared. The federal government was unwilling to support a city where Jim Crow laws still existed and the city was unwilling to accept funding that came with the condition that it fully embrace civil rights for its black citizenry. The restoration of the colonial city would never regain the momentum it had achieved earlier.

One of the principal historic buildings in St. Augustine was Henry M. Flagler's Ponce de Leon Hotel. Many experts believe it to be Florida's most architecturally significant historic building. In 1963, the Hotel was one of several St. Augustine sites that served as a backdrop to events in the civil rights movement. At first blacks were excluded from the banquet at the hotel in which Vice President Lyndon Johnson was invited to launch the celebration of St. Augustine's upcoming 400th birthday as the nation's oldest permanent European settlement. When civil rights activists like Dr. Robert Hayling and others protested the exclusion of blacks from the event, negotiations took place and two tables were designated for local black residents.[43]

On March 31, 1964, more than a hundred students from all-black Richard J. Murray High School marched downtown and held a sit-in at the elegant dining room of the Ponce de Leon Hotel. They were met by police with dogs and cattle prods and arrested. It was the first mass sit-in of the civil rights movement in St. Augustine, and it was reported the next day in the *New York Times*.[44] Additional incidents took place at other segregated locations, including the Monson Motor Lodge and the Ponce de Leon Motor Lodge, all of which contributed to the momentum that led to passage of the landmark Civil Rights Act of 1964. A number of books recount the events of the civil rights movement that took place at the Ponce de Leon Hotel and other sites around St. Augustine, including David Colburn's *Racial Change and Community Crisis,* which received the 1986 Rembert Patrick Award as the best book on Florida history, and Pulitzer Prize-winner Taylor Branch's *Pillar of Fire.*[45]

In 1968 the Ponce de Leon Hotel was adapted for use as the principal building of the newly established Flagler College. The conversion of the Ponce for use by Flagler College and the similar adaption of the Plant Hotel in Tampa as the principal building of the University of Tampa were two of the most important adaptations of historic buildings in Florida. Beginning in 1976, with the nation's bicentennial anniversary, Flagler College embarked on an ambitious campaign to restore the hotel and other Flagler-era campus buildings. In 1988 the College celebrated the centennial of the hotel, and a decade later students created the Flagler's Legacy program, which provides guided tours of the hotel to thousands of visitors annually. It was added to the National Register of Historic Places in 1975, and became a United States National Historic Landmark on February 21, 2006.[46]

With the physical restoration and reconstruction of the colonial city at a standstill, the Historic St. Augustine Preservation Board shifted its efforts more to research, identification, evaluation, and designation of the city's cultural resources. The board's professional staff worked to keep St. Augustine in the vanguard of state preservation efforts in the 1970s, during a time when historic preservation in the United States experienced dramatic changes. The national movement, launched by Congressional passage of the 1966 National Historic Preservation Act, fed upon a growing national awareness of the negative impact of modern development on America's historic towns and cities and the energies generated by the 1976 national Bicentennial celebration of the "birth" of the United States. The board's staff prepared applications to list many local historic buildings and sites in the expanded National Register of Historic Places, including, in 1971, the St. Augustine Historic District. The St. Augustine Historic District extended beyond the colonial city and included the Ponce de Leon and Alcazar hotels.[47] In 1970, the National Historic Landmarks Program had designated the (circa 1600) St. Augustine Town Plan Historic District, the González-Alvarez House, the Llambias House, and the Cathedral of St. Augustine as National Historic Landmarks.[48] Three years later, in 1974, the City Commission adopted an ordinance demarcating for architectural control five local historic districts, essentially within and around the colonial city. To supervise change within those districts, the Commission authorized creation of the Historic Architectural Review Board (HARB), a citizen panel appointed by the Commission and charged with the responsibility of exercising those controls.[49]

Although the Restoration initiative faltered for lack of funding in the 1970s, historical and archaeological research and investigations flourished. Professional historians and archaeologists, funded by the Historic St. Augustine Preservation Board, the National Park Service, and the St. Augustine Restoration Foundation, which briefly considered the reconstruction of the 1580 colonial settlement, produced a rich and abundant body of scholarship. In little more than a decade's time, archaeologists Hale Smith, Charles Fairbanks, John Griffin, Kathleen Deagan, and Robert Steinbach, and historians Albert Manucy, Luis Arana, Eugene Lyon, Paul Hoffman, Michael Gannon, Michael Scardaville, Thomas Graham, and Amy Bushnell established a base of knowledge that will support a generation and more of research and preservation efforts.[50]

The preservation initiative also expanded in the 1970s to embrace resources outside the colonial city. The Preservation Board completed a three-year archaeological and building survey in 1981, compiling information about historic resources that permits agencies, property owners, and, especially, the Historic Architectural Review Board to make informed preservation judgments. Employing the information gathered from the survey, the Board's staff wrote nominations embracing two historic neighborhoods, the Abbott Tract Historic District, located north of Castillo de San Marcos, and the Model Land Company Historic District, comprising of the residential blocks situated west and north of the Ponce de Leon Hotel. Both were listed in 1983.[51] In 1986, Historic Property Associates, Inc., the state's oldest historic preservation firm, updated the 1971 St. Augustine Historic District National Register nomination. Until that time only the approximately forty colonial structures in the city had been considered to be historic under federal guidelines. The new nomination expanded the period of significance of the district through 1935, when the Government House Post Office and Customs House were rebuilt. The updated district brought recognition and historic preservation protections and benefits to hundreds of buildings dating from the Territorial Period, Flagler Era and Florida Boom period of the city's history.[52] The nomination papers for listing in the National Register of a fourth historic district within the city, Lincolnville, prepared at the request of the City in 1988, recognized the community's historic black neighborhood.[53] A later attempt, sponsored by the City Planning Department in 1992, to add the Lighthouse neighborhood to the National Register of Historic Places failed because of objections from residents.[54]

One of the great historic preservation success stories in St. Augustine was the restoration of the St. Augustine Lighthouse Keeper's Quarters. In 1980, a group of fifteen women in the Junior Service League of St. Augustine (JSL) signed a 99-year lease with St. Johns County for the keeper's house and surrounding grounds. They undertook a massive restoration project. Shortly after the JSL adopted the restoration, the League signed a 30-year lease with the Coast Guard to begin restoration of the lighthouse tower. The lighthouse was subsequently placed on the National Register of Historic Places in 1981.[55]

Restoration of the Lighthouse's antique Fresnel lens was an important component of the restoration. The antique lens was functional until it was damaged by rifle fire in 1986, and nineteen of the prisms were broken. As the lens continued to weaken, the Coast Guard considered removing it and replacing it with a more modern, airport beacon. Championed by the JSL, this plan was dismissed and the nine-foot tall lens was restored. This was the first restoration of its kind in the nation. Today, the St. Augustine Light Station consists of the 165-foot (50 m) 1874 tower, the 1876 Keepers' House, two summer kitchens added in 1886, a 1941 U.S. Coast Guard barracks and a 1936 garage that was home to a Jeep repair facility during World War II. The site also became a National Oceanic and Atmospheric Administration weather station.[56]

The discovery of the physical remnants and preservation of the second Fort Mose was another important preservation achievement of the 1980s. In 1738, the Spanish Governor, Manuel de Montiano, ordered the creation of the first defense work at Gracia Real de Santa Teresa de Mose about two miles north of St. Augustine. Escaped slaves from British colonies were directed there. They were recognized as free, and men who passed inspection were taken into the Spanish militia and placed into service. The military leader at the fort was Francisco Menéndez. Fort Mose was the first free African-American settlement legally sanctioned in what would become the United States. The fort was destroyed in 1740 by British invaders. A new fort for free blacks was built in 1752 near the location of the first fort, and uncovered in a 1986 archaeological excavation. It had a total population of about one hundred people. The village had a walled palisade around it, with dwellings, a church, and an earthen fort.[57] The site was designated as a National Historic Landmark on October 12, 1994. The 24-acre site came under protection as a Florida State Park, administered through the Anastasia State Recreation Area and became the premier site on the Florida Black Heritage Trail.[58]

Since the late 1970s, the City of St. Augustine has become increasingly involved in historic preservation. In 1987 the city adopted a Historic Preservation Element as a part of its Comprehensive Plan. This document provided an outline of goals and objectives for preserving cultural resources and suggested policies for achieving them. In response to one of the plan's declared objectives, the City Commission in 1988 approved an ordinance requiring property owners who were undertaking development that impacted a defined below-ground level to have the property's archaeological resources assessed. The City employed a professional archaeologist to perform the investigations. St. Augustine remains the only city in Florida with such an ordinance in place.[59]

The Historic St. Augustine Preservation Board withdrew from sponsorship of community historic preservation research and advocacy in the late 1980s. Preserving buildings and other historic resources was left to property owners and market forces. A relatively small number of property owners have taken advantage of federal tax laws that allow an investment tax credit for the rehabilitation of historic buildings. These have included the former Exchange Bank at 24 Cathedral Place, the Casa Monica Hotel on Cordova

Street, and the former Record Building on Bridge Street. Many eligible public agencies and non-profit entities have received state and federal grant assistance for historic preservation improvements to historic buildings. However, only within the historic districts controlled by municipal ordinance were changes to the historic architecture or landscape officially monitored.[60]

In the mid-1990s, as the St. Johns County Board of County Commissioners and its staff prepared to move into a new courthouse on the northern outskirts of the city, St. Augustine faced the renewed possibility of having a vast, empty building in the heart of the city. In the early 1960s, the same building, originally constructed as the Casa Monica Hotel in the late nineteenth century, had remained vacant for over 30 years before its conversion to the county courthouse. In the same period, its two companion buildings, the Ponce de Leon Hotel and the Alcazar Hotel, likewise empty or about to be vacated, found useful new lives, the first as a centerpiece for a four-year college and the second as a museum and municipal office building. The Casa Monica was rescued a second time through adaptive use, and returned to its original purpose as a hotel. The facility breathed new economic vitality into the city, like the two other Flagler-era hotels. Both St. Johns County and the City of St. Augustine adopted a State-authorized ad valorem tax relief provision to encourage rehabilitation of the Casa Monica Hotel and other eligible historic buildings.[61]

The Historic St. Augustine Preservation Board experienced some fitful years after 1988. The apathy of state officials toward maintaining the historic program became increasingly apparent. Faced with growing evidence that the board's years were numbered, St. Augustine's mayor and city manager began quietly in 1993 to inquire about the costs and problems associated with the City's assumption of the program's management. When the State Legislature ended the Preservation Board program in 1997, the Florida Department of State gave the City a lease for the buildings and properties that had been assembled during the State's 36 years of operation and responsibility for managing the museums associated with those properties. After a decade of City oversight,the University of Florida in 2007 took responsibility "to ensure long-term preservation and interpretation of state-owned historic properties in St. Augustine."[62]

By default, the City's Planning Department became the only identifiable entity in the city that exercised an active historic preservation role, responsible for the Historic Architectural Review Board and the archaeological program, as well as review of ad valorem tax relief applications. Architectural preservation outside of the historic districts controlled by municipal ordinance essentially relies on incentives provided under state and federal tax laws. Archaeological research continued under the auspices of the City and the University of Florida, which conducted annual field studies that for over a decade centered on early settlement patterns. Historical research within the city that might contribute to interpretation of archaeological findings and to architectural preservation suffer from an absence of any sponsored professional historian dedicated to that work.[63]

On April 1, 2001, King Juan Carlos I and Queen Sofia, the reigning monarchs of Spain, visited Saint Augustine. The King's visit symbolized the strong relationships between St. Augustine and Spain, particularly Avilés, the home of Pedro Menéndez. In 1924 a delegation from St. Augustine visited Avilés and helped normalize relations between Spain and the United States in the aftermath of the Spanish-American War. During the 400th anniversary celebration the Spanish government agreed to participate in the celebration. As part of the commitment, the Spanish Government built the Casa del Hidalgo at the corner of Hypolita and St. George streets. For a time the building housed an official Spanish tourism office. Also during the 400th Anniversary celebration, King Juan Carlos, then the Prince of Asturias, visited St. Augustine. The King's visit was without precedent in the long history of St. Augustine. No reigning monarch had ever previously visited St. Augustine.[64]

Another major preservation accomplishment was the restoration of the Bridge of Lions, which occurred between 2006 and 2010. The Bridge of Lions was begun in 1925 and completed in 1927 during the height of the Florida Land Boom. Its construction was a major impetus for D. P. "Doc" Davis' Davis Shores development. The bridge is a double-leaf bascule bridge that spans the Matanzas Bay, a part of the Intracoastal Waterway System. It is a part of State Road A1A and connects downtown St. Augustine to Davis Shores and the rest of Anastasia Island. It is named for a pair of marble lions that guard its western approach. The lions were a gift of Dr. Andrew Anderson, a physician, philanthropist, and friend of Henry M. Flagler. Anderson spent the last decade of his life funding public art in the Ancient City and the lions at the base of the bridge were his last contribution.[65]

Upon completion, the Bridge of Lions was hailed as "The Most Beautiful Bridge in Dixie" and has long been a landmark of the nation's oldest city. However, over time with age and increased traffic loads, the Florida Department of Transportation declared the bridge structurally deficient and functionally obsolete. Similar to the bayfront expansion of the 1950s, the community was divided over what to do with the bridge. The Department of Transportation eventually approved a restoration plan and awarded a $77 million contract to Jacksonville-based Reynolds, Smith & Hills for design and engineering services.[66]

The Bridge of Lions was officially closed in 2006. A temporary bridge was erected while the historic bridge was restored. The restoration was completed on March 17, 2010, when an official ceremony was held and the bridge was reopened for use. Following the removal of the temporary bridge to an offshore reef, and landscaping, the restored lion statues were returned on March 15, 2011, after a six-year absence. After five years of work, the bridge renovations were complete. In 2010 *Roads & Bridges* magazine named the Bridge of Lions as fourth in the nation's top ten bridges projects for the year.[67]

By the time of St. Augustine's 450th anniversary, the city remained a highly popular heritage tourism destination, offering a historic center anchored by St. George Street and lined with historic buildings from various periods, as well as the Castillo de San Marcos National Monument. A privately funded Freedom Trail of Historic Sites focused on the civil rights movement. Historic Excelsior School, built in 1925 as the first public high school for blacks in St. Augustine, has been adapted as the city's first museum of African-American history. In 2011, the St. Augustine

Spain's King Felipe VI and Queen Letizia, with permission of *The St. Augustine Record*, September 19, 2015.

Foot Soldiers Monument, a commemoration of participants in the civil rights movement, was dedicated in the downtown plaza a few feet from the former "Slave Market," where white supremacists rallied in the 1960s. Robert Hayling, the leader of the St. Augustine movement, and Hank Thomas, who grew up in St. Augustine and was one of the original Freedom Riders, spoke at the dedication. Another corner of the plaza was designated "Andrew Young Crossing" in honor of the civil rights leader, who received his first beating in the movement in St. Augustine in 1964. Bronze replicas of Young's footsteps were incorporated into the sidewalk that runs diagonally through the plaza, along with quotes expressing the importance of St. Augustine to the civil rights movement. That project was publicly funded. Some important landmarks of the civil rights movement, including the Monson Motel and the Ponce de Leon Motor Lodge, were demolished in 2003 and 2004.

For many years after World War II, some thought of St. Augustine as one of America's best kept secrets. For better or worse, the city now is nationally known and has continuous year round tourism. On September 8, 2015, the City of St. Augustine commemorated its 450th anniversary as the oldest continually occupied European settlement in the United States. Ten days later the reigning monarchs of Spain, King Felipe VI and Queen Letizia, visited St Augustine to commemorate the anniversary and spearhead the Spain-US Economic Forum. They greeted St. Augustine's citizens and visitors from the same balcony at Government House as did his parents in 2001. In the words of St. Augustine historian Albert Manucy, the challenge of St. Augustine is to use its historic resources while still preserving them.[68]

NOTES

1 Thomas Graham, *The Awakening of St. Augustine: The Anderson Family and the Ancient City, 1821-1924* (St. Augustine: St. Augustine Historical Society, 1978), 166-190 passim; Jean Parker Waterbury, ed. *The Oldest City, St. Augustine Saga of Survival* (St. Augustine: St. Augustine Historical Society, 1983), 197, 199, 203, 206, 211.

2 *St. Augustine Record*, July 4, 1937. This issue was devoted exclusively to the 1930s restoration program.

3 William R, Adams, Robert H. Steinbach, Michael Scardaville, David Nolan and Paul L. Weaver, *Historic Sites and Buildings Survey of St, Augustine, Florida*. (St. Augustine: n.p., 1980), 125-126.

4 James E. Wise and Anne Collier Rehill, *Stars in Blue: Movie Actors in America's Sea Services*. (Annapolis: Naval Institute Press, 2007), 163; "Jacob A. Lawrence (1917-2000)" see http://www.uscg.mil/history/faqs/Jacob_Lawrence.asp at United States Coast Guard Website.

5 Klyne Nowline, "Historians Share Stories About Florida in WWII," *The Intercom, Journal of the Cape Canaveral Chapter of the Military Officers Association of America* no. 34 (8) (August 2011): 9.

6 St. Augustine Alligator Farm Historic District, "National Register of Historical Places - Florida (FL), St. Johns County". National Park Service, reference #92001232; Andrew A. Rooney, *Andy Rooney: 60 Years of Wisdom and Wit*. (Washington, DC: Public Affairs, 2010), ix; Sloan Wilson, *What Shall We Wear to This Party?: The Man in the Gray Flannel Suit Twenty Years Before & After*, (Westminster, MD: Arbor House., 1976), 133–134.

7 Florida Master Site File form, 8SJ60; see also Website http://staugustine.com/

history/lightner-museum.

[8] *Record*, June 18, 1954.

[9] Ibid., *Florida Times-Union*, September 15, 1976; *Record,* September 14, 1976.

[10] *Record*, September 6, 2000 advertising supplement, p. 2.

[11] Leon Odell Griffith, *Ed Ball: Confusion to the Enemy* (Tampa, FL: Trend Publications, 1975), 37-45.

[12] Ed Long and Brendan Burke, *Shrimp Boat City* (St. Augustine: St. Augustine Lighthouse & Museum, 2013), 146.

[13] Adams, et al, *Historic Sites Survey*,12; *Record,* September 16, 1953, p. 18.

[14] Thomas F. King, *Cultural Resource: Law and Practice*, 2nd ed. (New York: Altamira Press, 2004), 21-22; Adams, et al, *Historic Sites Survey*, 15.

[15] *Record*, September 16, 1953, p.18.

[16] Ibid., October 11, 1957.

[17] Adams, et al, *Historic Sites Survey*, 12, see also St. Augustine Historical Society, 1952 and 1953 Annual Reports, SAHS Library.

[18] Thomas Graham, "The St. Augustine Historical Society, 1883-2008," *El Escribano* 45 (2008): 21-22. In September of 2014 the Fornells House collapsed during renovations and was demolished.

[19] Bradley Brewer, "A Synopsis of Restoration," unpublished manuscript, Historic St. Augustine Preservation Board Files in Adams, et al, *Historic Sites Survey*, 12.

[20] *Record*, July 4, 1937.

[21] Adams, et al, *Historic Sites Survey*, 11.

[22] William R. Adams, "Preserving the Ancient City," *El Escribano* 39 (2002): 154-155.

[23] Ibid.

[24] Ibid., 155.

[25] Ibid., 155-156.

[26] *Record* August 5, 2013.

[27] Michael Gannon, ed., *The History of Florida* (Gainesville: University of Florida Press, 2013), 35-37, 130.

[28] Adams, "Preserving the Ancient City," 154-155.

[29] Steve Rajtar and Kelly Goodman, *A Guide to Historic St. Augustine, Florida*. (Stroud, Gloucestershire, England: The History Press, 2008), 52–53.

[30] Ibid., 53.

[31] Michael V. Gannon, *The Cross in the Sand: The Early Catholic Church in Florida, 1513-1870*, (Gainesville: University of Florida Press, 1965), 20-30.

[32] "Father Francisco Lopez Statue National Register Nomination" reference #12000317 (2012), 35-36.

[33] See David R. Colburn, *Racial Crisis and Community Conflict: St. Augustine, Florida, 1877-1980*. (New York: Columbia University Press, 1985).

[34] Ibid., 32-34, 189. See Flagler College Civil Rights Library Timeline at http://civilrightslibrary.com/collections/timeline/

[35] Ibid.

[36] Department of Justice, Federal Bureau of Investigation, June 28, 1963, Jacksonville Field Office Report to FBI Director; City of St. Augustine, City Commission Minutes, Friday, June 28, 1963, Regular Meeting; *Record*, June 30, 1963, p. 8B.

[37] Ibid.

[38] City of St. Augustine, City Commission Minutes, Friday, June 28, 1963, Regular Meeting; *St. Augustine Record,* June 30, 1963, 8B.

[39] Ibid.

[40] City of St. Augustine Miniature Golf Course National Register Nomination, November 19, 2014 (#14000953).

[41] "Racial and Civil Disorders in St. Augustine, Report of the Legislative

Committee," (February, 1965), 6-9 in collection of the St. Augustine Historical Society Library; Colburn, *Racial Crisis,*111.

42 *Daytona Beach News Journal*, June 16, 1964; *Record*, April 19, 2013; Colburn, *Racial Crisis,* 97-98, 111.

43 Flagler College Civil Rights Library Flagler College Digital Collections. March 31, 1964 at http://civilrights.flagler.edu; Ponce de Leon Hotel, Vertical File, St. Augustine Historical Society.

44 "Racial and Civil Disorders," 28-29.

45 "Racial and Civil Disorders," 24; Colburn, *Racial Crisis;* Taylor Branch. *Pillar of Fire* (New York: Simon & Schuster, 1998).

46 Hotel Ponce de Leon National Historic Landmark, February 17, 2006 (#75002067) Flagler College. "Historical Background on the Hotel Ponce de Leon", Flagler College website.

47 Adams, "Preserving the Ancient City," 156-157.

48 "St. Augustine Cathedral National Historic Landmark", April 15, 1970 (#70000844); "González-Alvarez House National Historic Landmark," April 15, 1970 (#70000845); " Llambias House National Historic Landmark," April 15, 1970 (#70000846)

49 Adams, "Preserving the Ancient City," 156.

50 Ibid., 156-157

51 Ibid., 157

52 St. Augustine Historic District National Register Nomination, 1970 (#70000847)

53 Lincolnville Historic District National Register Nomination, November 29, 1991 (#91000979)

54 Adams, "Preserving the Ancient City," 157.

55 St. Augustine Lighthouse and Keeper's Quarters, Vertical File, St. Augustine Historical Society Library.

56 Ibid.

[57] Patrick Riordan "Finding Freedom in Florida: Native Peoples, African Americans, and Colonists, 1670–1816", *Florida Historical Quarterly* 75 (1996): 30–32.

[58] Fort Mose Site, National Historic Landmark, October 12, 1994 (#94001645).

[59] Adams, "Preserving the Ancient City," 157.

[60] Ibid., 158-159.

[61] Ibid.

[62] Ibid., 158; *Record* July 22, 2007, ; http://www.staugustine.ufl.edu/govHouse.html, accessed February 9 2017..

[63] Adams, "Preserving the Ancient City," 159.

[64] "The Royal Visit to St. Augustine, Juan Carlos I, King of Spain, & Queen Sofia, April 1, 2001," (St. Augustine: Third Millenium, 2001).

[65] Bridge of Lions National Register Nomination," November 19, 1982 (#82001040).

[66] Vertical Files, "Bridge of Lions File, Folder 4, Replacement, Restoration, Newspaper Clippings, 2000s," St. Augustine Historical Society.

[67] Ibid.

[68] *Record,* September 19, 2015; Planning and Building Department, City of St. Augustine, *Architectural Guidelines for Historic Preservation,* 4th edition (2011), 1

Epilogue

A City's Glorious Past, "Growing up in History's Playground"

Michael Gannon

When I was a high schooler growing up in St. Augustine during the World War II years I reveled in the physical remains of that city's Spanish colonial past. Many days I could be found clambering over the battlements of Spain's old coquina stone castle, then called Fort Francis Marion, after a South Carolina Revolutionary War hero. Few residents of the town seemed to know, or to care, that four score years before the Revolution that castle stood as the northernmost sentinel of Spain's New World empire, a stern remnant of the cordon of fire that once ranged from Panama to Colombia, Cuba, Puerto Rico, and Florida.

On other days I bicycled down the city's narrow streets such as Treasury and Artillery Lane, imagining myself a helmeted horseman in service to King Philip V. Or I cast my mullet net in waters off the old Franciscan mission *Nombre de Dios* (Name of God), the first site permanently established by Europe from which to serve North America's native people. Or I stood among the old Spanish residences on Avilés, Charlotte, and Marine Streets, and watched artists of the Provincetown and Rockford schools recreate from the oils on their palettes the age-mellowed gray and ochre of stucco ground floor exteriors, and, on the second floors above, the darker hues of the wood-plank balconies that formed arabesques over the pavement below. These were the architectural features brought to San Agustín from Spanish home provinces centuries before.

In addition to the "fort," as everyone called the castillo, tourists (mainly military personnel on weekend leaves) were directed by locals to the city's "attractions," such as the Fountain of Youth, the Old Spanish Inn, and the Oldest Schoolhouse. It was a catchpenney town, and any place advertised as "oldest" could count on making money. Local artist Norman MacLeish, brother of poet Archibald, showed me his fanciful watercolor of ''The Oldest Shipwreck, Now Under Construction."

But hold on! There was one attraction called "oldest" that, in my young estimation, rose above the rest. It was the González-Alvarez house, which stands on St. Francis Street in the little-visited south side of town, a site that has been continually occupied since the early 1600s. Popularly advertised as the Oldest House, the building was maintained and accurately interpreted by the St. Augustine Historical Society, which, seemingly alone among St. Augustine's organizations, provided the public with well-researched information about the city's Spanish past. From the Society a visitor learned that St. Augustine was founded one year after the death of Michaelangelo and the birth of William Shakespeare, and was the first permanent European settlement on the continent north of Mexico. It boasted our country's first church, school, and hospital; first European institutions of government, banking and commerce; first courts and city plan.

Among the Society's other contributions was its advocacy in the mid-1930s of an effort to obtain national funding for the purpose of restoring the city's 36 surviving colonial buildings. An institute with Andrew Carnegie money responded positively, undertook some still-important historical and archaeological research, then, with the onset of World War II, abandoned the project.

Following high school, I worked and studied mostly outside the state. On my return to St. Augustine in 1962, I found that the city had made dramatic strides in the understanding of its 236 years under the flag of Spain, and of its 21 years under King George III and Parliament. Two events in particular had put the citizens on this new trajectory: The U.S. Department of the Interior had changed the name of the Spanish castle from Fort Marion to its original cognomen Castillo de San Marcos (Castle of St. Mark). And, responding to the leadership of Governor LeRoy Collins, in 1959 the Florida Legislature had created the St. Augustine Historical Restoration and Preservation Commission (later the Historic St. Augustine Preservation Board). Its purpose: preserving, restoring, and reconstructing, as far as that was possible, the old colonial walled city. I quickly became caught up in the excitement.

In 1965, the city and the Roman Catholic Parish of St. Augustine observed the 400th anniversary of their founding. In the run-up to that date a great amount of scholarship was generated; historical conferences took place; and important government officials visited from Spain and Washington, including Vice-President Lyndon B. Johnson. Archbishop Joseph P. Hurley asked me to produce and direct the church's ceremonies. In that connection, in 1963 I met with President John F. Kennedy in Tampa. I was to show him certain historical documents and maps and to invite him to participate in the quadracentennial events scheduled for September 8th, 1965. From the 15 minutes we met together I remember two things that he said to me: "Certainly St. Augustine is a national historical treasure," and "I'll keep in touch." But four days later he was dead.

At the Mission *Nombre de Dios,* where it was believed the Spanish founders came ashore and the first pastor of St. Augustine celebrated a Mass of Thanksgiving, the Catholic Diocese of St. Augustine erected a votive church dedicated to the Prince of Peace and a 208-foot-high stainless steel cross, the highest in the hemisphere. It was my responsibility to oversee the construction of those monuments, which marked the approximate place where Christianity formally began in what is now the United States. In 1993 archaeologist Kathleen Deagan uncovered on the mission site the remains of the Spaniards' *casa fuerte,* or block house, dating from 1566. Six years earlier, she had found, on the neighboring Fountain of Youth grounds, the colony's first encampment. It was a blessing, she told me, that the Fountain of Youth Park was created where it was, since the undisturbed soil, not having been built upon, was readily available to the archaeologist's trowel.

Michael Gannon continued his love and concern for St. Augustine and its past through his efforts and contributions as a member of the Historic St. Augustine Preservation Board for twenty years. He served on the board of directors of the St. Augustine Historical Society during the 400th anniversary and again fifty years later during the 450th anniversary commemoration.

Excerpt reprinted from *Forum* v. 29 (Spring 2005) with permission of the Florida Humanities Council.

Contributors

Amy Turner Bushnell is a Researcher in Residence at the John Carter Brown Library in Providence, Rhode Island, and an adjunct Associate Professor in the Brown University Department of History. Since publishing *The King's Coffer: Proprietors of the Spanish Florida Treasury, 1565-1702* (1981), and *Situado and Sabana: Spain's Support System for the Presidio and Mission Provinces of Florida* (1994), she has been writing essays on a variety of topics, from the politics of food shortage to the relation between missions and mobility. Her next book to come out will be a new edition of Jonathan Dickinson's Journal, with Jason E. Daniels.

James G. Cusick is curator for the P.K. Yonge Library of Florida History at the University of Florida. His previous works include *The Other War of 1812* (2007) and *Andrew Jackson in Florida* with Sherry Johnson (2016).

Kathleen Deagan is a historical archaeologist and Distinguished Research Curator Emerita at the University of Florida's Florida Museum of Natural History. She has been studying Spanish colonial occupations in St. Augustine and the Caribbean for more than four decades. and is author of eight books and more than 70 scientific papers.

Thomas Graham taught at Flagler College from 1973 to 2008. He received his PhD from the University of Florida and his MA and BA degrees from Florida State University. He is the author of *Mr. Flagler's St. Augustine* (2014), *Silent Films* in St. Augustine (2017), and *The Awakening of St. Augustine* (1978). He is a past president and life member of the Saint Augustine Historical Society. He is a Florida native and can trace his ancestry back to 1602 in St. Augustine.

Patricia C. Griffin, historical anthropologist, received a PhD from the University of Florida. Her publications include *Mullet on the Beach: The Minorcans in Florida* (1991), *Fifty Years of Southeastern Archaeology: The Selected Works of John W. Griffin* (1995), and *The Odyssey of an African Slave: Sitiki* (2009).

Carl Halbirt was the city archaeologist of St. Augustine, Florida, from 1990 to 2017. He established the City of St. Augustine's Archaeology Program and conducted more than 800 investigations in response to the City's Archaeological Preservation Ordinance. He examined sites encompassing the past 10,000 years. He has published in various books, professional journals, local newsletters, the program's website, and developed exhibits. He received his MA in anthropology from Northern Arizona University, Flagstaff, and MPA from the University of North Florida. He is a past president of the Saint Augustine Historical Society.

Eugene Lyon is a Florida native and a specialist in Spanish Colonial Florida and the Spanish Maritime System. He holds a PhD from the University of Florida His publications include *The Enterprise of Florida* (1974), *The Search for the Atocha* (1985) , and *Pedro Menéndez de Avilés, a Sourcebook* (1995).

Eugene Lyon received the grade of *Oficial* in the Order of Isabella from the King Juan Carlos of Spain, and has been honored by the President of the Dominican Republic and the City of St. Augustine. The Florida Historical Society presented him with Jillian Prescott Award for lifetime service to Florida history.

Susan Richbourg Parker specializes in the Spanish presence in the colonial Southeast. Her publications appear in *The Yamasee Indians: from Florida to South Carolina* (2018), *The Tulane European and Civil Law Forum*, Vols. 37-38 (2017), *Signposts: New Directions in Southern Legal History* (2013), *The History of Florida* (2013), and *From La Florida to La California: Franciscan Evangelization in the Spanish Borderlands* (2013). She served as Executive Director of the Saint Augustine Historical Society from 2007 to 2016.

Daniel Schafer is professor emeritus and University Distinguished Professor, the University of North Florida. The author of numerous journal articles and book chapters on African American and Florida history, he has recently published the following books with the University Press of Florida: *Thunder on the River: The Civil War in Northeast Florida*; *William Bartram and the Ghost Plantations of British East Florida; Zephaniah Kingsley Jr. and the Atlantic World: Slave Trader, Plantation Owner, Emancipator*; and a revised and expanded edition *of Anna Madgigine Jai Kingsley: African Princess, Florida Slave, Plantation Slaveowner.*

T. W. (Tracy) Upchurch is an associate professor of law and history at Flagler College where he teaches American history and directs the Frank D. Upchurch, Sr., Endowed Law Program. He holds a MA in American History from the University of North Florida and a JD from the University of Florida and is a member of the Florida Bar. His family has resided in St. Augustine since the 1920s.

Paul L. Weaver, III, holds a BA in American History with High Honors and a MA in Latin American History/Historic Preservation Magna Cum Laude, both from the University of Florida. He has held professional positions at the Museum of Florida History, Library of Florida History, Florida Bureau of Historic Preservation, and Historic St. Augustine Preservation Board. He is a founder and the President of Historic Property Associates, Inc., Florida's first historic preservation consulting firm. He has served as Chairman of the City of St. Augustine Historic Architectural Review Board and is a member of the Board of Directors of the St. Augustine Historical Society.

Index

St. Augustine Historical Society

(904) 824-2872	Jan 31, 2020
www.oldesthouse.org	3:12 PM

PURCHASE

Authorization 348115
Receipt XHGu

New Oldest City	$28.95
Subtotal	$28.95
Sales Tax	$1.88
Total	**$30.83**
Visa 2139 (Swipe)	$30.83

Gerald O Deer

